Advance Praise for *Farmstead Chef*

Farmstead Chef stirs up revolution, moving us back into the gardens and local farmers markets. It captures the renaissa and homegrown cooking where key ingredients include fresh, seasonal and local food along with a deep-rooted conviction that our every bite can make a difference in transforming our world.

— Nell Newman, Co-founder and President of Newman's Own Organics

With farmers finally emerging as the new rock stars, Kivirist and Ivanko possess the creative talents and authenticity as growers themselves to not only connect with individual readers and eaters, but help foster a new generation of farmers who are restoring and revitalizing America.

— Curt Ellis, King Corn and FoodCorps

We need to view food as something important again, worth taking the time to seek out and to cook. I'm eager to try the recipes in *Farmstead Chef* — they promise a taste at once refreshing and deeply hopeful.

— Bill McKibben, author of *Eaarth* and *The End of Nature*

This book put a big smile on my organic farmer face. Why? With playful people like Lisa Kivirist and John Ivanko kissing off corporate America, the serious nature of taking back our food supply becomes a belly-laugh, belly-full party that even the most skeptic will want to attend. For good food and good laughter, *Farmstead Chef* is the place to be.

— MaryJane Butters, publisher of *MaryJanesFarm*

Kivirist and Ivanko uniquely "connect the dots" between the food system and what's on your family's plate. By blending practical ideas with broader contexts, *Farmstead Chef* uniquely and positively challenges us to change our perspectives on the everyday act of eating, with results that are simply delicious.

— Mark Muller, Director of the Food and Community Program, Institute for Agriculture and Trade Policy

Kivirist and Ivanko redefine traditional definitions of health. Rather than focus on deprivation, *Farmstead Chef* celebrates abundance and the fulfilling joy and pleasure of knowing where our food comes from and savoring every bite with those you love.

— Melinda Hemmelgarn, Registered Dietician, writer,
FoodSleuth Radio host

Collaborative to the core, Kivirist and Ivanko possess an ability to connect the various grassroots organizations and efforts working toward improving our food system. This skill, enhanced by their prolific writing and engaging speaking abilities, will bring their latest book, *Farmstead Chef*, to a wide national reach.

— Denise O'Brien, Founder, Women, Food and Agriculture Network

Tapped into both what's growing on their farm and what's brewing on Capitol Hill, this dynamic and prolific duo represent the new face of food in America: individuals who seek connections to their food source and celebrate the potential of eating fresh, local and seasonal, one June strawberry at a time.

— Aimee Witteman, Former Executive Director,
National Sustainable Agriculture Coalition, Washington, DC

Farmstead Chef is compelling, practical and sumptuous. Kivirist and Ivanko prove that you can eat local, and well, year round, even in a four season climate.

— Brian Halweil, author of *Eat Here* and
senior fellow with the Worldwatch Institute

For more, please see
farmsteadchef.com and innserendipity.com
or join on
facebook/farmsteadchef

Farmstead Chef

John Ivanko & Lisa Kivirist

NEW SOCIETY PUBLISHERS

Cover design by Diane McIntosh.
Illustration: iStock (Matthew Hertel)
Photographs by John D. Ivanko unless otherwise credited.
Book design and layout: Greg Green and John McKercher.

Printed in Canada. First printing September 2011.

Paperback ISBN: 978-0-86571-703-9
eISBN: 978-1-55092-491-6

Inquiries regarding requests to reprint all or part of *Farmstead Chef*
should be addressed to New Society Publishers at the address below.

To order directly from the publishers, please call toll-free (North America) 1-800-567-6772,
or order online at www.newsociety.com

Any other inquiries can be directed by mail to:

New Society Publishers
P.O. Box 189, Gabriola Island, BC V0R 1X0, Canada
(250) 247-9737

New Society Publishers' mission is to publish books that contribute in fundamental ways to building
an ecologically sustainable and just society, and to do so with the least possible impact on the
environment, in a manner that models this vision. We are committed to doing this not just through
education, but through action. Our printed, bound books are printed on Forest Stewardship Council-
certified acid-free paper that is **100% post-consumer recycled** (100% old growth forest-free),
processed chlorine free, and printed with vegetable-based, low-VOC inks, with covers produced
using FSC-certified stock. New Society also works to reduce its carbon footprint, and purchases
carbon offsets based on an annual audit to ensure a carbon neutral footprint. For further information,
or to browse our full list of books and purchase securely, visit our website at: www.newsociety.com

LIBRARY AND ARCHIVES CANADA CATALOGUING IN PUBLICATION

Ivanko, John D. (John Duane), 1966–
Farmstead chef / John Ivanko & Lisa Kivirist.

Includes indexes.
ISBN 978-0-86571-703-9

1. Seasonal cooking.   2. Cookbooks.
I. Kivirist, Lisa II. Title.

TX714.I93 2011   641.5'64   C2011-905466-3

NEW SOCIETY PUBLISHERS
www.newsociety.com

Join the Conversation

Visit our online book club at NewSociety.com to share your thoughts
about *Farmstead Chef*. Exchange ideas with other readers,
post questions for the authors, respond to one of the sample questions
or start your own discussion topics.
See you there!

Books for Wiser Living recommended by *Mother Earth News*

Today, more than ever before, our society is seeking ways to live
more conscientiously. To help bring you the very best inspiration and
information about greener, more sustainable lifestyles, *Mother Earth News* is
recommending select New Society Publishers books to its readers. For more
than 30 years, *Mother Earth* has been North America's "Original Guide
to Living Wisely," creating books and magazines for people with a passion
for self-reliance and a desire to live in harmony with nature.
Across the countryside and in our cities, New Society Publishers and
Mother Earth are leading the way to a wiser, more sustainable world.

For more information, please visit MotherEarthNews.com

AUTHORS' DEDICATION

To our mothers, feeding us until we could feed ourselves.
To the farmers and food artisans, without you, most of us would be dead.
To anyone who knows great food and eats that way.
Finally, to our son, Liam, who nourishes and inspires us every day.

Contents

Acknowledgments

There are many who have nourished us, both in ideas and edibles, who inspired us to take the road less traveled, and who continue to challenge us in every way, from how we generate our energy to what we serve on the table.

In particular, we'd like to give thanks to the many inspiring people and visionary grassroots organizations we've had the honor to partner with, including but definitely not limited to: Faye Jones and the amazing staff at the Midwest Organic & Sustainable Education Service (MOSES); Jan Joannides and Brett Olson at Renewing the Countryside; Mark Muller, Abby Rogosheske, Jim Harkness and all the folks involved with the Kellogg Food & Community Fellows program and the Institute for Agriculture & Trade Policy; the energizing staff at the Midwest Renewable Energy Association; the staff with our Wisconsin Department of Tourism, especially those involved with the Travel Green Wisconsin program; BowTie Publications, publishers of *Hobby Farms*, *Hobby Farm Home* and *Urban Farm*. Jamie Lamonde and *Edible Madison*; Bill McKibben at 350.org; MaryJane Butters of MaryJanesFarm; Kat Steele and the Esalen Institute, all those creative editors and art directors at Ogden Publications, publishers of *Mother Earth News* and *Natural Home* magazine; Brian Halweil and the rest of the staff at World Watch Institute; Alisa Gravitz and Denise Hamler the rest of the tireless worker bees at Green America; Guillermo Payet at LocalHarvest.org; Donna Neuwirth at the Wormfarm Institute; Bill and Becky Wilson at Midwest Permaculture; Peter Nicholson and Foresight Design;

Rodney North (the Answer Man) and the rest of the folks at Equal Exchange; Mark Shepard; Mary Bergin; Terese Allen; Jim Slama at Familyfarmed.org; Nell Newman; Michael Pollan and Curt Ellis.

Kudos, likewise, to the farmers, food entrepreneurs and culinary artisans who grace our kitchen with the fresh, seasonal, local or sustainable ingredients not found in our gardens. Thanks to Organic Valley Family of Farms, Equal Exchange, the cheesemakers and brewmasters of Green County, our Willy Street Co-op, Jordandahl Farm, Scotch Hill Farm, Dreamfarm, Heartland Mills, Wholesome Sweeteners, Florida Crystals and Sugar River Dairy, Circle M Farm, Shady Blue Acres, Grassroots Farm, among many others.

We are graced by the kindred spirits at New Society Publishers, especially Chris and Judith Plant, Ingrid Witvoet and the rest of the talented crew there. We are changing the world, one kilowatt, lightbulb and potato pancake at a time.

We recognize a few of the many people who have influenced our culinary and life journey, not least of which are our parents, Aelita and Valdek Kivirist, Susan Ivanko and especially our own son, Liam Ivanko Kivirist. Deep appreciation goes out to our local mentors, Phil and Judy Welty (a Kitchen Table Talk feature in this book), and global mentors, Jack Matson and Elizabeth Goreham. Special thanks, too, to organic dairy farmers Rick and Mary Stanek, Mimi Tilmanis, Leslie Van Gelder, Chris Barth, Matt Urban, the Zettles, the Burkhalters, the Colemans, the Engelberts, Joy and Delbert Rohde, Steve and

Deb Schroeck and Karl and Nadine Schmidt, Chris Sandvig, John and Mary Frantz, Karen and Dave Yaney, Kara Belew, Adria Goodson, Jenni Taylor, Cheryl Toth, Marshall King, Bethany Swope and Jen and Scott Lynch. Our growing fields would not be what they are today, were it not for the "management interns" over the years with our Cooperative Enterprise Program with the Michael Fields Agriculture Institute; they include Amy Kremen, Dave Stanger, Kristen Vetterlein, Janet Kruse and Andrea Weimer.

For our Kitchen Table Talks with local farmstead visionaries and global food game-changers featured in the pages of this book, you helped us express a new food story of abundance, ecological restoration, nourishment and health. Thanks to Todd and Jordan Champagne, Roger Doiron, Severine von Tscharmer Fleming, Jai and Joel Kellum, Beth and Jody Osmund, Bryant Terry, Nancy Vail and Jered Lawson, Poppy Tooker and Jonathan Fagan (for sharing his soup recipe). And if we're ever lost in the woods or urban jungle, we'd be in good hands with wild food foragers Georgia Pelligrini, Sam Thayer and Cindy Rosen. We're also grateful for the early discussions regarding the ideas for this book provided by Kristina Holmes, for the masterful design of our farm steadchef.com website by Ann Foley Design, and for the book trailer created by Shouting Mountain (Taldish Castle) with the original music by Giovanni Paris (Giovanni-Paris.com).

Lisa thanks her amazing network of women working to transform our food system: Liz Johnson (The White House Project), Leigh Adcock and Denise O'Brien (Women, Food & Agriculture Network), Erin Schneider, Katie Peterman, Aimee Witteman, Sue Roberts, Rose Hayden-Smith, Angie Tagtow, Melinda Hemmelgarn, Alissa Hamilton, Margaret Krome, Martha Davis Kipcak, Gini Knight, the Green County Women in Sustainable Agriculture Cocktail Club and Stateline Homeschoolers.

Our local tribe of kindred spirits gifts us deep friendships and perpetual potlucks — and soup nights. Thanks to some amazing families: Vestin, Krieger, Carus, Giaimo, Carper, Lynch, Bubenzer, Endres, Stern-Hickey and Smith. Thanks, too, to our tribe of families spread far and wide, many of whom opened their kitchens as test kitchens for this cookbook: Meister-Sylvester, Rue-Scholin, Cohen, Ambo, Abatangelo, Lilly and Morrison-Sang.

Finally, our culinary enterprise would not have thrived had it not been for the never-ending arrival of hungry guests appearing at the back door of our Inn Serendipity Bed & Breakfast. We can't wait to whip up something new in the kitchen, just for you.

Savoring the Good Life,
Lisa Kivirist and John D. Ivanko

Introduction

First, we kissed off corporate America as twenty-somethings, pledging to never again let dysfunctional executives walk all over us while greed runs wild. You might say our premature mid-life crisis may have been caused by indigestion. That's way before we realized an inconvenient truth or the dark side of Food, Inc. Back then, we overdosed on lattes with our cubicle clones and chowed down on fast food.

Then we did the unthinkable at age 30, freaking out our parents. We became farmers. Not the hundreds-of-acres and chemical- and fossil-fuel-addicted kind, but small, self-reliant, diversified and sustainable, focused on food crops and the health of the land, water and air, not dependent upon the USDA's commodity subsidies for corn and soybean row crops to survive.

Eating What We Grow

That's right. On our Green Acres in Green County, Wisconsin, you can actually eat what we grow on our farm, a farm that's completely powered by the wind and sun. Sometimes we use the sun to bake our bread in a Sun Oven or a woodstove to simmer our soups. Mostly, we try to eat from our gardens, from our community or from those growers who share our passion for making this world a better place.

We share our abundance through our award-winning Inn Serendipity Bed & Breakfast, now well entrenched on the foodie highway as road food (and a bed) that nourishes the mind, spirit and body. When we tour our gardens with visitors, we taste as well as talk, sometimes returning to the house with armfuls of cucumbers. Our ethnic upbringing (ever heard of stir-fry made with bratwurst?) and 1970s suburban roots (remember TV dinners?) led to a culinary awakening in our 20s, enticed by urban ethnic restaurants, foreign exchange student housemates in college and discovering the tastes of the places we visited when we traveled around the world. Our life, we realized, unfolds through our food.

Inn Serendipity farmhouse with solar thermal system on roof, used to heat domestic hot water.

Return of the Farmstead and the Kitchen

Farmstead Chef is the first cookbook to capture the return to our nation's farmstead roots of independence, self-sufficiency and frugality, blended with the spice of modern living and a passion for transforming our planet. Whether you're a dedicated urbanite or live at the end of a country road, here's your chance to rediscover homegrown and homemade cooking, preserving the harvest, stocking the pantry and building local community around your kitchen table.

This cookbook redefines healthy eating in a way that reaches out to a more balanced worldview on food beyond calorie counts and fat-free or "meat-free" fake food. There's sugar, flour and salt in many of our recipes. Cheese and butter, too. No swearing off alcohol or caffeine, but the vodka draws flavor from raspberries picked at their peak ripeness and our version of a frozen mochaccino, made with organic Fair Trade coffee, won't suck your bank account dry. The use of tofu, soy milk and nutritional yeast is done selectively, because the recipes taste better and are more nutritious with them. Our Wisconsin Cornucopia Beer and Cheese Soup recipe is a Wisconsin State Fair award-winner for good reason: our selection of the best local, fresh, seasonal and chemical-free ingredients we could find.

For a decade and a half we've been experimenting, learning to let Mother Nature headline our show in the kitchen. We creatively blend textures, colors and smells with our recipes that appeal to all the senses, based on the abundance of nature, not scarce or hard-to-find ingredients. Once we rediscovered the tastes of garden-fresh, seasonal ingredients, no amount of flashy, food-styled advertising could bring us back into the industrially grown, processed food fold.

Our great food formula strives to restore balance and encourages moderation, paired with an active and mindful lifestyle and workstyle (read: cut out the stress). For more about how our cooking is connected to the rest of our lives — to the energy we use, gardens we tend, work we love and community we share — you can look to the first two books we penned together, *Rural Renaissance* and *ECOpreneuring*. They distill the specifics on sustainable living and detail our triple bottom line approach to running a green business, respectively.

Rethinking Eating

Starting with breakfasts and finishing with mouth-watering desserts, *Farmstead Chef* showcases the creative and budget-friendly side to eating lower on the food chain more often, while taking responsibility for the food we put into our bodies — by growing it, sharing it, savoring it. By lower on the food chain we mean more fruits and vegetables and less meat. Not, no meat. Included is a chapter on beverages, like fruit cordials and smoothies, and "Liam's favorites," recipes inspired by our son who loves his spinach and broccoli. This "farmsteadtarian" cookbook — preparing healthy meals with ingredients sourced as close as possible from a farm, ranch or artisan food purveyor — is anything but prescriptive, proclaiming you will die an early death if you touch an ounce of sugar, eat meat or unwind with a strawberry daiquiri at the end of the day.

Most of us live on a continuum, swinging like a pendulum back and forth between successes and failures, accomplishments and setbacks. So, too, is there a continuum of cooking that can respect nature, our fellow farmers and, in the case of animals that may end up on our plate, the life that ceases so that ours may be nourished. There's plenty of evidence that too much of anything can lead to trouble. You alone must walk the line, armed now with the information to make more informed decisions regarding the world we live in and the foods we eat.

We learned it first in elementary school: our ancestors started out as roaming hunters and gatherers who feasted on wild animals and plant-based wild foods. Food crops eventually came from our discovery of agriculture — saving and planting seeds for wheat and grains, vegetables and fruits — forever transforming our relationship with the land and allowing us to build houses in permanent settlements. Next came domestication of animals and selectively breeding the wildness out of them. Today, we have cows, pigs and goats that would unlikely survive on their own if not for our care.

We've come a long way from such nomadic eating, having discovered and refined agriculture over the past 10,000 years to such a degree that the vast majority of us live in the city with only 2 percent of Americans providing enough "food" to feed the remaining 98 percent of us. We write "food" because much of the processed, zap-to-eat, grown-to-ship-well and last-on-the-shelf meals smack of convenience and corporate profits, not health or nutrition.

This reality of third-party food providers, combined with a growing awareness of what's happening to the planet and how we treat our animals, the land and the farmers, has spawned a diverse range of declared dietary preferences, from omnivore to vegan to locavore to flexitarian — and now, there's someone we call the farmsteadtarian, a person who eats as much as possible from their own gardens,

community and, when necessary, from carefully selected sources as close to the farmers, ranchers, food artisans, beekeepers, brewers or growers as possible. Permaculturists, market growers and small-scale sustainable agriculture advocates share in common the belief that local food systems operate within and should nourish the living systems of which they're a part.

Rather than focus on what's not on the plate, we give thanks for what is. This cookbook is, in part, for all of you, though not every recipe will be for you.

The Kitchen

Illustrated by John's alluring, unpretentious photography that captures both the sense of place and

simple beauty found in potatoes and tomatoes, *Farmstead Chef*'s recipes provide a delicious roadmap to restore the planet and revitalize our lives. It's written to be accessible to all levels of cooking experience, so we've sprinkled some cooking tips wherever there might be a question on an ingredient, technique or process (remember, we're still learning ourselves). We know you know how to Google it; Enough said. For those who have just arrived back in the kitchen — other than knowing where to find the cereal or corkscrew for the wine — or have recently arrived to the local and organic food scene, we've created introductory cooking information on our website, farmsteadchef.com.

Just getting started? Don't panic if you don't have a chef's knife. Neither do we. We have an assortment of different knives, including one for paring, a serrated one for cutting breads and a large one to get through those watermelons. Our recipes are meant to be starting points for you to add to or subtract from, with your own five senses — and, of course, with whatever nature's bounty offers.

As for the rest of our kitchen, we have a nice collection of pots and pans, a few pots (including our workhorse, an inherited Le Creuset), wooden cutting boards, tongs, mixing spoons and spatulas, the Cadillac of any farmstead kitchen — a KitchenAid MixMaster — and a couple of drawers of both the low-tech and high-tech hand-me-down gadgets.

On the low-tech front, to work through buckets of apples, grapes and pears, we have a hand-crank peeler, a Foley Food Mill for apple sauce and grape juice, a hand-crank pasta maker and the essentials to hot water bath process a year's supply of applesauce. For pizza-parlor-quality crusts, we use an oven cooking stone, and to roll our sushi and spring rolls, we employ a bamboo sushi mat. We have a few attractive white serving dishes or platters, too; who wants to serve up soup out of a glass mixing bowl? Farmsteads aren't bachelor pads, after all.

On the high-tech end, we whip it up in a food processor or blender, fry it in a deep fryer and use a microwave to efficiently warm things. For perfect rice, every time, pick up a rice cooker; it can't get easier than this: add rice and water, then turn on; when a tune plays on our Zojiruchi Rice Cooker, it's ready (or will stay warm for when you need it). A chef's showplace or licensed commercial kitchen, our farmstead kitchen is not. We're a farmstead. Our focus is the output. Our eclectic array of tools helps us get from garden to plate.

The Return of the Farmstead

Why farmstead? Because for those wishing to reclaim sanity when it comes to providing a healthy, ecologically responsible meal for themselves or their family, we're going to need to return to our farmstead: in the city, suburb or at the end of a country lane. Our current food system is simply unsustainable: when as many as 20 calories of energy or resources goes into every 1 calorie of food nutrition that we end up eating; when government policy, like the US Farm Bill, provides cash entitlements for farmers that reward, in part, monoculture corn crops for animal feed, fuel (ethanol) and food (mostly in the form of high-fructose corn syrup used by the food processing industry); when 2 percent of the population feeds the other 98 percent.

Thomas Jefferson's agricultural ideal — a nation of yeoman farmers — is as useful an idea today as it was in 1776. What he didn't foresee, or perhaps couldn't imagine, is more than 80 percent of Americans

Inn Serendipity Farm and Bed & Breakfast. Credit: Valdek Kivirist

choosing to confine themselves to urban living and entrust their food supply to farmers and large corporate processors they'll never know, often thousands of miles way.

But today's version of yeoman farmers — unlike Jefferson's idyllic vision of the small farmer in the countryside — are picking up the hoe and planting food gardens by the hundreds of thousands, but they live in the inner cities, eat the former lawns of their McMansions-turned-food-plantations or intervene in the disease of sprawl, ruining developers' plans for growing houses on fertile farming land by purchasing these farms and renewing the rural renaissance filled with local, self-reliant, community-based enterprises.

About the Cookbook

The temptation to organize a seasonal cookbook by the seasons speaks to Spock's sense of logic. But we tend to prepare meals based first on what type of meal we're looking to make — breakfast or dinner, a snack or a refreshing beverage — then examining what we have in abundance. True, sometimes it's obvious: with 200 perfectly ripe tomatoes sitting on the counter, eat Tomato Pie (recipe page 15) for breakfast or the Fried Green Tomato and Basil Sandwich (recipe page 149) for lunch or dinner. Maybe you just received a box of fresh fruits and vegetables from your CSA, and instead of a couple of beets, you have 15. What to do? Try the Beet Burgers (recipe page 155), since they're great right out of the oven as well as reheated after they're frozen (months later). The first eight chapters provide a collection of recipes that speak to a general classification, like drinks or bread. Both may be paired with a main dish or breakfast instead.

Eating seasonally means letting nature's abundance direct your meal plan, allowing you to serve meals that contain only the highest quality, most nutritious ingredients, sometimes harvested just minutes before you eat them if you grow a kitchen garden on your patio, rooftop or backyard. Sometimes the ingredients are so fresh, you merely need a dash of balsamic vinaigrette and a few spices to savor the subtle flavors of your first salad of the season. But after gorging on strawberries for two weeks, or if you came home from the farmers market with ten pints on special from your favorite farmer there, you can freeze them whole (see page 31 on tray freezing) and lock in nearly all the fresh fruit flavor and nutrition.

Each chapter features an introductory narrative addressing the why or how we ended up cooking the way we do. Then scattered throughout, like seeds planted in fertile soil, are informational sidebars on food storage, frugal home cooking, hosting potlucks and stocking the pantry, as well as slice-of-life profiles of farming friends or urban gardeners, kitchen canners and a vegan chef — Kitchen Table Talks — most containing a recipe to try. The final chapter is a digest version of our son's favorite recipes and pantry-stocking specifics so you'll be prepared for even the snowiest snowstorm. Like the recipes in the Kitchen Table Talks, these recipes are easily cross-referenced throughout the other eight chapters.

The recipes in this book draw inspiration from our journeys to far-flung locales where we rediscovered the joys of cooking and sharing meals slowly in the camaraderie of others. You'll find a classic eggs Benedict recipe as well as an Indonesian-influenced peanut sauce for asparagus or a Grecian souvlaki with home-baked pitas. We celebrate the diversity of culinary influences resulting from the melting pot we know as America, featuring a New Orleans seafood gumbo and an avocado dip from a soul-food vegan chef in Oakland, California.

As for the recipes themselves, they pass the "grandmother's test." For starters, most of the recipes fit on one page and have ingredients or names you can pronounce and, usually, could find in your backyard garden or chicken coop. We're all creative, have some degree of green thumbs and can cook in the kitchen. In the case of farmstead cuisine, it's mostly harvesting, washing, chopping, cooking in a pan or oven — not brain surgery.

With this cookbook, you can eat well, save money and restore the Earth. Real food rots, so eat it fresh! And remember, there's always a place for you at our farmstead table!

FARM FRESH EGGS

BREAKFAST ENTRÉES

Zucchini Feta Pancakes

Asparagus Goldenrod

Breakfast Burritos

Eggs Benedict

Cocoa Pancakes (vegan)

Fresh Tomato Breakfast Pie

Tofu Scrambler (vegan)

Savory Zucchini Bake

Frittata of Leeks

Baked Potato Pancakes

Fried Potato Latkes

Winter Squash Quiche

Kitchen Garden Quiche

Baked Omelet Roll

Applicious Pancakes

"Granolaheads" Crunch

Raspberry Cream Cheese French Toast (aka "Breakfast Cake")

Savory Frittata (vegan)

** see Liam's Favorites (page 211) for:

Rolled Pancakes with Fresh Fruit or Chocolate Filling

Liam's Apple Omelet

Farming Without Fossil Fuels

It was during the Great Depression, in April of 1930, that Delbert Rohde was born in one of the upstairs rooms of our farmhouse, the way it was done back then. Over the next sixty-six years, he'd eventually come to take over and own his family's farm with his wife, Joy, at his side. Like so many, they more than made do with a bountiful garden overflowing with fruits and vegetables, cheese and butter from the cheese factory where the milk from their cows went and an occasional butchered animal raised on the farm providing beef, pork or poultry for special occasions. They ate fresh, from a root cellar, or canned produce year-round.

By the middle of the 20th century, however, the face of farming had changed. The USDA proclaimed: Get big or get out. The era of post-World War II agriculture ushered in the big chemical and seed companies — and farmland that demanded tractors to work it. At the Rohde farm, there was the year without Concord grapes, accidentally wiped out by pesticides applied on the corn crops that drifted onto the kitchen gardens located a few feet from the back door of their farmhouse. It was the era of productive land use and chemical agriculture, followed a couple decades later by Genetically Modified Organisms (GMOs), like strawberries with animal genes or corn that can withstand poisons.

We imagine the time when Delbert's grandfather Henry Rohde first set eyes on these rolling green Wisconsin hills back in 1887. He saw more than rich topsoil, streams for splashing in and trees for kids masquerading as monkeys. Gazing at the landscape, he must have sensed a place where he and his family could turn the soil and embrace the American pursuit of happiness, complete with cabbage, chickens and community.

Like at many family farms around the country, Del and Joy's own kids moved on — to the city and into careers with paychecks. Few were interested in milking cows, picking berries or canning tomatoes. They traded self-reliance for paychecks, small-town community for supermarket convenience. It appeared that another family farm would become a statistic, with the farmhouse turned into a residence for a truck driver or doctor who welcomed a rural commute to town.

Our ending up with the Rohde farm came down to the floppy straw summer hat Lisa wore when she first visited. John was still finishing up grad school at Penn State, studying leisure, of all things. And ecotourism, for we both yearned to transform our homestead into a country inn called Inn Serendipity, one where we could turn the soil and till up the good life in our pursuit of happiness in much the same way as Henry Rohde did more than 100 years ago — though we traded Henry's windmill for a wind turbine, and we mostly freeze our fruits and veggies instead of canning them.

Del and Joy could have sold this place to a higher bidder. Even "common sense" suggested to the Rohdes that two twenty-something urbanites — college-trained in the arts of advertising deception — would not likely survive their first winter on a farm. It's true: we never planted a seed in our life. We couldn't identify a potato plant for all the French fries in the world.

But the Rohdes sensed our passion and commitment to plant roots, homestead and share the farm with others. Perhaps Joy could see a younger version of herself in Lisa — in that straw hat — puttering in the gardens or changing laundry hung on the line. No doubt, they may have been perplexed by the amount of time we spent walking in and out of closets on the second floor (we had been sizing them up for the B&B bathrooms). They realized we'd be doing new things to their place, trading the well-manicured parklike lawns for a wilder version of English gardens, planting trees to buffer what quickly became an organic farm. Chemicals were forbidden while mounds of compost piles took form. Suddenly, one year, we planted a wind turbine to spin our electricity meter backwards, sending more power back onto the grid than we use. With a sense of familiarity given the still omnipresent, but out of action, windmills used for pumping water in the old days, the Rohdes stopped by to celebrate the commissioning of our wind turbine on their farm. Rice crispy treats for all.

When Del and Joy first walked this land with us in 1996, our toes tingled and spirits lifted by the fresh start on our lives, having escaped the cubicle world and many of the entanglements that urban life brings: the commutes, takeout food, smog. We felt the heartbeat of the farm that sustained the Rohde family for over 100 years. Who ever thought that living in a place where you didn't have to lock your doors every night could be so freeing?

Our bed and breakfast magnifies this gift of a fresh start as we share with guests a morning meal overflowing with the farm's bounty in the form of breakfast burritos, potato pancakes or a range of other house specialties. We serve an experience of what life was once like for more than half of Americans who lived on farms back at the turn of last century, with neighbors dropping by, kids foraging in the raspberry patch, apples and cinnamon simmering on a wood cookstove. By the end of a decade of transforming this 5.5 acres, we had largely severed our dependency on fossil fuels to make our farm go. We work the soil mostly by hand, secure our electricity completely by the wind and sun, heat and cook with

wood. Garden nutrients come by way of compost and green manures. Out are the pesticides and fertilizers made from oil and natural gas.

We like to think of our breakfasts as cultivating the next chapter in our guests' lives. Maybe they will head home and start a garden or try growing something new, like rutabagas. Perhaps they'll put together that backyard composter that's still sitting in a box in the garage or host a community potluck. Maybe they will quit that job void of meaning or purpose and finally launch a dream business of their own. Whatever their next step, we love being part of the process, one breakfast at a time.

Inn Serendipity's 10 kW Bergey wind turbine, completely powering the farmstead.

Inn Serendipity's breakfast of zucchini feta pancakes, muffin and smoothie, served on the front porch of the farmhouse.

Zucchini Feta Pancakes

SOMETIMES THE TEACHER APPEARS before the student is ready. Or in our case, sometimes the recipe appears before the kitchen is ready. Lisa found this zucchini feta pancake recipe while flipping through a magazine at a youth hostel in New Zealand during our backpacking days after escaping our cubicles. Some recipes, like seeds, must be saved, set aside for just the right time to try out. So we jotted this one down in our travel journal before heading south to Milford Sound.

Years later and after more than a decade of experiences on the farm, zucchini and summer squash started piling up on the counter like they often do. We needed breakfast ideas to savor this abundance. Fast. More squash were on the way. Then we remembered the New Zealand sunrise, and zucchini recipe. After relocating the travel journal, we headed to the kitchen.

The savory flavor combo of zucchini and feta results in a pancake that helps us fly through the zucchini with gusto. The light flavor of the squash is accented by the richness of farm-fresh eggs and brininess of the cheese. This recipe works best with tender and succulent young summer squash or zucchini.

INGREDIENTS

4   eggs, separated
4   c. fresh zucchini (or any summer squash), shredded
1   c. feta cheese, finely crumbled (about 1 lb.)
½   c. green onions or chives, finely chopped
1   T. fresh mint, finely chopped (or 1 t. dried)
½   t. salt
½   c. flour
    Canola oil for frying

DIRECTIONS

❶ In a large bowl, combine egg yolks, zucchini, feta cheese, onions, mint, salt and flour. Mix well.

❷ Beat egg whites until stiff. Fold into batter mixture.

❸ Heat oil until very hot in a 6-inch skillet; we sometimes use an electric fry pan so we can fit more pancakes at once. Drop about ⅛ cup batter for each pancake. Cook on both sides until browned and crisp.

❹ Serve immediately and garnish with edible flowers such as nasturtiums or a sprinkle of bee balm flower petals.

YIELD: 5 servings.

COOKING TIP — Vegetable-based Canola Cooking Oil

Many commercial cooking oils use chemicals and solvents to separate the oil from its vegetable source. Expeller pressed (sometimes called mechanically pressed or cold pressed) uses pressing or grinding to more healthfully coax the oil away from the plant matter. This is why these oils, often made from canola (or mustard rape), may appear cloudy. Because GMO-based canola or mustard rape is so widely grown, we purchase only certified organic Spectrum Canola Oil. Spectrum even tests its seed and oil to eliminate the small (but growing) possibility of wind drift contamination from GMO fields. While we love the flavor of olive oil, for sautéing at medium and high heat, we like the neutral flavor of canola oil.

Asparagus Goldenrod

"WHAT ARE YOUR HOBBIES?" a guest asks us. While the question may have been sincere, we stared back a little dumbfounded to come up with a reply. Then we remembered that core ingredient of the good life we created: Love what you do. Our creativity is expressed with every breakfast plate. We may not do watercolors or doodle, but every time we plate a breakfast, we tap the colors and textures of everything from the tomatoes to the tablecloth and arrange them in an appealing way. Asparagus Goldenrod provides the perfect springtime elements that, when plated, looks like a work of art. Like art, this one takes a little time in the set-up — cue the grated egg yolk. To keep the dish hot, it's best to create it on a heated plate.

INGREDIENTS

- 3 eggs, hard-boiled
- 1 lb. fresh asparagus spears, trimmed
- 2 T. butter
- 2 T. flour
- ½ t. salt
- ½ t. pepper
- 1 c. milk
- 1 T. fresh tarragon (1 t. dried)
- 4 thin slices toast, cut in half diagonally
- 1 T. chives, chopped

DIRECTIONS

❶ Peel the eggs and cut them in half. Scoop out egg yolks and set aside. Chop egg whites and set aside.

❷ Cut asparagus spears diagonally into 2- to 3-inch pieces. Place the pieces in a steamer basket over, but not touching, boiling water. Cover and reduce heat. Steam 5 to 8 minutes until the asparagus are crisp-tender.

❸ While the asparagus are steaming, prepare the white sauce. In a medium saucepan, melt the butter. Stir in flour, salt and pepper. Slowly stir in the milk. Cook and stir over medium heat until the mixture is bubbly. Cook and stir for a few minutes more. Add the tarragon and chopped egg whites. Heat through.

❹ Arrange 2 toast points on each warm serving plate. Divide asparagus evenly over the 4 plates. Spoon the white sauce evenly over the asparagus. Press the yolk through a sieve over each serving. Top with chives as a garnish.

YIELD: 4 servings.

Breakfast Burritos

*A*MONG OUR MOST versatile breakfast items, this dish features whatever is in seasonal abundance or frozen from an earlier harvest. Perfect for non-morning people, breakfast burritos need to be prepared the night before. This recipe can be readily doubled for larger groups (use a 9 × 13-inch baking pan). Leftover burritos taste great the next day — just be sure to reheat them in the oven, not the microwave.

INGREDIENTS

- ½ c. onion, chopped (1 small)
- 2 cloves garlic, minced
- 2 c. mixed veggies, chopped (any combo of spinach, broccoli, bell peppers or summer squash will work)
- 1 T. canola oil
- ¼ t. salt
- ½ T. fresh dill (½ t. dried)
- 4 whole wheat flour tortillas, 8-inch round
- 1½ c. cheese (cheddar, havarti or mozzarella), shredded, separated
- 2 eggs, lightly beaten
- 1 c. milk
- 2 t. flour
- ½ t. mustard powder
- ½ c. salsa (optional as condiment)
- ½ c. sour cream (optional as condiment)

DIRECTIONS

❶ To prepare veggies, sauté onions and garlic and add spinach, broccoli, peppers, zucchini and other vegetables of choice. Season with salt and dill.

❷ Place approximately ½ c. of the cooked and seasoned veggies down center of tortilla. Top with ¼ c. cheeses.

❸ Roll up tortillas and place them seam side down in a lightly oiled 8-inch-by-8-inch pan.

❹ Mix eggs, milk, flour and mustard powder. Pour over tortillas.

❺ Cover pan with foil and refrigerate overnight.

❻ Let stand at room temperature for 30 minutes prior to cooking. Bake uncovered at 350° for about 45 minutes or until eggs are set.

❼ Sprinkle additional cheese on top and cover for last 5 minutes of baking.

❽ Serve with salsa and sour cream.

YIELD: 8 servings.

COOKING TIP

Veggie Tales

For some of our recipes, we like to mix it up by featuring whatever vegetables we have fresh at the time. Try blending some firmer vegetables like broccoli and bell peppers with a leafy green like spinach for a tasty flavor combination. In most cases, leave out the root crops or starchy spuds; they usually make a better side dish.

Eggs Benedict

WHILE PERFECTLY SEASONED sausage links or lean strips of bacon can be served as sides to most of our breakfast entrées, there's nothing more enticing to the eye, nose and palate than eggs Benedict, especially when made with a couple of slices of Canadian bacon and poached farm-fresh eggs with their nutrient-rich orange yolks. Eggs Benedict is mostly a matter of assembling several distinct steps to create a masterpiece. If a spouse, friend or partner can join you in the kitchen, the tango of sharing some cooking responsibilities makes the whole process a delight.

INGREDIENTS

4 **eggs**

1 **lb. Canadian bacon, thinly sliced**

2 **English muffins (see recipe page 58)**

1 **c. Hollandaise sauce (see page 104)**

1 **t. paprika**

DIRECTIONS

❶ Fry bacon in a pan until fully browned on both sides. Drain off fat and cover the bacon to keep warm.

❷ Poach eggs, cooking for about 2 minutes, or until the white of the egg is solid but the yolk remains runny.

❸ Prepare the Hollandaise sauce.

❹ Toast each English muffin, then place on the plate. Add a strip or two of Canadian bacon to each muffin half, then a poached egg on top, covering the stack with several spoonfuls of Hollandaise sauce.

❺ Garnish with a light sprinkle of paprika. Serve immediately.

YIELD: 4 servings.

COOKING TIP

Omnivore, Vegetarian and Pescatarian Benedicts

Closer to ham in flavor, texture and appearance, Canadian bacon is leaner and doesn't crisp in its own fat when cooking, so it works well for this dish. But Eggs Benedict can be easily modified to be vegetarian with a bed of fresh, sautéed spinach, Swiss chard (called Eggs Florentine) or thinly sliced avocados with fresh bean sprouts layered underneath the poached egg instead of the Canadian bacon. It can also incorporate other regional specialties, like smoked salmon or fresh crab.

Cocoa Pancakes

*J*OHN DRESSES THESE PANCAKES up with the raspberry sauce from the Raspberry French Toast recipe (page 33) and a light "snow sprinkle," as Liam calls it, otherwise known as powdered sugar sifted through a fine strainer. For easy breakfast fixings, premix the dry ingredients the night before.

INGREDIENTS

- 2 c. soy milk (plain, vanilla or chocolate)
- ⅓ c. sugar
- 1½ T. molasses
- 1 c. flour
- ¾ c. soy flour
- 2½ T. cocoa powder
- 1 t. baking powder
- ½ t. baking soda
- 4 T. maple syrup (optional)
- Fresh raspberries or strawberries (optional)
- 1 T. canola oil

DIRECTIONS

❶ In a large bowl, combine soy milk, sugar and molasses. Mix well.

❷ In a separate bowl, mix flours, cocoa, baking powder and baking soda.

❸ Gradually stir dry ingredients into soy milk mixture until a batter forms, thick but still smooth and able to be poured.

❹ Heat lightly oiled skillet over medium heat. Ladle about ¼ c. batter for each pancake. Cook about 2 minutes on each side, until lightly browned and bubbles start to form around edges.

❺ Serve pancakes immediately with maple syrup or with fresh fruit topping of strawberries or raspberries.

YIELD: 4 servings.

Eating with the fullest pleasure — pleasure, that is, that does not depend on ignorance — is perhaps the profoundest enactment of our connection to the world.

WENDELL BERRY, IN *WHAT ARE PEOPLE FOR?*

Fresh Tomato Breakfast Pie

*F*RESH TOMATO DEVOTEES ABOUND — but why don't we see more tomatoes on the breakfast table? You will in our farmhouse, thanks to this Fresh Tomato Breakfast Pie. Part quiche, part pizza, this treat readily accepts heirloom varieties of all shapes, sizes or colors. Definitely something meant for breakfast, this recipe is a summer standard that we fantasize about as the winter winds howl outside. As a recipe that desperately demands fresh tomatoes, don't attempt it in January.

CRUST INGREDIENTS

- ¾ c. flour
- ½ c. cornmeal
- ½ t. salt
- ⅓ c. butter (5⅓ T.)
- ¼ c. cold water
- ½ t. canola oil

FILLING INGREDIENTS

- 3 c. tomatoes, chopped (3 medium tomatoes)
- 1 t. salt
- 1 T. fresh basil, finely chopped (1 t. dried)
- ½ c. green onions, chopped
- ½ c. cheddar cheese, shredded
- ½ c. Swiss cheese, shredded
- 2 T. flour
- 1 c. evaporated milk
- 2 eggs
- 1 t. canola oil

DIRECTIONS

❶ Chop tomatoes and place in a colander. Let the tomatoes sit while you make and refrigerate the crust (see next step) to let some of the water drain from the tomatoes. This will make your crust less soggy.

❷ For the crust, in a mixing bowl, combine flour, cornmeal and salt. Cut in butter until crumbly. Add water, tossing with a fork until the dough forms a ball. You may need to add more water to provide enough moisture for a ball to be formed. Refrigerate for 30 minutes. You can also do this tomato and crust step the night before and refrigerate overnight for easy morning prep.

❸ On a lightly floured surface, roll out dough to fit in a 9-inch pie pan. Transfer pastry to a lightly oiled pie pan. Trim dough to ½ inch beyond edge of plate; flute edges. Bake at 375° for 10 minutes. Remove from oven and let cool completely.

❹ Place tomatoes in the crust; sprinkle with salt, basil, onions and cheeses. In a bowl, whisk flour, milk and eggs until smooth. Pour over filling. Bake at 375° for 40 to 45 minutes or until a knife inserted near the center comes out clean. Let stand for 10 minutes before cutting and serving. Top individual slices with a sprig of fresh basil or sprinkle of dried parsley.

YIELD: 6 servings.

Tofu Scrambler

V Vegan

G Gluten free

*T*OFU FALLS INTO its own special category; think of it as a neutral base, a nutrient-rich palette that readily soaks up other flavors. This scrambler showcases that idea with seasonings to wake up your taste buds. The texture closely resembles scrambled eggs, satisfying egg-lovers and vegans alike.

INGREDIENTS

- 1 T. olive oil
- 1 c. onion, chopped (about 1 medium)
- 2 cloves garlic, minced
- 2 c. bell peppers, chopped
- 2 t. dried thyme, crushed with fingers
- 2 t. cumin, ground
- 1 t. paprika
- 1 t. turmeric
- 1 t. salt
- ½ c. water
- 1 lb. extra-firm tofu, drained
- ⅓ c. nutritional yeast
- 1 c. salsa

DIRECTIONS

❶ To prepare veggies, sauté the onions and garlic in olive oil in a 6-inch skillet until tender. Add peppers and sauté until soft.

❷ In the skillet, stir in the thyme, cumin, paprika, turmeric, salt and water and mix well. Cook for 5 minutes.

❸ Crumble tofu into the veggie mixture and mix well. You want the tofu to remain chunky.

❹ Cook for 10 minutes over low heat, stirring occasionally and adding splashes of water if necessary to keep the mixture moist. Mix in the nutritional yeast.

❺ Add the salsa at the end, cooking for 2 more minutes until the salsa is heated through.

❻ Serve in ramekins or small bowls with a side of Oven Roasted Potatoes (see page 92).

YIELD: 3 servings.

You never change things by fighting the existing reality.
To change something, build a new model that
makes the existing model obsolete.

BUCKMINSTER FULLER

Curing Your Summertime Culinary Rut

Even with the fresh garden abundance that gifts us with a daily cornucopia of seasonal produce for ingredients, we can get into a culinary rut. We grow tired of the tossed salads while our zucchini and tomato harvest piles up on the kitchen counter. For CSA shareholders, it's often the reality of what to do with not one but ten daikon radishes. We feel overwhelmed. After all, the goal in growing our own food or supporting a CSA is to enjoy it, not make compost. Even the zucchini and green beans given away seem to find their way back in a potluck casserole. Others share our great problem. We need a fresh cooking groove.

We've learned that any artist needs time to rekindle a creative muse. We home-cooks (and gardeners) need a dose of cooking inspiration too, especially when we have a bounty of fresh fare to savor.

Here are three tips to cure any summer cooking rut that ails you:

1. Flip Savory and Sweet

Twist the expected menu and serve a familiar item category in a new way. For example, most folks expect pancakes to be bread-like and sweet, swimming in a pool of syrup. Zucchini Feta Pancakes provide a savory alternative to traditional pancake fare, served "naked" with no syrup or toppings. While we serve these for breakfast, you could readily twist things further and serve them for a quick supper.

2. Add a Strong Companion Flavor

Adding in a distinct, unexpected flavor to a dish perks up the palette. The fennel in the Savory Frittata or acidic kick from the salsa in the Tofu Scrambler showcases flavors unexpected on the breakfast table.

3. Blend in Fresh Company

Sometimes it isn't the ingredients or the recipe that grows a bit stale. It's the company around the table. Add a splash of newness around the table and share the summer garden abundance by inviting someone new over to share a meal. Living in the country with near weekly potlucks along with the B&B activities, we're blessed with a daily dose of interesting and inspiring people coming through our kitchen, providing the ultimate in keeping life, and food, fresh.

Savory Zucchini Bake

ZUCCHINI SHOWS UP in multiple forms on our breakfast table during peak harvest season. We try to see how many different ways we can prepare zucchini, since it's best fresh. We've learned to experiment, trying everything from tempura to this savory bake. That doesn't mean, however, we won't stick a few zucchini in your car if the doors are left unlocked.... This dish also works well as an appetizer, cut into small pieces with a cookie cutter in whatever shape you fancy. Wheat-free baking mix versions make an easy adaptation for gluten-free dietary needs.

INGREDIENTS

- 3 c. zucchini, shredded (or other summer squash)
- 1 c. onion, chopped (about 1 medium)
- 1 c. quick baking mix (see recipe page 232)
- 2 garlic cloves, minced
- ½ c. hard granular cheese, grated (Parmesan)
- ½ t. salt
- 2 T. fresh parsley, chopped (optional)
- ½ t. seasoning salt
- 1 T. fresh oregano (½ t. dried)
- ½ c. canola oil
- 4 eggs, lightly beaten
  fresh parsley or chives (optional)

DIRECTIONS

❶ In a large bowl, combine zucchini, onion, baking mix, garlic, cheese, seasonings, oil and eggs. Pour into a lightly oiled 9 × 13-inch baking pan.

❷ Bake at 350° for 30 minutes or until golden brown. Let cool for several minutes.

❸ Serve in the shape of squares, hearts, stars or your favorite Pokémon character. Garnish with finely chopped parsley or chives on top.

YIELD: 8 servings.

Farmers are our heroes.

BE A LOCAL HERO
DRINK AND EAT LOCAL!
NATIVE OWNED AND OPERATED
OFFERING AN ARRAY OF LOCAL,
FRESH, AND HOMEMADE FOOD
ALONG WITH CRAFT BEERS,
WINES, AND SODAS. CHEERS!
100+ CRAFT BEERS

Frittata of Leeks

*W*HAT STARTED AS growing a few leeks just for Potato Leek Soup quickly evolved into a leek love affair. The sweetest and most delicately flavored of all onions, the tiny transplants that arrive by mail look like blades of grass. Don't be fooled, though. They can grow into hearty leeks the diameter of baseball bats. We harvest ours only after several frosts since each frost helps make them even sweeter. Keeping a bit of the soil on the leeks for storage come early November, we set them in plastic 5-gallon buckets in the basement where they'll readily keep through February.

INGREDIENTS

1½ c. potatoes, peeled and cubed (1 large potato)

3 c. leeks, cleaned and thinly sliced (1 large leek)

½ t. salt

3 eggs, lightly beaten

2 T. olive oil

½ c. hard granular cheese, grated (Parmesan)

1 egg yolk

1 T. olive oil

DIRECTIONS

❶ Bring a pot of water to a boil and add potatoes and leeks together. Cook over medium heat until potatoes are tender but still firm and leeks are soft, about 10 to 15 minutes, then drain.

❷ Mash the potatoes and leeks together in a bowl. Add salt and eggs and most of the cheese.

❸ Place 2 T. oil in an 8-inch baking dish. Place in the oven for just a minute or until the oil sizzles.

❹ Remove hot baking pan from oven, then pour the potato-leek mixture into the pan. Mix the remaining 1 T. oil with egg yolk and brush over potato-leek mixture.

❺ Sprinkle with remaining cheese and bake at 350° for about 20 minutes or until golden brown.

❻ Serve in pie-shaped wedges and garnish with a sprinkle of fresh chopped chives or dried parsley.

YIELD: 4 servings.

COOKING TIP

Cleaning Leeks
To clean leeks, cut in half and hold under cold running water while separating each of the layers of the leeks to rinse out any soil trapped between the layers.

OUR LOCAL HOMESCHOOL GROUP organized an enlightening potluck series one year: Reasons for the Seasons. We intended to explore and expose the kids to other cultural traditions and holidays that we might not otherwise encounter in our rural area, but quickly realized it's the food that ties us all together. From a Rosh Hashanah feast to a Cinco de Mayo fiesta, we came home inspired to add more cultural flavor to our kitchen. This latke recipe came from a compilation of an amazing number of Jewish grandmothers posting their varied techniques on the Web. The combinations of mashed with shredded potatoes gives the pancake its firm texture. We enjoy two variations of potato latkes, both traditionally served with sour cream and home-made applesauce. The first version is healthier since the pancakes are baked instead of fried. But a bumper potato crop one year along with some mid-winter cravings for fried comfort food led to the second version.

Baked Potato Pancakes

INGREDIENTS

- 2 t. canola oil
- 5 medium potatoes, peeled (about 5 c. when shredded)
- 1 c. onion, finely chopped (1 medium onion)
- ¼ c. flour
- 1 t. salt
- 2 eggs, lightly beaten
   applesauce and sour cream for toppings (optional)

DIRECTIONS

❶ Shred potatoes and onions. In a large bowl, combine onions, flour and salt. Toss with 2 forks to mix well or mix using clean hands.

❷ Drop heaping tablespoons of this mixture onto 2 lightly oiled baking sheets and press with spoon to make a flat pancake.

❸ Bake at 400° for 15 minutes or until pancakes are golden brown on bottom. Flip the pancakes over, switch positions of baking sheets and bake for about another 10 minutes, or until golden brown on both sides.

❹ Serve immediately, garnished with a dollop of sour cream or applesauce.

YIELD: 5 servings.

Fried Potato Latkes

INGREDIENTS

2   medium potatoes, peeled and cubed (about 2 c.). You can also use 2 c. of leftover mashed potatoes.

3   medium potatoes, peeled (about 3 c. when shredded)

1   medium onion, shredded (about 1 c.)

2   eggs, lightly beaten

3   T. flour

4   T. cornmeal

1   t. salt

6   T. vegetable oil
    applesauce and sour cream for toppings (optional)

DIRECTIONS

❶ Bring a pot of water to a boil and add cubed potatoes. Cook potatoes until tender but still firm, about 10 to 15 minutes. Drain and mash.

❷ Shred remaining 3 potatoes and onion.

❸ In a large bowl, mix shredded potatoes, mashed potatoes and shredded onion. Add eggs, flour, cornmeal and salt; mix well. Feel consistency of the dough; mixture should hold together without being sticky. If it sticks to your hands, add more flour until dough is no longer sticky.

❹ In a large skillet over medium heat (or electric fry pan), warm enough oil to cover ¼ inch deep. When hot, drop mixture by heaping tablespoon to oil; flatten with a spatula and cook on both sides until golden brown.

❺ Serve immediately, garnished with a dollop of sour cream on top or a side of applesauce.

YIELD: 5 servings.

Food is our common ground, a universal experience.

JAMES BEARD

Winter Squash Quiche

*I*N A WORLD where the majority of restaurant ingredients namelessly fall off the Sysco truck, it's hard to find the story — much less the flavor — behind our food. Everything may be cut, processed and packaged to perfection, but we're losing the connection to what's real. In most parts of our country, you can get carefully stored winter squash directly from the farmers, if not from your root cellar or a cool corner of your own basement. Celebrate fall flavors with this Winter Squash Quiche, a fabulous recipe for beginning cooks since it doesn't have (or need) a crust. Just mix up the ingredients and pour it into the pan.

INGREDIENTS

2   T. onion, chopped

1   T. canola oil

2   c. Swiss cheese, shredded

1½ c. milk

3   eggs, lightly beaten

1   c. winter squash purée

¼   t. salt

⅛   t. nutmeg

DIRECTIONS

❶ In a skillet, sauté onion in oil until tender. Transfer to a lightly oiled 9-inch pie plate. Sprinkle with cheese.

❷ In a large bowl, whisk milk, squash, eggs, salt and nutmeg until smooth. Pour over cheese.

❸ Bake at 325° for 50 to 60 minutes or until a knife inserted near the center comes out clean.

❹ To serve, cut into pie-shaped wedges and sprinkle with a dash of paprika on top.

YIELD: 5 servings.

Kitchen Garden Quiche

*R*EAL MEN NOT ONLY eat quiche, they make it. At least that's the tempting kitchen scene in our home where John is the king of crusts and quiches. There's nothing like harvesting fresh vegetables, adding some collected eggs from the hens (if you have one or two) and stirring in rich cream to make a quiche. This dish is not just for breakfast; try it for dinner, paired with a fresh salad.

INGREDIENTS

One 9-inch prepared pie crust (see page 180)
½ lb. melting cheese (cheddar, mozzarella, fontina, or Swiss)
1 clove garlic, minced
1 c. broccoli florets, chopped (or other seasonal veggie)
3 eggs
1½ c. half & half cream
⅛ t. nutmeg
⅛ t. salt
1 c. Swiss chard or spinach, chopped and sautéed

DIRECTIONS

❶ Sauté garlic with vegetables on medium heat for about 5 to 7 minutes, until vegetables are tender.

❷ In a large bowl, beat eggs and combine with cream, nutmeg and salt. Add shredded melting cheeses.

❸ Pour mixture into a 9-inch pie pan with crust dough in place. Do not over fill pan to prevent your creation from over flowing in your oven.

❹ Bake at 375° until filling is puffed up and golden brown, about 30 to 35 minutes.

❺ Remove from oven and either serve cut wedges immediately hot or let cool to room temperature.

YIELD: 4 servings.

Mosquitoes remind us that we are not as high up on the food chain as we think.

TOM WILSON

DELIVERING THE DIVERSE TASTES OF THE SEASONS

**Jai and Joel Kellum,
King's Hill Farm,
Mineral Point, Wisconsin**

A flock of turkeys perch on the railing along the steps leading up to the front door of Jai and Joel Kellum's house at King's Hill Farm, located about an hour's drive northwest of our place. It's a farm seeped in diversity: of crops, animals, people and approaches to living closer to the land.

Chickens, ducks and geese roam in a field behind the house while a bunch of kids dart behind a teepee, our son not far behind. Two pigs root around in a pasture, along with a llama and a goat. Their dogs manage to keep the wildlife out of the crops and away from the livestock — in itself a remarkable feat. A cadre of farm interns has gathered in a kitchen on the lower level of the house, putting the final touches on whatever dish they're planning to pass for the potluck. There's oven-roasted acorn squash with a wild rice filling, an Indian curry with peas and potatoes and loaves of multigrain harvest breads. In their packing shed, the Kellums' son, Cedar, is jamming with his yet to be named band — a name we've been invited to come up with.

It was our fifth visit to Jai and Joel's certified organic farm and definitely a most delicious one given the autumn harvest potluck at hand. We dragged along our deep fryer to share some winter squash fritters. Every spring, we usually swing by King's Hill to pick up some transplants and check on the progress of their "edible forest."

Despite the abundance of animals, the farm is most known for its beautiful, high-quality fresh vegetables, delivered to more than 140 CSA shareholders. They also sell their produce at two farmers markets from June through October: the Green City Market and Glenwood Sunday Market, both in Chicago. In all, the farm feeds over 700 people each year on about 40 acres of rented cropland, a 7-acre food forest and an acre of woods where more than 1,300 logs are inoculated with spores to produce hundreds of pounds of shiitake mushrooms every year.

The feathered animals, as it turns out, are prolific egg layers (one of the special add-ons available to CSA shareholders or at market) and an important part of how the Kellums care for their land. The animals meander about freely, eating insects. Or they're relocated to work up the soil in their fields or inside the Kellums' two greenhouses before next year's transplants get started. Of course, they provide plenty of manure, too. The farm is buffered by more than 790 acres that are largely woods, pasture and set-aside lands in the Conservation Reserve Program (CRP).

"We're trying to get as close to sustainable as we can," smiled Jai, wearing a sunhat that covers most of her tanned arms when we arrived in late May to pick up our transplants. "We grow over a hundred different cultivars of vegetables alone. Plus we have nut trees, fruit trees, herbs and small fruit bushes. When we certified our edible forest as organic, they said we had more species of plants than any other farm they've certified."

Much of King's Hill Farm's growing fields employ alley cropping. Guided by Joel, the farm manager, they're contouring the land in a way that naturally promotes swales and ridges within the landscape where annuals grow next to perennials. As the trees and bushes mature, they'll deliver years of fruits and nuts — a seasonal cornucopia of fresh ingredients. They believe that providing a regular diet of seasonal foods and vegetables does more for developing minds and bodies than does an occasional purchase of California-grown organic spring mesclun.

"The land was organic and the ideas were already here," explains Joel, who, if you get him going, will have you pulling up a chair and hastily taking notes. "All that was required was some molding and patience. Failure balanced with success is the perfect recipe for 'Keep Going For It Farm Pie.'" He's wise beyond his years, but not content to rest on his laurels. We wouldn't be surprised to visit one day when their place is powered by the wind.

In the spring, the floor of their edible forest supports an early harvest of plants that take advantage of the yet undeveloped forest canopy. By mid-summer, hickory, hazelnuts, wild cherries, apples and plums will ripen, each to be harvested according to their own calendar. Ten beehives, besides yielding honey harvested for sale, are home to thriving colonies of these very important pollinators. Diverse and interconnected, the design of the farm is inspired by permaculture, something that Joel has received certification in, not so much to teach it as to draw from this knowledge base to help create a more viable and ecologically sound operation.

Few secrets are kept for long on King's Hill Farm, with Joel and Jai welcoming as many as seven farm interns every year, along with volunteers, short-term helpers, school groups and even some hard-working local Amish teenagers. The full-season interns work, eat and sleep onsite and take on just about every task imaginable over the course of the summer.

"It's the best way to give people a feel for what goes into farming," admits Jai. "We want them to have a clue as to what they're getting into. It's a lot of hard work with little result, at least early on in the season before things really get growing. We do everything we can to give them a taste of what farming is, whether they end up growing what they eat themselves or grow to feed others and sell at market." It's a recipe that has worked well for the couple, having gotten their start more than a decade ago as interns at Prairie Dock Farm in Watertown, Wisconsin.

Before arriving to King's Hill Farm, Joel and Jai became acquainted with the harsh new realities of

Teepee at King's Hill Farm.

farming on a warming planet at their first farm located about two hours north. "We operated quite successfully as Avalanche Organics for about nine years," explains Jai. "Then the floods hit our fields along the Kickapoo River over and over again. There are always risks in farming, having to deal with Mother Nature's droughts, storms and pest issues. Farmers and others in the area kept saying 'This is the 100-year flood' and 'This is the 500-year flood.' After these events unfolded year after year, we needed to adapt. With the third and worst flood in 2007, we started looking for another place." On a ridge with no threat of rising water, King's Hill it was.

Joel and Jai taste what they grow, perhaps the ultimate test for any farmer, something most commodity or chemical farmers can't even do. "I love preparing meals with fresh food," beams Jai. "My favorite is picking kale and walking it right into the kitchen. After a quick wash, the kale is tossed in a hot pan and sautéed with some onions. I don't use recipes much, just as guidelines when cooking. I love taking whatever's fresh at the time and combining them to make a seasonally inspired meal." She's a true farmstead chef.

"With all our interns and visitors, including some from as far away as France and Russia this past year, we get such an opportunity to taste the ways everyone cooks and prepares fresh from the fields," Jai continues. "Because we're often eating with a large group of people, our lunches are quite an experience, never eaten on the fly."

French Onion Soup with Shiitake Mushrooms

JONATHAN FAGAN, one of the full-season interns at King's Hill Farm, devised this vegetarian version of the traditional French onion soup, incorporating their delectable shiitake mushrooms to add the rich umami flavor to the sweetness of their yellow storage onions. No beef stock needed. "Music, people and food all have something in common," says Jonathan, summing up his take on life. "If you spend enough time around them in the right setting, you'll come to like them and miss them, should they no longer be a part in your life."

INGREDIENTS

- 4 c. fresh shiitake mushroom caps, thinly sliced, stems removed (½ lb.)
- 4 large onions, yellow or white (2½ lbs.)
- ¼ c. butter (½ stick)
- ¼ c. dry sherry
- 4 c. vegetable stock
- ½ t. salt
- ½ t. pepper
- ½ c. Gruyère cheese, grated
- ½ c. croutons (see recipe page 230)

DIRECTIONS

❶ Peel onions and slice in half. Then slice again into ⅛-inch slivers (not chopped).

❷ Melt butter into the bottom of a 4-quart pot, then add sliced onions, stirring to coat the onions. Let it sit at medium heat with lid on for 5 minutes. Then remove lid, stirring once again to begin to caramelize the onions to a very dark brown color, but not burnt.

❸ Turn the heat to medium-low, then for approximately 1 hour simmer the onions while stirring every 10 minutes to coat them in the butter. If the onions are not carmelizing, turn up the heat slightly but be careful not to burn them.

❹ When onions are almost completely caramelized, stir in the mushrooms and let simmer for about 5 minutes until mixture exudes the earthy aromas of the mushrooms.

❺ Add sherry wine. Simmer on medium heat for about 3 minutes, stirring occasionally as the sherry vaporizes. Then add vegetable stock and bring to a boil. Stir in salt and pepper to taste then turn down heat to keep soup warm for serving.

❻ To serve, divide soup evenly and ladle into four bowls. Top the soup in each bowl with croutons and grated Gruyère cheese, divided evenly among the bowls.

YIELD: 4 servings.

Caramelizing Onions

The magic of this beef-less French Onion Soup is the earthy flavor of the shiitake mushrooms when combined with the sweetness of the caramelized onions. When the onions start to appear evenly light brown and stringy, they are starting to caramelize properly. Too much stirring at this point and they will never heat up enough; too little stirring and they will burn and you will start to see browning stuck to the bottom of the pan. Blackened onions will make the soup bitter, but don't panic if they burn a little; just add some water and stir with a wooden spoon and try to reincorporate the sugars, allowing the water to simmer off.

Baked Omelet Roll

*T*HIS BAKED OMELET ROLL provides a "base" for various breakfast dishes, from slicing the roll into "noodles" to cutting out flat rectangular slices and serving it as a layered "breakfast lasagna." We like the "egg roll" twist with a Hollandaise sauce, though it requires a couple of extra steps right before serving. It's worth the effort.

INGREDIENTS

1   c. onion, chopped (1 medium onion)

2   cloves garlic, minced

5   c. mixed veggies, chopped (any combo of spinach, broccoli, bell peppers, summer squash work)

½   t. salt

6   eggs

½   c. flour

1   c. milk

1   T. fresh dill, crumbled (1 t. dried)

1   c. cheese (cheddar or mozzarella), shredded

1   c. Hollandaise sauce (see recipe page 104)

1   t. canola oil

DIRECTIONS

❶ To prepare veggies, sauté onions and garlic until onions are translucent and lightly browned. Add spinach, broccoli, bell peppers, zucchini and other vegetables of choice. Season with salt and dill. Set aside.

❷ In a large bowl, beat eggs until frothy, then beat in flour until smooth. Finally, add milk and salt and beat egg mixture until well-blended.

❸ Pour egg mixture into a lightly oiled 9 × 13-inch baking pan. Bake at 450° for 20 minutes or until eggs are set and top is puffed and golden brown. Remove from oven. Don't panic when the puffed egg dish quickly settles and flattens out — that's normal.

❹ Cut egg layer into approximately three 4-inch-by-9-inch slices. "Flip" slice upside down onto a temporary plate (not final serving plate) so that the golden-brown side will eventually show on the outside of the egg roll.

❺ Place cooked veggies evenly down center of roll. Sprinkle shredded cheese on top. Roll up from narrow end and place egg roll seam-side down on the same temporary plate. Place in warm oven (or microwave) until cheese melts.

❻ Transfer egg roll to serving plate and top with Hollandaise sauce and a sprinkle of paprika on top for garnish.

YIELD: 4 servings.

COOKING TIP

Transform the egg roll into a meat-lovers delicacy by adding ½ lb. cooked ground pork sausage (drain off excess fat) to the vegetables.

Applicious Pancakes

*I*N OCTOBER we always experience a couple of weeks of apple abundance when we're canning applesauce, baking pies, dehydrating apple snacks and crunching on apple slices in between. That's when we whip out this apple pancake recipe since it tastes best when using fresh crispy apples. Any apple varieties will work, so choose what you like best.

INGREDIENTS

1	c. flour
1	T. sugar
½	t. salt
2	eggs
1	c. milk
1	T. canola oil
4	c. apples, peeled and finely chopped (about 6 large apples)
4	T. maple syrup
1	T. powdered sugar

DIRECTIONS

❶ In a large bowl, combine flour, sugar and salt.

❷ In a separate bowl, beat eggs and add milk and oil.

❸ Gradually stir dry ingredients into egg mixture until a batter forms, thick but still smooth and pourable.

❹ Fold in apples.

❺ Heat lightly oiled skillet over medium heat. With a ladle, drop about ¼ c. batter for each pancake. Spread batter with back of spoon. Cook about 2 minutes on each side, until lightly browned and starting to bubble on edges.

❻ Serve with maple syrup and a dusting of powdered sugar.

YIELD: 4 servings.

"Granolaheads" Crunch

A WRITER ONCE DESCRIBED Inn Serendipity as a place that has such a "1960s feel to it that one half expects to find Mamma Cass crooning in the fruit cellar." *Newsweek* magazine pronounced us "granolaheads." But neither of us were raised in a Volkswagon Westfalia camper van or by hippie parents. We came of age in the early 1990s and entered the job market post-college. Staring at credit card bills and cubicle walls, however, we discovered our inner hippie—and granola. We closeted our power suits and plotted our rural escape, envisioning a lifestyle based on peace, love and duct tape. A place where independence and self-sufficiency trumped The Donald or Gordon Gekko. Cue the granola experiments, resulting in this house favorite that gets sprinkled over yogurt or quite often simply eaten by the handful.

INGREDIENTS

8 c. whole oats
1 c. chopped nuts (peanuts work great)
½ c. sesame seeds
1 c. wheat germ
1 c. flax seed, ground
⅔ c. vegetable oil
½ c. honey
½ c. brown sugar, packed
2 T. water
1 T. vanilla extract (see recipe, page 233)
1 c. raisins (or any dried fruit; optional)
1 t. canola oil

DIRECTIONS

❶ In a large bowl, combine oats, nuts, sesame seeds, wheat germ and flax seed.

❷ In a saucepan over medium heat, simmer oil, honey, brown sugar and water until well-mixed. Do not boil. Remove from heat and stir in vanilla. Pour honey mixture over oat mixture and stir to coat evenly.

❸ Pour into two lightly oiled 9 × 13-inch baking pans. Bake at 275° for 50 to 60 minutes or until golden brown, stirring every 15 minutes. Keep a careful eye on the granola during the final baking period—it can easily burn. Add raisins after you remove from oven.

❹ Stir the granola occasionally as it cools. Store in an airtight container.

YIELD: 8 cups.

No Sugar Coating It

We use sugar in our cooking. When our recipes call for granular, brown or powdered sugar, we use certified organic Florida Crystals sugar made from evaporated sugar cane juice from sugar cane that's grown and harvested in the US; the company is also certified carbon neutral by the Carbon Fund.org. We also use sugar from Wholesome Sweeteners. In *Little House on the Prairie*, Ma used to go down to the Olson's Mercantile to purchase "store boughten sugar," the bleached white stuff, a perceived sign then, and still today, of higher quality or better purity—in fact, the white of sugar (or flour) comes from the harsh chemicals and processing that make it that way. We also opt to use local sweeteners like honey and maple syrup as much as possible; don't be afraid to try alternative sweeteners like sorghum molasses, brown rice syrup or stevia if it's available near you.

Just Can It: Preserving the Harvest

What do you do when you've given away all the zucchini from your gardens that your neighbors can handle? Or perhaps you belong to a CSA that hosts a pesto-making party before the first frost, resulting in buckets of the fragrant green sauce. What then?

Just preserve it. Savor your abundance during the winter months by freezing or canning your fruits, veggies and herbs. The key is picking the freshest, most ripe produce — whether from a farmers market, your CSA box or your backyard plot — and getting them processed as quickly as possible.

Food preservation is more about recipes and techniques than years of training. It gives us time together in the kitchen with time-proven crafts — and saves us thousands of dollars on food costs. Most of our food preservation efforts are devoted to freezing, canning and cold storage. Like so many things in our life, preserving foods is balanced with our enjoyment of cooking and eating seasonally.

Savoring the fruits and vegetables that ripen throughout the growing season keeps our meals, tastes and attitudes fresh, diverse and creative. Because we eat a mostly vegetarian diet, we haven't done much preserving of meat or fish, though freezing it is the simplest approach.

While there is a wide variety of ways to preserve food, the one thing that unites them is their relatively low-tech approach. The following are a few of the methods we use to "put up" food — and a few tips to prevent you from going overboard. Unlike a fine aged wine or cheese, frozen foods don't get better with time.

Go for the "low-hanging fruit" first: cold storage or root cellaring. For winter squash, cooking pumpkins, onions and garlic, it doesn't get any easier than this: just place the harvested vegetables in a cool, dry place, away from the sunlight. Some produce requires different amounts of humidity. For effective cold storage, the temperature needs to be kept between 35–45 degrees, otherwise your potatoes may start sprouting if too warm, for example. In our old farmhouse, we can store potatoes, turnips, apples, beets and carrots in the corner of our basement. The north wall of our first floor works just fine for storing garlic, onions, pumpkins and winter squash because of the drier and warmer conditions (we keep a rather cool 62-degree house in the winter).

Freeze it. Freezing is another relatively easy option to preserve your produce. If you're quick to point out that a freezer takes energy to run, you're right. But so does simmering sauces, sanitizing jars and doing hot water baths — often during the heat waves of July and August — if you're canning. Certain foods, like strawberries, tomatoes or peppers, just need to be cleaned, set on trays and frozen whole (or cut into slices, in the case of peppers). Other foods, like spinach, Swiss chard and broccoli, need to be blanched first, to prevent the enzymes from ripening further, locking in flavors, nutritional value and color. Just because produce may freeze well, however, doesn't mean you can serve it the same way you might if it was just picked from the vine. So our frozen strawberries only go into fruit smoothies and daiquiris and our sugar snap peapods get cooked into pad

Thai. Fresh and frozen fresh are not the same thing when it comes to texture and taste.

By November of each year, our freezer is packed full with foods that will sustain us until June of the following year. Every year we freeze spinach, tomatoes, Swiss chard, apple slices, grape juice, raspberries, strawberries, broccoli, green beans, summer squash, sweet peas and rhubarb. This is in addition to prepared foods that also freeze well, like many of the soups and nibbles found in this cookbook.

Have a plan, before you can. Before you harvest buckets of cucumbers or pile the tomatoes on the counter, make sure you have the ingredients you need for whatever it is you may be canning. Canning involves using a boiling-water bath to destroy microorganisms and create a vacuum seal around the lid of the jar to prevent any remaining bacteria from reproducing. It requires sturdy canning jars, specially designed canning jar lids and choosing the method best suited for the acidity level of the food. We use the boiling-water bath method to can high-acid foods like pears, applesauce, salsa and pickled cucumbers. The combination of acidity and heat kills the harmful bacteria. Low-acid foods (most vegetables) must be pressure canned. Remember, though, the more you cook something the fewer the nutrients.

Check out the *Ball Blue Book Guide to Preserving*, Janet Chadwick's *The Busy Person's Guide to Food Preserving* or Carol Hupping's *Stocking Up: The Third Edition of the Classic Preserving Guide* for more details. All are accurate quick reference guides to put up foods for when the snow flies.

Out to dry. We line-dry our laundry, so why not our food? Drying, whether by air, sun or oven, is another simple means of storing foods and helps retain more nutrients than most other preserving options because the nutrients aren't cooked out. The goal is to remove the moisture from the foods so that the bacteria, molds and yeast that might cause the food to spoil cannot grow. Almost anything can be dried. Unless you're eating dehydrated foods as snacks, you'll need to rehydrate them before or while you're cooking.

Savor fresh, too. Sometimes we can get so overwhelmed by trying to keep up with the basil, we forget to eat it fresh. Balance pesto-making fiestas with delighting in a mozzarella sandwich with fresh basil leaves on top.

Experiment and ferment. Try your hand at fermenting pickles made with a homemade brine solution. A traditional food preservation method, fermentation can involve the use of yeasts to transform sugar into alcohol to make beer, for example. The use of certain bacteria creates lactic acid in some foods like sauerkraut. Fermentation allows foods to be stored while creating their distinctive flavors. Dill pickles, kimchee and soy sauce are all fermented. If this sounds like fun, check out our Kitchen Table Talk with Todd and Jordan Champagne (page 105) or Sandor Katz's book, *Wild Fermentation*.

Don't try to do it all in one year. Processing can be a demanding process, especially canning, so set aside some time if you're going to can a batch of pickles. That said, when you're canning, you won't be making just one jar, so there's economies of scale here that make it worth every bit of the effort. For more on fermentation and canning, and just about any other aspect of cooking and ingredient selection, check out *The New Food Lover's Companion* by Sharon Tyler Herbst or canningacrossamerica.com.

Raspberry Cream Cheese French Toast

*A*N IMPORTANT LESSON when cooking for kids: Call it what it is. The first time we hosted a family, we rightly thought this recipe would be a creamy, sweet, fruity treat, welcomed by the kids. The problem arose when we called it "French Toast"; the kids expected exactly that: A slice of plain bread dipped in egg batter and grilled, not the layers of raspberries and cream cheese on their plate. We learn fast. The next time we prepared this recipe for a family, we called it "Breakfast Cake"; the kids cheered in delight and ate the whole thing. This recipe makes a large batch to feed a hungry crowd of twelve. You can easily cut it half and bake it in an 8 × 8 pan for smaller groups.

FRENCH TOAST INGREDIENTS

½   t. canola oil
1   pkg. cream cheese (8 oz.)
8   c. fresh 1-inch bread cubes (about ½ loaf bread)
1   c. raspberries (or blueberries)
12 eggs
½   c. maple syrup
2   c. milk

SAUCE INGREDIENTS

1   c. sugar
2   T. cornstarch
1   c. water
1   c. raspberries (or blueberries)
1   T. butter

DIRECTIONS

❶ Place bread cubes in a lightly oiled 9 × 13-inch baking pan.

❷ Dot bread with scoops of cream cheese.

❸ Mix raspberries, eggs, syrup and milk and pour evenly over bread.

❹ Cover and refrigerate overnight.

❺ The next day, bake at 350° for 30 minutes, covered with foil. Then remove foil and cook for an additional 30 minutes uncovered.

❻ For the sauce, mix sugar, cornstarch and water in saucepan. Lightly boil until thick. Add berries and butter and cook again until warm and thick.

❼ Serve immediately, cutting the French toast into 3-inch squares with the raspberry sauce drizzled over the top of each square.

YIELD: 12 servings.

COOKING TIP

Leftover sauce?
This versatile raspberry sauce works well on chocolate cake or ice cream.

Savory Frittata

V Vegan

G Gluten free

*T*HE FENNEL, ROSEMARY AND TURMERIC give breakfast a dash of unexpected flavor. These flavors infuse a taste of place, something memorable that lingers long after the meal ends. This hearty breakfast is ideal for people dedicated to a vegan diet or need to go gluten-free, but worth a try as an adventurous alternative for anyone growing tired of eggs and sausage in the morning.

INGREDIENTS

- 2 c. potatoes, peeled and cubed (2 medium potatoes)
- 2 c. mixed veggies, chopped (any combo of broccoli, bell peppers, summer squash work)
- 1 c. onion, chopped
- 2 cloves garlic, minced
- 1 t. canola oil
- ½ t. salt
- ½ t. fennel seed
- 1 T. rosemary (1 t. dried)
- 1 lb. extra-firm tofu, drained
- ¾ c. water
- 1 T. arrowroot powder or 1 ½ T. cornstarch
- 2 t. nutritional yeast
- ⅛ t. turmeric

DIRECTIONS

❶ Steam potatoes until cooked through but firm enough to retain shape.

❷ To prepare veggies, sauté onions and garlic. Then add broccoli, peppers, summer squash and other vegetables of choice. Mix in salt, fennel and rosemary.

❸ In a blender, blend tofu, water, arrowroot, yeast and turmeric until smooth. Add more water as needed.

❹ In a large bowl, gently combine tofu mixture, potatoes and veggies.

❺ Pour mixture into a lightly oiled 8 × 8-inch baking dish and place baking dish into larger dish (a 9 × 13-inch baking pan works well), filled with several inches of water. Bake uncovered at 375° for about 50 minutes or until mixture is firm and lightly browned.

❻ Serve with a sprinkle of parsley and a side of salsa.

YIELD: 4 servings.

One of the greatest gifts you can give to the planet is to choose to become vegetarian, or even better, a vegan.

JULIA BUTTERFLY HILL

BREADS

Applesauce Muffins

Pear Ginger Muffins

Cocoa Muffins (vegan)

Winter Squash Spice Muffins

Cinnamon Raisin Biscuits (vegan)

Apple Coffee Cake

Peanut Butter Pumpkin Bread

Blueberry Crumb Coffee Cake

Zucchini Muffins

Chocolate Zucchini Bread

Oven-roasted Garlic for Bread Spread (vegan)

Winter Squash Fritters

Cheese Straws

French Baguette (vegan)

English Muffins

Potato Rolls

No-knead Dutch Oven Artisan Bread (vegan) (Roger Doiron)

Winter Squash Rolls

Homemade Pitas and Pita Chips (vegan)

Kneading Sustainability

My wife had me long before hello — or good morning. The aroma of freshly baked muffins will do it every time.

Like scents wafting through the house, beckoning us to the breakfast table, the concept of sustainability appeals to our sense of personal responsibility, accounting for how we live, treat others and make a living in relation to the planet that nurtures us. Trusting intuition and our personal experience, drawing more from our experiential knowledge than an overload of facts or figures, leads us to recognize that we're a vital part of the web of life. This ecological connection helps us become better stewards and eaters.

Sustainability is an ideal, a moving target, something we're always working toward and improving upon. It touches not just on food and agriculture, but energy use, land stewardship, transportation and waste — recognizing that we live within an interdependent and interconnected living system. Organic farmers know this, motivated less by profits and more by nourishing fellow beings while simultaneously restoring and improving the soil, water and air. In practice, sustainable living is less about the growth of property, wealth or stuff and more about valuing diversity and cultivating a passion for restoration. It's about creating local livable communities and fostering greater social and economic equity while preserving, and ideally restoring, the ecosystems upon which we depend for our very survival.

Our personal knowledge is not the same thing as "common knowledge," the flow of sound bites from "experts" in the media or government. The vast majority of food imported into the US has never been inspected. Thousands of chemicals, many approved for use in food products by the US FDA, have conten-

tious and often-conflicting research studies associated with them. But farmsteadtarians tend to operate under a version of the precautionary principle: when in doubt about what's in it or where it's from, don't eat it. We don't need to prove its harm before we take evasive action. There are more than 80,000 chemicals which are not fully studied or not studied at all, according to Urvashi Rangan at the Consumers Union, publisher of *Consumer Reports*. "Freedom" is not the fifty brands of cereal on the supermarket shelf — it's understanding exactly what we're eating; knowing that it's nourishing and safe; that it was harvested by fairly paid workers who didn't have to don a gas mask to work in the field.

While we can live more self-reliantly, we cannot live independently. Nature thrives on interdependences, with different species filling niches and maintaining symbiotic relationships. Our human species is not apart from this natural order, but a key part of it. Our life depends on several inches of topsoil with plenty of earthworms and micro-organisms, some sunlight and enough rain. Without the honeybees for pollination, about a third of all our food crops would be dust. Without enough rain, ditto.

There's no way around it, sustainability cannot be used in the same sentence as development, infinite growth and rampant consumerism, upon which the present global economy is based. Sustainable agriculture, then, closes ecological loops; restores and improves topsoil, air and water; localizes production; and respects farmers, rather than exploiting them. Robert Rodale, founder of the Rodale Institute, called it "regenerative agriculture." Those corporations proclaiming that we can "produce more, conserve more" are counting on enough people who have lost their connection to the land and those who work it to mask their profit motives and the kind of agriculture they foster instead: chemical-laden, large-scale, oil-addicted, genetically modified, industrial.

When baking, kneading is the step where it's all hands-on. You're turning over the dough, working it to make it more flexible and helping to distribute the yeast and other ingredients to form gluten, giving bread its texture and elasticity. There's no exact start or end time to kneading. It's done when you say so. Some of us will work vigorously and have a rhythmic technique, while others excel at pushing around the pile of flour and water for seemingly an eternity. Either way, kneading could be likened to mixing a pallet of watercolors — based on the eye of the beholder. Like sustainability. We know we need it, but how we get there is in our hands (as opposed to corporations or the government).

Most recipes are approximations — a pinch here and a dash there. Everyone has a different palate and preferences for sweet, sour, bitter, salty and savory. If you don't care for the hot, acrid taste of horseradish, just try the recipe without it.

But baking is different — it demands exact measurements. Otherwise the bread won't rise, yeast won't react, and those glutens go flat. Not all recipes in this chapter have this trait, but some do.

Any way you bake it, the planet needs us as much as we need her. We're a part of the tapestry of life, as imperfect or immeasurable as it may be.

Applesauce Muffins

*C*ALL US THE Johnny Appleseed of muffin distribution. Where Johnny planted orchards as he wandered Ohio, we scatter muffins, sending some home with guests or dropped off with friends in town. There's something about giving away things unexpectedly that instigates change. Drop a seed and something might grow. Give a friend a muffin and maybe they'll linger and talk over a cup of coffee. These Applesauce Muffins blend Johnny Appleseed inspiration in bread form. Bake some and share.

INGREDIENTS

1   t. canola oil
2   c. flour
½   T. cinnamon
½   T. allspice
1   t. baking soda
½   c. butter, softened (1 stick)
1   c. sugar
1   egg
1   c. applesauce
1   T. vanilla extract
½   c. raisins

DIRECTIONS

❶ Lightly oil 12 standard muffin cups.

❷ In a large bowl, combine flour, cinnamon, allspice and baking soda.

❸ In another bowl, cream butter and sugar. Beat in eggs, applesauce and vanilla. Stir into dry ingredients until just moistened. Fold in raisins.

❹ Fill prepared muffin cups almost full.

❺ Bake at 350° for 20 to 25 minutes or until a toothpick comes out clean. Let cool for about 10 minutes before removing from pan and placing on wire rack.

YIELD: 12 muffins.

COOKING TIP

Stocking your Pantry with Organic Flour

By buying bulk bags of organic flour (and sugar) through a local buying club or food cooperative, we never run out and we save money. Our organic flour comes from Heartland Mills, a farmer-owned company based in Kansas; it's unbleached and un-enriched. Typical commercial processing of wheat into white flour extracts a lot of the good nutrients; therefore, the millers have to chemically add back in the nutrients, hence enriching the flour. Enriched flour breaks down faster in your body causing elevated blood sugar levels. Organic flour companies like Heartland Mills use minimal processing, therefore they don't need to enrich and add the good stuff back in. The flour (and sugar) can be used as a one-for-one replacement for refined sugar or enriched flour in any recipe.

Pear Ginger Muffins

*B*ECOME A FRUIT FORAGER wherever you may live. Every early September, Mary Frantz calls us: "The pears are ripe. Come pick." Retired doctors, Mary and her husband John live in town and keep up the most prolific backyard urban homestead we've ever seen. They have more pears than they know what to do with, and we're happy to put the fruit to good use. We bet there's probably a tree you see every year in a yard near your home that overflows with fruit. Be a forager and rekindle community relationships by knocking on the door of its owner and ask to pick the tree; chances are your neighbors will be thrilled to know the fruit is going to good use rather than rotting on the ground. Then pay it forward. Return after the harvest bearing fruit pies or muffins to share, and you'll come to embrace the grace that results from your community's abundance. These muffins pair ginger with fresh pears, creating a fall flavor that can only be savored during the harvest season.

INGREDIENTS

- 1 t. canola oil
- 2 c. flour
- ½ c. brown sugar, firmly packed
- 2 t. ginger
- 1 t. baking soda
- 1 t. cinnamon
- 1½ c. fresh pears, peeled and finely chopped
- ½ c. raisins
- ½ t. salt
- ⅛ t. nutmeg
- ⅛ t. cloves
- 1 egg
- 1 c. plain yogurt
- ½ c. vegetable oil
- 3 T. molasses

DIRECTIONS

❶ Lightly oil 18 standard muffin cups.

❷ In a large bowl, combine the first ten ingredients. In another bowl, beat the egg, yogurt, oil and molasses until smooth.

❸ Stir the wet ingredients into the dry ingredients until just moistened. Fold in pears and raisins.

❹ Fill prepared muffin cups almost full.

❺ Bake at 400° for 18 to 22 minutes or until a toothpick comes out clean. Let cool for about 10 minutes before removing from pan and placing on wire rack.

YIELD: 18 muffins.

Cocoa Muffins

A NOT TOO SURPRISING CONFESSION: we love chocolate. But as we learned more about sustainability and Fair Trade issues, our chocolate options grew leaner and more expensive. Organic Fair Trade chocolate chips are hard to find, expensive and, we grudgingly admit, not a necessity of life. Our next best option is cooking more with baking cocoa, supporting companies like Equal Exchange. Much less expensive and processed than those chips, baking cocoa contains more of the good health benefits of chocolate, like antioxidants to lower blood pressure and cholesterol. A bonus with these muffins: Their taste closely resembles that of their cupcake cousin, so you can also pour the batter into a 9-inch cake pan (you may need to bake it a little longer) for a special birthday cake.

INGREDIENTS

1   t. canola oil
1½ c. flour
1   c. sugar
1   t. baking soda
½   t. salt
3   T. cocoa powder
1   t. vinegar
⅓   c. vegetable oil
1   t. vanilla
1   c. water
1   T. powdered sugar

DIRECTIONS

❶ Lightly oil 12 standard muffin cups.

❷ In a large bowl, combine all ingredients.

❸ Fill prepared muffin cups until almost full.

❹ Bake at 350° for about 20 minutes or until a toothpick comes out clean.

❺ Let cool for about 10 minutes before removing muffins from pan and placing them on a wire rack.

❻ To serve, place on serving plate and dust with powdered sugar.

YIELD: 12 muffins.

Mother Earth doesn't charge a penny for her fruits. Money is our invention, not hers, though to listen to many people you'd think it had the same status as water, food and oxygen. There is food for free everywhere. You just need to know where to look and what to look for.

MARK BOYLE, THE MONEYLESS MAN

Winter Squash Spice Muffins

*W*E'VE FOUND A LITTLE MORSEL of something goes a long way, like chocolate chips. The unexpected sweet tidbits you'll find when you bite into these muffins blend wonderfully with the other spices. In place of the winter squash, you can readily use pumpkin. The frozen pulp purée from either winter squash or pumpkin also works well in this recipe.

INGREDIENTS

1   t. canola oil
2   eggs
1   c. winter squash purée
½   c. butter, melted (1 stick)
2   t. cinnamon
½   t. ginger
½   t. nutmeg
½   t. allspice
1   t. baking soda
½   t. baking powder
¼   t. salt
¾   c. sugar
1¾ c. flour
¾   c. chocolate chips

DIRECTIONS

❶ Lightly oil 12 standard muffin cups.

❷ In a large bowl, combine eggs, squash and butter.

❸ Add spices, baking soda, baking powder, salt, sugar and flour. Mix until well-blended.

❹ Fold in chocolate chips.

❺ Fill prepared muffin cups until almost full.

❻ Bake at 350° for 25 minutes or until a toothpick comes out clean. Let cool for about 10 minutes before removing from pan and placing on wire rack.

YIELD: 12 muffins.

There is a great deal of truth to the idea that you will eventually become what you eat.

MOHANDAS GANDHI

Cinnamon Raisin Biscuits

V Vegan

*T*HESE BISCUITS ARE DELICIOUS WARM AND FRESH. Not so, a few hours later. The recipe can be cut in half for smaller groups. Butter can be substituted for the margarine and regular milk for soy for a non-vegan version.

BISCUITS

- ⅔ c. soy milk (plain or vanilla)
- 1 T. lemon juice or vinegar
- 2 c. flour
- ¼ c. sugar
- 2 t. baking powder
- 1 t. salt
- ¼ t. baking soda
- ⅓ c. vegan margarine (5½ T.)
- ⅓ c. raisins
- 1 ½ t. ground cinnamon
- 1 t. canola oil

FROSTING

- ¾ c. powdered sugar
- 1 T. vegan margarine, softened
- 1 t. vanilla extract
- 3 to 5 t. warm water

DIRECTIONS

❶ Place the 1 T. lemon juice (or vinegar) in a 1-cup glass measuring cup. Fill to ⅔ c. with soy milk. Let stand at least 5 minutes (milk will curdle).

❷ In a large bowl, combine flour, sugar, baking powder, salt and baking soda.

❸ Cut in margarine until mixture resembles coarse crumbs.

❹ Stir in soy milk until mixture is just moistened.

❺ In the same bowl, sprinkle in raisins and cinnamon. Knead 8 to 10 times in bowl (cinnamon will have a marbled appearance).

❻ Form batter into 12 mounds, 3 inches in diameter and 2 inches apart on a lightly oiled baking sheet.

❼ Bake at 425° for 12 to 16 minutes or until golden brown.

❽ For frosting, combine the sugar, butter, vanilla and enough water to achieve desired consistency. Frost the warm biscuits then serve immediately.

YIELD: 12 biscuits.

COOKING TIP Most margarine contains trace amounts of dairy products such as whey or lactose. We use Earth Balance for our vegan recipes.

Apple Coffee Cake

*T*ALK ABOUT A MULTI-PURPOSE RECIPE. We cut this up as a coffee cake in squares for breakfast. If you take an afternoon tea break, skip the cookies and try this fruity option instead. Packed full of apples, it stays moist and works great for travel snacks. Drizzle the cake with warm Caramel Syrup (see page 191) and share it as a dessert after dinner.

INGREDIENTS

½ c. butter (1 stick)
2 c. sugar
2 eggs
6 T. water
1 t. vanilla
4 c. apples, peeled and chopped
   (about 6 large apples)
2 c. flour
2 t. cinnamon
½ t. nutmeg
½ t. allspice
2 t. baking soda
1 t. canola oil

DIRECTIONS

❶ In a large bowl, cream butter and sugar. Add eggs one at a time.

❷ Mix in water and vanilla, then fold in apples.

❸ Mix together dry ingredients (flour, cinnamon, nutmeg, allspice, baking soda). Gently fold in dry ingredients to apple mixture.

❹ Pour into lightly oiled 9 × 13-inch baking pan. Bake at 350° for 1 hour.

YIELD: 12 servings.

COOKING TIP

Quick Breads

Both the Apple Coffee Cake and Peanut Butter Pumpkin Bread are quick breads—they don't use yeast and therefore don't need kneading and rise time before baking.

Peanut Butter Pumpkin Bread

*P*UMPKINS AREN'T JUST for jack-o-lanterns. After growing New England Pie and Long Pie (we stack these elongated pumpkins on our front porch like cordwood), we discovered that these varietals glow with flavors, not candles. Who knew a silken pumpkin purée and peanut butter made such good partners? This loaf-style recipe yields two loaves; if that's more than you need, these loaves freeze well or are always appreciated by neighbors. We've learned the hard way that lightly oiling and flour-dusting the pans are crucial steps to ensure the loaf smoothly pops out of the pan.

INGREDIENTS

1   T. canola oil
1   T. flour (for dusting pans)
3   c. sugar
2   c. pumpkin purée
4   eggs
1   c. vegetable oil
¾   c. water
⅔   c. peanut butter
3½ c. flour
2   t. baking soda
1½ t. salt
1   t. cinnamon
1   t. nutmeg

DIRECTIONS

❶ Prepare two 8 × 4-inch loaf pans by lightly oiling them, then dusting the inside of the pan with flour.

❷ In a large mixing bowl, combine the sugar, pumpkin, eggs, oil, water and peanut butter. Blend pumpkin mixture well.

❸ Combine the flour, baking soda, salt, cinnamon and nutmeg. Gradually add to pumpkin mixture; mix well.

❹ Pour into prepared loaf pans. Bake at 350° for 60 to 70 minutes or until a toothpick inserted into the centers comes out clean.

❺ Cool for 10 minutes before removing from pans to wire racks.

YIELD: 2 loaves.

Ah, Peanuts!
It's nutty. Peanuts are from the legume family, kin to pinto beans and lentils. Peanut butter provides plant proteins along with healthy non-hydrogenated fats.

Blueberry Crumb Coffee Cake

$\mathcal{W}$E WISH WE HAD highly acid soil on our farmstead to grow blueberries, but we don't. Happily, some local growers have managed to cultivate wonderful crops of these luscious berries, and we purchase them by the quart whenever we get the chance. They have the highest antioxidant capacity of all fresh fruit, lots of vitamin C and may even be a natural belly fat buster. For this recipe, you can use fresh or frozen blueberries; if using frozen, do not defrost them. We use this dish as a morning coffee cake, but it can easily masquerade as an evening dessert.

FRUIT FILLING INGREDIENTS

3   c. blueberries
⅔   c. sugar
¼   c. cornstarch
¾   c. water
1   T. lemon juice

CRUST INGREDIENTS

2   c. flour
1   c. sugar
1   T. baking powder
1   t. salt
1   t. cinnamon
¼   t. nutmeg
1   t. canola oil
1   c. butter (2 sticks)
2   eggs
1   c. milk
1   t. vanilla extract

TOPPING INGREDIENTS

½   c. flour
½   c. sugar
¼   c. butter (½ stick)

DIRECTIONS

❶ In a saucepan, combine fruit, sugar, cornstarch and water. Over medium heat, bring to a boil. Stir constantly and boil for about 5 minutes or until thickened.

❷ Remove from heat and stir in lemon juice. Let cool.

❸ Meanwhile, make crust. Mix flour, sugar, baking powder, salt, cinnamon and nutmeg in a bowl. Cut in butter until mixture looks like coarse crumbs. Beat together eggs, milk and vanilla. Add to flour mixture and mix well.

❹ Spread two thirds of the mixture into a lightly oiled 9 × 13-inch baking pan. It's simplest to use clean wet hands to evenly spread the mixture into the pan.

❺ Spoon fruit filling over crust to within one inch of pan edge. Top with remaining crust mixture.

❻ For topping, combine flour and sugar in bowl. Cut in butter until coarse crumbs form. Sprinkle over top of cake.

❼ Bake at 350° for about 1 hour or until lightly browned.

YIELD: 12 servings.

COOKING TIP

Berry Friendly, But Not For Strawberries
Many different small berries, like raspberries, cloudberries, blackberries and black raspberries, can easily replace the blueberries in this recipe, making it quite versatile throughout the various berry-abundant seasons. The recipe will not, however, work well with strawberries due to their texture.

Zucchini Muffins

W E DID THE IMPOSSIBLE. Our first couple of years in the gardens, we killed our zucchini. So while everyone else in our town would lock their car doors in the summer for fear of their front seat becoming a depository for unwanted surplus, we left our doors unlocked — and windows open. After a few years working on our soil and realizing that the squash bugs were ruining our day, we've managed to join other growers with over-zealous crops. Thankfully, this muffin recipe blows through any varieties of summer squash or zucchini — eight balls, patty pans, curly necks — they all work well in this recipe, but it's best to get the zucchini before they get too big.

INGREDIENTS

1   t. canola oil

1⅓ c. sugar

2   eggs

1   t. vanilla

3   c. fresh shredded zucchini
    (or summer squash)

⅔ c. butter, melted

3   c. flour

2   t. baking soda

¼ t. salt

2   t. cinnamon

1   t. nutmeg

DIRECTIONS

❶ Lightly oil 18 standard muffin cups.

❷ In a mixing bowl, combine the sugar, eggs and vanilla. Stir in zucchini and melted butter.

❸ In a separate bowl, combine flour, baking soda, salt, cinnamon and nutmeg. Add flour mixture to zucchini mixture and blend well.

❹ Fill prepared muffin cups until almost full. Bake at 350° for about 25 to 30 minutes or until a toothpick inserted in the center of the muffins comes out clean. Let stand for about 5 minutes before removing from pan and placing on a wire rack to cool.

YIELD: 18 muffins.

Chocolate Zucchini Bread

*L*ONG BEFORE THE BIG GULP, SUPER SIZE OR JUMBO PACK, there was the single serving: a portion meant to satisfy our appetite or quench our thirst, not overstuff or drown it. We take this same approach to anything with chocolate in it. With a high-quality baking cocoa, you just need enough cocoa — when prepared with rich farm-fresh eggs and our vanilla — to create decadent bread without having to use a whole bag of chocolate chips or a pudding mix in it. Like the Zucchini Muffins, any summer squash or zucchini will work in this recipe. This bread freezes well and can be quickly retrieved for those impromptu soup nights or potlucks.

INGREDIENTS

1   T. canola oil
1   T. flour (for dusting pans)
3   eggs
1   c. vegetable oil
2   c. sugar
1   T. vanilla extract
2   c. shredded zucchini (about 1 medium)
2½ c. flour
½   c. baking cocoa
1   t. salt
1   t. baking soda
1   t. cinnamon
¼   t. baking powder

DIRECTIONS

❶ Prepare two 8-inch-by 4-inch-by 3-inch loaf pans by lightly oiling, then dusting the inside of the pan with flour.

❷ In a mixing bowl, beat eggs, oil, sugar and vanilla. Stir in zucchini.

❸ In a separate bowl, combine flour, baking cocoa, salt, baking soda, cinnamon and baking powder. Add flour mixture to zucchini mixture and blend well.

❹ Pour into prepared loaf pans.

❺ Bake at 350° for 1 hour or until a toothpick stuck in center of bread comes out clean.

❻ Before serving, let the bread fully cool for easier slicing.

YIELD: 2 loaves.

Sprouting Hope with Your 100-foot Diet

We should never lose hope, give up, toss in the towel when faced with a seemingly insurmountable problem/obstacle. We saw the movie, *The Road*, a disturbing look into a future where some undefined calamity forces a father and his son onto a road for their very survival. Their situation seemed hopeless, yet they kept moving forward, down the road. Around our town today, it's not that bad, but some folks are without a job, without a house or without a family. Hope seems to be the buzzword of late. But to hope without action is like passion without a purpose — or planting seeds in poor soil, forgetting about weeding, watering and nourishing them with compost and care. As Anna Lappé and her mom, Francis Moore Lappé, like to say: "Hope is not what we find in evidence. It is what we become in action."

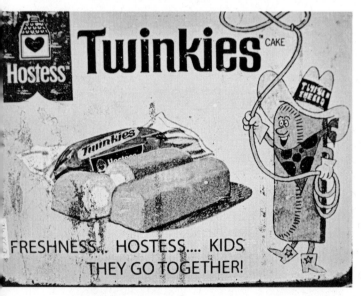

A sign of the processed times. "Fresh" Twinkies?

Every new growing season ushers in a hope for a great harvest by American gardeners now numbering into the millions, according to the National Gardening Association. With rooftop gardens, patio container plantings and backyard kitchen gardens, the 41 million Americans who grow at least some of their own food (12 million of them do it without any chemicals) are reclaiming the power that comes with being able to feed yourself and your family with little or no involvement from multinational corporations or government. Forget the 100-mile diet — say hello to the 100-foot (or less) diet.

In many parts of the country — including Detroit, Pittsburgh, Atlanta and San Diego — urban farmers are growing more healthy food than their farming folk in the country. This underground farmer movement has more Americans each day picking up the shovel and potato fork, starting a compost pile and growing some fruits, vegetables and herbs. Some of this growth stems from simple economics: it's easier, more affordable and healthier to eat from our own gardens, for both us and the planet. This agriculture tradition is uniquely human, one that the corporate food industry has failed to extinguish.

At the turn of the 20th century, more than half of all American families worked the land. During World War II, more than half the US population (and many Canadians and Europeans, too) grew at least some of their food as a part of taking responsibility for their nourishment and to make a contribution to the war cause. Today, nearly 1 in 7 of us may grow a tomato plant, harvest basil from a potted plant or tend to a small flock of chickens in our backyard. And millions more are getting into the game before their food stamps run out. As we quickly discovered: plant a seed in the spring and witness the miracle of nature's abundance as your countertops overflow with cucumbers, tomatoes and, of course, zucchini.

Sunlight, access to a water supply, some soil and a little space is all that's needed to get started with your own garden. You'll quickly discover that there are many organic gardening strategies that help add a bump to your bumper crops, including building your soil with compost, rotating crops to deter garden pests and preserve soil balance and mulching for weed control and moisture retention. But the most important thing for organic growers is keeping the natural-gas-derived and oil-based chemicals out of the gardens and away from your food by avoiding synthetic fertilizers, fungicides and insecticides. Organic growing means that nothing is being poisoned: not the soil, the water, the farmers or the eaters. It's farming with nature rather than waging war against it.

More and more research has emerged documenting, too, that crops grown organically have higher levels of minerals, nutrients and, most important to any great cook, flavor. Flavor remains the most compelling reason to grow, and eat, organically, ideally from produce grown or raised nearby where you live. Less than a 100 feet from your back door is best.

There are many approaches you may take to growing some of your own food, such as:

French-style intensive raised beds: It's a favorite of ours, since it builds soil tilth: the soil structure that's nutrient dense and loose, airy and crumbly. It also efficiently uses a small space to produce a large yield of edibles. Soils vary by geography and climate, but all soils have a mixture of clay, sand and organic matter to meet the growing needs of the plants. Raised beds help focus your energy into nutrient-rich soils, minimize soil compaction (which prevents root systems from developing) and, because the beds can be built above ground with a wooden framework, reduce the backbreaking efforts of gardening. Our raised beds are four feet wide, double-dug and mounded, increasing the depth of the soil that helps the plants thrive better.

Permaculture-designed gardens: A term coined by Bill Mollison and David Holmgren, permaculture is the melding of permanent human settlements and agriculture, creating designs based on viable, natural ecological systems where what's produced by one element of the system becomes the input for another. The ethics of permaculture are simple: care for people, care for the planet and share the surplus. In nature there is no waste, so permaculture-inspired gardens recycle or reuse all nutrients and energy sources, regenerating natural systems while boosting the self-sufficiency of human settlements and reducing the need for industrial production systems that demand cheap, polluting energy sources to thrive. "We're not stealing from nature, we're actually providing for it," explains permaculturalist Mark Shepard with Forest Agriculture Enterprises, where he has created a food forest on his farm in Wisconsin through permaculture design. Plants are selected and planted according to how they help one another. Free-ranging chickens, for example, can help fertilize, work up the soil and control insect pests while providing nutrient-packed eggs (we humans provide shelter, security, a water source and supplemental food in the winter). There are numerous go-to places for more information, including the Permaculture Activist (permacultureactivist.net) or the Urban Permaculture Guild (urbanpermacultureguild.org). For a more personal, hands-on experience, consider taking one of the growing number of permaculture design courses, perhaps from Midwest Permaculture (midwestpermaculture.com), Glacial Lakes Permaculture (glaciallakespermaculture.org) or the Esalen Institute (esalen.org).

Lasagna gardening: A no-till, no-dig approach to planting a garden, particularly suitable if you live in a suburb where grassy lawns are abundant. The gardens can be of any size or shape, but involve placing layers of organic material such as leaves, grass clippings and old newspaper that will decompose to create a rich, loose soil perfect for growing plants of any kind. The first layer is always cardboard or several sheets of newspaper, to smoother the grass or weeds underneath. After that, it's basically a compost pile, with earthworms working their magic as they wiggle their way up through the decomposing matter. For more about lasagna gardening, visit www.no-dig-vegetablegarden.com.

Container planting.

Container planting: Almost any container can be used to grow fruits, vegetables or herbs for fresh, seasonal cooking, from large flower pots to old wooden barrels. With a sunny enough patio or rooftop space, you're good to go. Five or more hours of direct sunlight a day is needed for proper growth for most plants, but many plants, such as tomatoes, require more. Whatever container you use, make sure there are holes at the bottom to allow the water to drain out (cover with old cracked ceramics, terracotta pots or newspaper) and start out by using an organic "soilless" potting mix that's appropriate to your plant's needs (some plants need more sand, compost or the soil to be more or less acidic). Along with sunlight, mindfully watering the plants (containers often lose moisture quickly) and adding fertilizer (an organic liquid fish emulsion works great) based on the types of plants grown is a must. For more, check out *From Container to Kitchen*, by D. J. Herda.

New gardening approaches come about as more of us explore new ways to meet our daily food needs. In New York City, for example, Homegrown Harvest founders Rebecca Bray and Britta Riley manage to use the available window space in apartments and condos to create a prolific vertical garden year-round with a hydroponic system. They call it window farming (windowfarms.org). If you don't have enough windows, try growing something on the roof, like they do on the Eagle Street Rooftop Farm, a 6,000-square-foot farm atop a warehouse in Brooklyn, New York (rooftopfarms.org). For a more general introduction to farming in the city, check out Urban Farm Online (urbanfarmonline.com) or in Canada, City Farmer News (cityfarmer.info). Community gardens are transforming empty city lots, church lawns and schoolyards into a cornucopia of fresh food; go to the American Community Gardening Association (communitygarden.org) to find one near you.

We use organic or heirloom seeds — seeds that are passed down from numerous generations with unique characteristics, most notably flavors, colors or shapes. Great sources for seeds to get your gardens underway include: Fedco Seeds or West Coast Seeds, for a wide selection of affordable organic and heirloom seeds (fedcoseeds.com and westcoastseeds .com); Seeds of Change, for over 1,200 varieties of organic seeds (seedsofchange.com); Seed Saver Exchange, for heirloom, mostly organic, seeds from fellow gardeners dedicated to saving and sharing heirloom seeds (seedsavers.org); Johnny's Selected Seeds, offering a wide selection of certified vegetable, herb and flower seeds (johnnyseeds.com); National Sustainable Agriculture Information Service, for a directory of organic seed suppliers (attra.ncat.org). Most local garden supply stores sell organic growing media for container plants, or can special order it for you.

As for what to grow, try something — anything. You might start with what grows best in your part of the country. The USDA breaks the country down into growing zones that reflect the frost dates and historical weather patterns that dictate what will, and will not, survive or thrive in your area. Cross-reference this zone number with the seed packets you're considering. An easier and simpler option: talk to neighbors or the farmers at your local farmers market and take advantage of their knowledge.

Space is usually a limitation, so consider this when planning your garden. You'll need plenty of sunlight and have a source of water for irrigation. Soil quality can be built up over time, but it helps that you have a supply line for compost or garden waste (a local restaurant or coffee house may happily assist). It's natural to grow what you love eating, like tomatoes, and avoid going overboard on crops that may overwhelm you on their prolific fruiting potential, like zucchini or cucumbers. We started by focusing on what we love to eat and what we eat the most of. For those in the city or suburbs challenged with space, you may want to grow what's least available fresh or affordable, like basil, which is rather pricey for small, one-ounce packages; growing your own makes pesto affordable and flavorful — and it's something that freezes well so can be savored year-round.

Community gardens in... San Francisco (top) or Santa Monica (bottom).

Oven-roasted Garlic for Bread Spread

OKAY, SO IT'S NOT A BREAD RECIPE. This garlic recipe is the best way to savor a freshly baked French Baguette (see page 55) — and the mouth-watering aroma will fill your house in the most delicious way. Garlic is a wonder plant, if there ever was one; it boosts our immune system, among many other benefits, and can help ward off a cold. It's a prebiotic, an important bacterial fuel for the beneficial probiotic bacteria that help maintain our intestinal health. To make the roasted garlic, we have an enclosed terra cotta baking dish we use for roasting garlic, but any shallow, covered casserole dish will do.

INGREDIENTS

4   whole garlic heads (not cloves)
2   T. olive oil
1½ c. water

DIRECTIONS

❶ Using a sharp knife, cut the top of the garlic head to expose the inner cloves.

❷ Brush heads with olive oil and place in a shallow casserole dish. Fill dish with 1 inch of water and cover.

❸ Bake at 350° for 45 to 60 minutes until garlic is very soft and light brown. Check garlic for softness since oven temperatures may vary.

❹ Serve with French baguette slices. To eat, remove the garlic from its skin with a knife and spread onto baguette rounds with butter.

YIELD: 4 servings.

Tomatoes and oregano make it Italian; wine and tarragon make it French. Sour cream makes it Russian; lemon and cinnamon make it Greek. Soy sauce makes it Chinese; garlic makes it good.

ALICE MAY BROCK

Winter Squash Fritters

*F*RITTERS BRING SMILES, and they're the ultimate winter comfort food. Any combo of winter squash works well, like butternut or acorn. The fritters make a nice accompaniment with a savory breakfast or as a side with soups. Serve with a honey-mustard dipping sauce.

INGREDIENTS

- 1   c. winter squash purée
- 1   egg
- ¼   c. onion or chives, chopped
- 1   c. corn
- ½   c. self-rising flour
- ½   c. self-rising cornmeal
- 1   t. sugar
- ½   t. salt
- 6   c. canola oil (for frying)
- 1   c. honey
- 1   T. Dijon mustard

DIRECTIONS

❶ In a bowl, combine the squash, egg, onion and corn.

❷ In another bowl, combine dry ingredients of flour, cornmeal, sugar and salt; add dry ingredients to squash mixture and beat well.

❸ In a skillet (an electric skillet works well) or deep fryer, heat ¼ inch of oil to 400°. Drop about ⅛ cup of batter and cook about 4 minutes or until crisp and golden, turning often. Cooking time will vary based on frying temperature. Drain on paper towels.

❹ For honey-mustard sauce: Heat honey over low heat until soft. Stir in 1 T. Dijon mustard, adding more to taste.

❺ Serve fritters with honey-mustard dipping sauce. Left-over fritters are best reheated in the oven to keep them crispy.

YIELD: 8 servings.

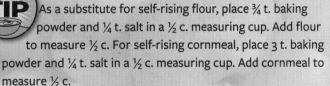

As a substitute for self-rising flour, place ¾ t. baking powder and ¼ t. salt in a ½ c. measuring cup. Add flour to measure ½ c. For self-rising cornmeal, place 3 t. baking powder and ¼ t. salt in a ½ c. measuring cup. Add cornmeal to measure ½ c.

Cheese Straws

*T*HESE CHEESE STRAWS break every rule of our modern food system: They take time to make, need to be made by hand and break easily so they don't transport well. That's reason enough for us to celebrate the Cheese Straws and let taste triumph over the industrialization of our food. Like a delicate cracker, these Cheese Straws make a beautiful hostess gift when placed in a wide-mouth canning jar (and will at least make it to a party if you hold them between your knees in the car).

INGREDIENTS

- 1 c. flour
- 1½ t. baking powder
- ½ t. salt
- ½ c. cheddar cheese, shredded
- 2 T. butter
- ⅓ c. milk
- 1 t. canola oil

DIRECTIONS

❶ In a large bowl, stir together flour, baking powder and salt.

❷ Cut in cheese and butter using a pastry blender until dough looks like coarse cornmeal.

❸ Add milk and mix well. Lightly knead dough into a ball, adding more milk if needed.

❹ Roll dough on lightly floured surface to about ⅛-inch thickness, cut into strips 3 inches long and ¼ inch wide.

❺ Bake on a lightly oiled cookie sheet in a 425° oven for 8 to 10 minutes. Watch during last minutes of baking. Straws should be removed from oven just about as they start to brown.

YIELD: 6 servings.

Pastured cows in the fields of Green County, Wisconsin, where there are more cows than people.

French Baguette

THE FRENCH HAVE A FLAIR FOR FLAVOR; ingredients are the key and their idea of *terroir*—or taste of place—helps define farmstead cuisine. Their wines are named by the growing regions; cheeses are named after their small towns. Most beekeepers understand this, knowing full well that their honey will imbue the flavors of what the bees themselves eat. We've found the baguette a perfect companion to a meal, a snack or to keep the kids quiet before the entrée arrives. If the baguette dries out, use it in fondue or toast it to make your own bread crumbs or croutons.

INGREDIENTS

2¼ t. dry active yeast (one .25 oz. package)

1 c. warm water (warm to the touch)

2 T. sugar

2 T. canola oil

1½ t. salt

3 c. flour

1 T. canola oil for the pans and baking sheet

DIRECTIONS

❶ In a large bowl of an electric mixer, dissolve yeast in warm water. Beat in the sugar, oil and salt.

❷ With the dough hook of mixer on low speed or by hand, gradually add in flour to form a soft dough. Mix (or knead by hand) until smooth and elastic, about 6 to 8 minutes. Place in a lightly oiled bowl, turning once to oil the top. Cover and let rise until doubled in size, roughly for 1 hour.

❸ Punch dough down and return to bowl. Cover and let rise for another 30 minutes. Punch dough down.

❹ Turn out onto a lightly floured surface. Shape into two loaves 12 inches long and 2 inches wide. Place loaves on lightly oiled baking sheet. Cover and let rise until doubled, about 30 minutes.

❺ With a sharp knife or kitchen shears, cut diagonal slashes two inches apart across top of loaf.

❻ Bake at 375° for 30 minutes or until golden brown. Remove from pan and place on a wire rack to cool.

YIELD: 2 loaves.

Sun Oven Cuisine: Cooking Unplugged

"Where do you plug it in?" asked my father-in-law, staring at the boxy thing with aluminum reflectors that focused the sunlight down into the black glass-covered chamber known as the solar Sun Oven, placed on the ground, facing south, in front of our garage.

"Don't need to," I replied, as his daughter (Lisa) sent an icy, watch-what-you-say glare my way. Her father was 83, so give him a flippin' break; he rode to school on a horse-drawn buggy.

"We just point it toward the sun, adjust the tilt so that the sun hits perpendicular to the glass-covered chamber and give it a little time to heat up to 350 de-grees," I continued pleasantly, pointing to the built-in thermometer. "When we're done, we just fold down the aluminum reflectors and put it away."

Thus began, in 2008, our adventure in cooking with the sun. We should have invested $150 in one years earlier. Since we use the sun to completely power our homestead, it was about time we did some of our cooking with it.

As long as it's at least partially sunny out — and not too windy (the wind will topple over the reflectors) — we use the Sun Oven to bake our bread, simmer our soups, steam our green beans, cook our appetizers and reheat our leftovers. All without a penny

Sun Oven with bread baking.

of purchased energy. On a bright, warm summer day, the Sun Oven (sunoven.com) does it in just about the same time as in our kitchen oven. The Sun Oven has no moving air, and the oven temperatures rise slowly and evenly, so the foods stay moist, tender and flavorful.

The key to success with a solar oven is, simply, the sun. Point it toward the sun and leave it be. The challenge is remembering that (a) the sun moves across the sky during the day and (b) the sun is higher in sky, almost directly overhead, in the summer and hangs lower in the sky as you head through the winter. Instead of the timer ringing in the house, you'll need to pass by the solar oven about every 30 minutes to check on cooking progress and refocus the oven on the sun by turning it. A leg in the back of the box lets us adjust the tilt appropriate for the season. Things can occasionally burn in the oven, so you'll need to keep an eye on it.

You'll be able to cook the most during the longer days with plentiful sunshine around the summer solstice (June 21); we've managed an egg dish in the late morning, fresh bread for a mid-day lunch, and a warm-up of some nibbles in the early evening. But don't count on much cooking during the winter solstice (December 21) period, especially if you're in the more northern climates; you'll be lucky to reheat some leftovers mid-day — if it's sunny, that is.

In general, most items you'd cook in a kitchen oven can be done in the solar one. For the better part of late spring, summer and early fall, we can achieve an average oven temperature of about 325 degrees, pretty good for most items you may be cooking. There are times, however, when we get the oven just right and the thermometer breaks 400 degrees. Chocolate Chip Zucchini Bread, anyone?

Using the solar oven may, however, create problems if you have a rambunctious dog or an overly curious child. The inside oven chamber does get hot, so it's wise to keep a couple of hot pads nearby. But cutting down on heat in the indoor kitchen and saving money on electricity or natural gas more than compensates for the inconvenience. That said, we tend to do more cooking outside anyway come summer, so we create a mini-outdoor kitchen area in the gardens. Nothing fancy, just functional, with a small table, a couple of chairs, hot pads and a spoon (for tasting).

You may need to invest in a few small pans that easily fit into the oven. The glass 9 × 13-inch Pyrex baking pans will stick out, thanks to their glass handles, which don't fit. Any oven-safe pots that fit will work. Some people also use the Sun Oven to dehydrate foods, yet another way you can eat what you grow year-round.

English Muffins

ON OUR FOOD JOURNEY away from the processed, we still had some packaged baggage in the pantry. English muffins, for example — they looked so perfectly browned when toasted and shaped in a way we could never do at home, right? Wrong. The British were eating these at teatime long before supermarkets came along. Not only are English muffins easy to make, they have a fun factor unlike any other bread recipe in this cookbook — you get to grill them, not just bake them. These muffins freeze well; pop the frozen muffins in the refrigerator before you hit the sack, and you'll wake up to English muffins ready to toast. While these English muffins are terrific, they're not as holey as those you'll buy in the store. Does it matter? Not to us — they taste better.

INGREDIENTS

- 1   c. milk
- ¼   c. butter (½ stick)
- 2   T. sugar
- 2¼ t. dry active yeast (one .25 oz. package)
- 1   c. warm water
- 5   c. flour
- 1   t. salt

DIRECTIONS

❶ In a small saucepan, heat milk until it bubbles. Add butter and mix until melted. Remove from heat. Mix in sugar until it dissolves. Let cool until lukewarm.

❷ In a small bowl, dissolve yeast in warm water. Let stand until creamy, about 10 minutes.

❸ In a mixer bowl, combine milk butter mixture, yeast mixture and 3 cups of the flour. Beat until smooth. Add salt and slowly add rest of flour. Using the dough hook, mix until a soft dough forms, about 6 to 8 minutes.

❹ Place dough in a lightly oiled bowl. Cover and let rise until doubled, about 1 hour.

❺ Punch dough down. Try not to handle the dough much more after this point in order to keep air bubbles in the dough to help make nooks and crannies. Roll dough to about ½ inch thick. Cut rounds with a wide-mouth Mason jar ring (or something about that shape). Sprinkle a baking sheet with cornmeal and place rounds on top to rise. Dust tops with cornmeal. Cover and let rise about 1 hour.

❻ Heat lightly oiled griddle or electric fry pan. Cook muffins about 10 minutes on each side over medium heat or until nicely browned. Then move to oven and bake at 350° for about 10 minutes.

❼ To use, split with a fork (not a knife) to preserve nooks and crannies.

YIELD: 18 English muffins.

Potato Rolls

*P*OTATOES ARE A BIG SOURCE of our homegrown carbohydrates. By Good Friday every spring, we plant several rows of Red Norland potatoes for an early harvest around the Fourth of July. We also plant Yukon Gold, Satina and sometimes a Russet variety—all of which store exceptionally well if you can keep them cool (around 35 to 45°) and dry. Not just for French fries, hash browns or baked potatoes, our richly flavored spuds make hearty rolls for sandwiches or a basket on the dinner table. Medium-starch spuds, like our Yukon Gold and Satina, work best in this recipe.

INGREDIENTS

7   c. flour, divided
½   c. sugar
2¼ t. dry active yeast (one .25 oz. package)
1   t. salt
2   c. milk
1½ c. butter (3 sticks), softened
½   c. water
1   c. cooked and mashed potatoes (you could also use 1 c. of leftover mashed potatoes)
2   eggs
1   t. canola oil

DIRECTIONS

❶ In a large bowl of an electric mixer, mix 2 c. flour, sugar, yeast and salt.

❷ In a saucepan over medium heat, heat milk, butter and water to just boiling. Add heated milk mixture to dry ingredients and beat until moistened.

❸ Add mashed potatoes and eggs. Beat until smooth. Stir in enough remaining flour to form a stiff dough. Do not knead. Put dough in a lightly oiled bowl and turn once to grease top. Cover and refrigerate overnight.

❹ Turn out dough onto a lightly floured surface and punch dough down. Divide dough in half. Shape each half-section into 12 balls. Roll each ball into an 8-inch rope and tie it into a knot.

❺ On a lightly oiled baking sheet, place bread knots two inches apart. Cover and let rise about 2 hours until doubled. Bake at 375° for 25 to 30 minutes or until golden brown. Remove and cool on wire racks.

YIELD: 24 rolls.

FOLLOW YOUR SEED

Roger Doiron,
Kitchen Gardeners International,
Scarborough, Maine

Zucchini? Peapod? Cucumber? If we had to give Roger Doiron a vegetable name, it would have to be something with a long vine and lots of fruit. With strong roots in supporting the home gardening revolution, he's got a wandering, prolific vine side — harvesting ripe, creative opportunities to entice people into rethinking what's on our plate and how can we grow more of it right outside our back doors. Roger is the founder of Kitchen Gardens International (KGI), a non-profit based in Maine.

Courtesy of Kitchen Gardeners International

"I'm a home gardening evangelist," Roger says with a modest smile. "We all have good intentions and want to make a difference, but the challenges and problems can seem so large today that it is even more important that we each feel we can contribute something, and growing your own fruits and vegetables provides that opportunity," explains Roger in a conversation with Lisa. He's been spending a year abroad with his Belgian-born wife, Jacquie, and their three sons, and running KGI virtually. "Home gardening is an accessible way we can contribute to being part of the solution and enjoy the fruits of our labor."

"I worked in Europe in the 1990s for Friends of the Earth, and experienced how Europeans strongly connect with their food and how gardening is so much more a part of their daily culture," reflects Roger on the roots of his gardening passion. "During my travels I saw so many home gardens with every available space used to grow food. That left quite the impression on me. When I got back to the States and walked around my old childhood neighborhood in Maine, I realized how few gardens were left. I had an epiphany that sparked my work today, helping people access tangible and practical information for home gardening."

He's filling up the gardening revival tent, that's for sure. KGI brings together over 20,000 people from 100 countries who are getting their hands dirty through gardening and sharing information and advice prolifically over the Web, answering questions like "Can backyard chickens and a garden peacefully co-exist?" or "How do I organize my seeds?"

"I realized there were a lot of garden clubs already, but I saw a need to start an organization that brought together people specifically dedicated to raising food and who saw their kitchen gardens in a bigger global frame of sustainability," Roger explains. "My Maine backyard garden is tied to gardens in Australia, India and beyond."

"The Internet does an enormous job of bringing people together and enabling the spontaneity of messages," Roger adds. He's earned a reputation as the MacGyver of new social media, a self-taught guru who creatively taps into innovative communication tools to spread the gardening and healthy food message. From Facebook campaigns aiming to turn the Fourth of July into "Food Independence Day" by encouraging local food picnic fare, to launching a "Real Food" page campaign in reaction to the 1 million fans on the Cheetos Facebook page, Roger packages complex food issues in a way anyone can relate to.

"With the increasing volume of information on the Web, the opportunity to get your message out is still there, but I've found how you frame it needs to be something a bit unexpected and new to get people thinking," advises Roger. The cherry on his social media sundae to date is his successful proposal and petition effort to replant a kitchen garden at the White House. The "Eat the View" campaign garnered over 100,000 signatures, and bushels of international media coverage. Through the use of Facebook and personalizing the gardening message, Roger brought home gardens to the forefront of the White House agenda.

"The success of the 'Eat the View' campaign reminds me of the power and potential of collective voices and how together we can change how Americans perceive and value food," Roger explains. "The White House recognized the impact of home gardeners through our efforts. By tearing out part of the

Roger Doiron in his kitchen garden.

White House lawn and planting fruits and vegetables for the President's family's meals, this sends a message to the world that we can all contribute to food security."

No-knead Dutch Oven Artisan Bread

(V Vegan)

$\mathcal{A}$N AVID, ECLECTIC HOME COOK, Roger Doiron dabbles in the international, doing Japanese one night and Moroccan the next. But bread remains a staple at every meal. His recipe for no-knead artisan bread, adapted from his *New York Times* article, changed our kitchen forever. No bread recipe tops the simplicity and taste of this one. You may react like we did the first time we made it, swearing that this recipe could never work as we stuck the wiggly bowl of dough in the hot oven. Behold, a miracle will appear when you open that lid 30 minutes later.

INGREDIENTS

- ¼ t. active dry yeast
- 1½ c. warm water
- ½ c. whole wheat flour
- 2½ c. white flour, plus more for dusting
- 1½ t. salt
- cornmeal or wheat bran for dusting

DIRECTIONS

❶ In a large bowl, dissolve yeast in water. Add the flour and salt, stirring until blended. The dough will be shaggy and sticky. Cover bowl with plastic wrap. Let the dough rest at least 8 hours, preferably 12 to 18 hours, at a warm room temperature (about 70°).

❷ The dough is ready when its surface is dotted with bubbles. Lightly flour a work surface and place dough on it. Sprinkle dough with a little more flour and fold it over on itself once or twice. Cover loosely with plastic wrap and let it rest for about 15 minutes.

❸ Using just enough flour to keep the dough from sticking to the work surface or to your fingers, gently shape it into a ball. Generously coat a clean dish towel with flour, wheat bran or cornmeal. Put the seam side of the dough down on the towel and dust with more flour, bran or cornmeal. Cover with another towel and let rise for about 1 to 2 hours.

When it's ready, the dough will have doubled in size and will not readily spring back when poked with a finger.

❹ At least 20 minutes before the dough is ready, heat oven to 475°. Put a 6- to 8-quart heavy covered pot (cast iron, enamel, Pyrex or ceramic) in the oven as it heats. When the dough is ready, carefully remove the pot from the oven and lift off the lid. Turn the dough over into the pot, seam side up. The dough will lose its shape a bit in the process, but that's okay. Give the pan a firm shake or two to help distribute the dough evenly, but don't worry if it's not perfect; it will straighten out as it bakes.

❺ Cover and bake for 30 minutes. Remove the lid and bake another 15 to 20 minutes, until the loaf is beautifully browned. Remove the bread from the pot and let it cool on a rack for at least 1 hour before slicing.

YIELD: One 1½-pound loaf.

Winter Squash Rolls

Every October, Anu visits us. No, the Celtic goddess of abundance, fertility and well-being doesn't ring the doorbell and walk in. But we sense her presence in the piles of butternut and acorn squash lining our porch. Life feels abundant and prolific, a sense that all will be right with the world because we sit on a pile of winter squash. We cook it, mash it and secretly stick it in just about anything. These rolls are a great way to savor your squash, adding a moist tenderness and deep orange color. They're perfect for any holiday table.

INGREDIENTS

4½ t. dry active yeast (two .25 oz. packages)
1½ c. warm water
⅓ c. sugar
2 t. salt
2 eggs
1 c. winter squash purée
7 to 7½ c. flour
⅔ c. butter, melted
2 T. butter, softened
1 t. canola oil

DIRECTIONS

❶ In a large mixing bowl, mix yeast in water. Let stand 5 minutes.

❷ Beat in sugar, salt, eggs, squash and 3½ c. flour. Beat in melted butter.

❸ With dough hook of mixer on low speed or by hand, gradually add in enough remaining flour to form a soft dough. Mix or knead until smooth and elastic, about 6 to 8 minutes. Place in a lightly oiled bowl, turning once to oil the top. Cover and refrigerate overnight.

❹ Turn dough out onto a lightly floured surface and punch down. Divide in half and roll each half-section into a 16-inch circle. Spread with two remaining tablespoons softened butter. Cut each circle into 16 wedges, like slices of a pie. Roll up each wedge starting with the wide end and place with pointed end down on lightly oiled baking sheet. Cover and let size about 1 hour until doubled.

❺ Bake at 400° for 15 to 20 minutes or until golden brown.

YIELD: 32 rolls.

Homemade Pitas and Pita Chips

PITAS AND PITA CHIPS are a healthier alternative to store-bought processed crackers and chips laden with preservatives and hard-to-pronounce ingredients usually having something to do with a bad-for-you fat. When we bake pita bread, it can go directly to the next step of making pita chips — our version of a healthier, unprocessed salty snack to crunch on.

INGREDIENTS FOR PITAS

- 2¼ t. dry active yeast (one .25 oz. package)
- 1¼ c. warm water
- 2 t. salt
- 3 c. flour
- 1 t. canola oil

DIRECTIONS FOR PITAS

❶ In the large bowl of an electric mixer, mix yeast in warm water. Let stand 5 minutes. Stir in salt and enough flour to make a soft dough.

❷ With dough hook of mixer on low speed or by hand on a floured surface, knead about 8 minutes until smooth and elastic. Do not let rise.

❸ Divide dough into 6 equal pieces. Knead each piece individually for 1 minute.

❹ Roll each piece into a 5-inch circle. Sprinkle flour on a baking sheet. Place circles on baking sheet and let rise in a warm place until doubled, about 1 hour.

❺ Flip circles and place upside down on lightly oiled baking sheets. Bake at 500° for 5 to 10 minutes. Remove from baking sheets and cool on wire racks.

YIELD: 6 pitas.

DIRECTIONS FOR PITA CHIPS

❶ Cut each pita into 6 wedges.

❷ Take olive oil (about ½ c. for 6 pitas) and add 2 t. salt (garlic salt or seasoning salt works well) and about 2 t. dried herbs like oregano and basil to taste.

❸ Brush chips on one side with oil mixture using a pastry brush.

❹ Place on cookie sheet and bake at 350° until they start to crisp. Watch closely — probably about 10 minutes — to avoid making them too crispy or burnt.

❺ Flip chips over, brush again with olive oil mixture, bake for about 5 more minutes until crispy.

❻ When out of oven, brush one more time lightly with olive oil.

YIELD: 36 crunchy, salty chips.

SOUPS

Cornucopia Beer and Cheese Soup

Cream of Asparagus Soup

Cucumber Soup

New Orleans Seafood Gumbo (Poppy Tooker)

Potato Soup

Cream of Carrot Soup

Zucchini-Summer Squash Bisque

Danish Potato Leek Soup

Tomato Dill Soup

Winter Butternut Squash Bisque

** see page 27 for:
French Onion Soup with Shiitake Mushrooms (Jonathan Fagan at King's Hill Farm)

** see page 236 for:
Lentil and Polish Sausage Soup (Brenda Carus)

Herbs

Our Food. Our Farm. Our Rules.

We're first to admit, rules, regulations and policies, as well-intentioned as some may be, get in the way of what we'd argue is a more viable, sustainable and local food system.

We're not alone. Joel Salatin is no fan of governmental regulations and policies either. In his book *Everything I Want to Do Is Illegal*, farmer Joel Salatin calls it the way he sees it. He's the operator of Polyface Farm in Virginia's Shenandoah Valley, where he and his family raise pastured poultry, "pigaerator pork," "salad bar beef" and forage-fed rabbits, among many other edibles. And this family farm does it within a system that's "beyond organic," as Joel says. His non-industrial approach to raising food has been the target of many a regulating agency that would rather the food be irradiated, treated with chemicals or fumigated before it touches the tongue of an American. Naturally, his approaches have been a boon for the media, always looking for a good fight, catapulting him to rock star farmer status. He's one prizefighter, too. For him, it's definitely about relationships, and local ones at that.

Meanwhile, in our county, the University of Wisconsin-Extension put the kibosh on a local effort to host a community potluck that they cosponsored. Evidently, you can't expect your neighbors to produce a dish safe for human consumption. This, despite a Wisconsin "potluck law" on the books that exempts such functions from government oversight. So we had a picnic instead.

We like to think that cooking is less about rules and more about guidance. So view our recipes as a compass to healthier eating. How you get there, your food route, is up to you. Our food route, while fresh and seasonal, tends to be inspired by the Mediterranean diet with an abundance of vegetables, legumes, nuts and olive oil in place of prime rib and pork chops. We replace salt with herbs, butter with olive oil (in some cases) and focus on whole grains, like couscous or oats found in our Granolaheads Crunch.

So here's our food compass, to serve as a guide. You'll notice a few directional points have everything to do with great health and nothing to do with food. Eating right is one aspect of living well and staying healthy.

- Use the best quality ingredients, period. Whether it's from your gardens, a CSA share, farmers market or supermarket that showcases local, seasonal produce or meats, the premium you might pay will make your meal taste gourmet.
- Go with your food preferences, or taste. If you don't like fennel — or don't have it in the house — just leave it out. If you want to cut down on fats, try swapping olive oil for butter when the recipe calls for it.
- Substitute at will. Many of our recipes are perfect for modification — create your own version.
- Using frozen ingredients is not evil; proper freezing techniques will keep your food at its nutritional best. We eat through our freezer in the winter and early spring, practically eliminating the need to buy anything at the grocery store.
- Share your kitchen, but there may be times to consider a time-of-use policy so there's no traffic jam on the counter. Baking, for example, can take up a lot of space. Our farmhouse kitchen has plenty of space to spread out, but we still draw a line in the sand to preserve our sanity as we work together preparing a feast. (We each have a side of the kitchen.)

- Who eats with our eyes? Or with our nose? Of course, we eat with our mouth. But we also realize that there's nothing like the anticipation that comes with the aromas drifting from the kitchen to whet the appetite. And when the serving platter, plate or bowls arrive with the meal, it should feel like Christmas morning in front of the tree. Like a three-dimensional canvas, let the table setting bring out the best in what you've prepared. Tablecloths, vibrant napkins and candles on the table can turn functional meals into dining experiences.

- Leftovers are good, sometimes great. Many of our recipes taste even better the next day, usually having something to do with the way the spices mellow out or blend with the ingredients. We've found that having leftovers can make cooking more efficient, allowing the busiest of busy people the time to make meals without resorting to the processed corporate kind. Saves lots of money, too. We often prepare a dish or two so that we're good to go for several days' meals. A batch of our muffins will last half a week if they're just for the two of us.

- Avoid preservatives. They do nothing for flavor; they're there because corporations must put them there to prevent what they make from rotting on the shelves. Skip them all. We're always reading labels and asking questions since these preservatives can show up in the strangest places.

Why eat something that may be a derivative of natural gas or coal? For example, the FDA-approved food additive BHT (butylated hydroxytoluene) is a fat preservative found in Domino's Pizza deep-dish pepperoni pizza that's made from a petrochemical process and is surrounded by controversy related to its possible toxicity and link to cancer; this preservative can also be found in other meat products.

- Skip the empty calories coming with high-fructose corn syrup and other flavor enhancers found in processed shelf-stable foods, like MSG and excessive salt. These calories go nowhere other than around your waist, hips and thighs while contributing to a host of other health problems.

Community potluck at Inn Serendipity.

Here are a few non-food, non-cooking compass readings:

- Exercise. Most of the healthiest people, no matter where they live and the diet they've chosen, exercise regularly and strenuously, just about every day. Walking to the car or the dog doesn't really count. The Amish plant fields, nearly 8 percent of commuters in Portland, Oregon, bike to work, and we work in the gardens with hand tools and our backs (not tractors). In the winter, we hit the gym.
- Drink lots of water during the day, but not the bottled type. Heck, Coca-Cola's Dasani is nothing more than filtered tap water from municipal water sources, but with salt added. At about $8.25 per gallon, we hardly wonder why Danone Group's Evian bottled water, while sourced from natural springs in Switzerland, spelled backwards is naïve (the math: 33.8 oz. bottle × $1.29/bottle × 6.4 bottles to make a gallon = $8.25)
- Well-being has less to do with how much money — or stuff — we own, but more to do with connections to family and friends, in short, relationships. It's often those who have the happiest lives are the same people with the greatest number of friends and strongest connection to community. Added to this is the joy and happiness garnered by strong connections to the outdoors, to nature: watching it (like the birds), growing it (as in your backyard gardens) and, of course, savoring it through a meal prepared with fresh ingredients and shared among friends.

There's a lot to be said for the comfort of soup and the versatility of ingredients harvested months ago that retain their delicious taste and hearty nourishment. For most of us, we don't just make one bowl of soup, we make a pot to share with others, to warm them up after walking home from school or satisfy our craving for summertime sunshine. Soup is love in liquid form. This sharing of food and companionship builds bonds, fosters security, provides a sense of stability, boosts our happiness and proffers a feeling of well-being. That's our experience and perhaps yours too, whether we're taking in a potluck before a community musical event or joining friends for their soup nights.

We like to think that our approach to making soups resembles an the old stone-soup story that has circumnavigated the globe, perhaps due, in part, to the universality of soups in every culture — and the existence of the haves and have-nots, the rich and poor, the fortunate and the less so. The stone-soup story starts with a pot of boiling water and a stone tossed into it. Then, as a community comes together, adding this or that ingredient to the pot, the soup is transformed from the bland to the magnificent, with each ingredient and its contributor playing an important role in making something delicious out of nothing at all.

It's in this spirit of getting together and feeding each other that we offer a taste of the soups found in this chapter.

Cornucopia Beer and Cheese Soup

L AST SUMMER we felt up for the long-standing culinary competitive showdown: entering our Wisconsin State Fair. The whole experience, from following the specific rules, to the judging of the event itself, ignited a competitive cooking side we never knew we had. The Cornucopia Challenge category had to feature local Wisconsin-produced ingredients, hence the abundance of beer and cheese. This Cornucopia Beer and Cheese Soup recipe took home a third-place green ribbon! The base of this soup uses two cups of flour to keep it thick and hearty — it's perfect for a winter warm-up, even if you don't live in America's dairyland.

INGREDIENTS

- ¾ c. butter (1½ sticks)
- 1 c. onions, chopped (about 1 medium)
- 3 cloves garlic, minced
- 1 c. broccoli florets, cut into small pieces
- 1 c. carrots, finely chopped
- 2 c. flour
- 2 c. chicken stock
- 1 bottle (12 oz.) locally made beer (dark or light work fine)
- 3 t. Worcestershire sauce
- 4 c. milk
- 3 T. maple syrup
- 2 t. dry mustard
- ½ t. fennel seed
- 2 t. salt
- ⅛ t. pepper
- 4 chicken sausages, cooked and cut into small pieces
- 5 c. cheddar cheese, shredded

DIRECTIONS

❶ In a large saucepan over medium heat, melt butter. Add onions and garlic. Sauté until onions are soft and translucent.

❷ Add broccoli and carrots. Cook about 5 minutes.

❸ Stir in flour, making sure vegetables are coated.

❹ Stir in chicken stock. Bring to a boil over medium heat.

❺ Stir in beer, Worcestershire sauce and milk. Reduce heat to low, simmer 10 minutes and add maple syrup, mustard, fennel, salt, pepper and sausage.

❻ Cook 5 minutes longer, then slowly add cheese by the handful, stirring constantly until cheese is melted and soup begins to bubble. If the soup seems too thick, add a bit more milk or water. Add salt to taste.

YIELD: 12 servings.

Cream of Asparagus Soup

*A*SPARAGUS IS ONE of the few perennial food crops — most of what we eat comes from annual food crops. But not asparagus. The tough work of planting it once results in years of harvests of the shoots, over and over again, that come from the plant's crown deep underground. We cherish the one crop we can always count on, year after year. With a creamy base, this soup adds a richness to the mild flavor of asparagus that makes it the perfect special occasion soup for spring holidays.

INGREDIENTS

- ½ c. onion, chopped (1 small onion)
- 1 T. canola oil
- 3 c. vegetable stock
- 2½ lbs. asparagus, trimmed and cut into 1-inch pieces
- 1 t. tarragon
- ¼ c. butter (½ stick)
- ¼ c. flour
- ½ t. salt
- 3 c. half & half cream or evaporated milk
- 1½ t. lemon juice

DIRECTIONS

❶ In a large saucepan over medium heat, sauté onion in oil until tender.

❷ Add broth, asparagus and tarragon; simmer until the asparagus is tender, about 8 to 10 minutes.

❸ In a blender or food processor, purée the asparagus mixture and set aside.

❹ In a large kettle, melt the butter. Stir in flour and salt. Cook, stirring occasionally, for 2 minutes or until golden. Gradually add cream.

❺ Stir in the puréed asparagus and lemon juice. Heat through.

❻ Serve with croutons and sprinkle of Parmesan cheese shavings on top.

YIELD: 6 servings.

COOKING TIP Cream makes soups rich in taste with every spoonful feeling luxurious. For lighter eating, use evaporated milk that is fresh milk with 60 percent of the water removed, creating a creamier substitute without the fat and calories. Make your own "evaporated milk" by reconstituting ⅔ c. dry milk with only ¾ c. water for the equivalent of 1 can of evaporated milk found at the store.

Cucumber Soup

*T*HIS RECIPE BEGS EXTRA FANFARE since it's the only cucumber recipe, aside from pickles, that preserves a bumper crop of cucumbers. When we have too many 5-gallon pails full of cukes, we turn them into soup.

INGREDIENTS

2	large cucumbers
1	medium onion
¼	c. butter (½ stick)
1	T. soy sauce
¼	t. salt
¼	t. pepper
1	c. vegetable or chicken stock (optional)

DIRECTIONS

❶ Peel cucumbers. Cut cucumbers in half and deseed.

❷ Shred cucumber and onion in food processor.

❸ Sauté cucumber and onion in butter until slightly brown.

❹ Return to food processor and purée.

❺ Return to pot. Add stock (optional, depending on your preference for thickness), soy sauce, salt and pepper, and bring to a boil.

❻ Serve immediately with a few homemade croutons on top.

YIELD: 4 servings.

COOKING TIP | **Freezing Cucumber Soup Pulp Base**

After puréeing the cooked cucumber and onion, pack in freezer containers and freeze. To thin the soup when defrosted before serving, reheat and add the optional broth. The completed soup will also freeze just fine—however, freezing only the pulp will take up less freezer space.

EAT IT, TO SAVE IT

Chef Poppy Tooker,
host of WWNO's *Louisiana Eats!* and author of
***Crescent City Farmers Market Cookbook*,**
New Orleans, Louisiana

Add one part culinary activist, five parts cooking instructor, three parts TV and radio personality and two parts food reporter and you have Chef Poppy Tooker, someone nearly everyone in New Orleans has eaten with at some point, whether listening to her *Louisiana Eats!* radio show, watching her on TV or sampling a treat at one of her culinary presentations.

New Orleans Chef Poppy Tooker in the kitchen.

It was at one of her presentations that Lisa discovered Poppy's uncanny ability to transform fresh, local ingredients into dishes that celebrated the taste of place. Poppy articulated through her food how food preservationists are essential to the survival of not only traditional recipes and regional food culture — but the very foods themselves.

"Instead of saying 'Clean your plate,'" begins Poppy, "my great grandmother used to say, 'Poppy, eat it, to save it.' A food preservationist is about restoring and recovering the heirloom fruits and vegetables and the heritage breed animals by cultivating the interest in and taste for them at the dinner table. We're interested in preserving this rich diversity and the food traditions that surround them, their story, so to speak, on how they came to be. If you want to understand food, you have to understand the people behind the recipes and the farmers who grow or raise it."

"As industrialized farming becomes ever more prevalent, the availability of a diversity of foods has shrunk precipitously," continues Poppy. "We risk losing the taste and flavors of the foods that have come to define us as humans — and specifically, people who live here in New Orleans. While we may come from different faiths, ethnic backgrounds and political leanings, we all have to eat. The beliefs and perspectives don't really matter when you sit down at the table to enjoy authentic foods that may be found in your community, sometimes only in your community."

America's melting pot has produced a zillion different ways to enjoy pizza, few resembling the crust and lightly cheesed pizza napoletana that you'd find in Rome. We have grits in the south, bagels in New York, crab cakes in Maryland, sushi in California, brats in Wisconsin, seafood gumbo in New Orleans — to name just a few.

The confluence of ethnicities, cultural traditions, religious preferences and geographically specific ingredients yields a dizzying array of delightful dishes and menus. Added to this are the dietary preferences or requirements of more Americans, from gluten-free to vegan. Today's kitchen is never boring as more of us explore new tastes, flavors and combinations — the Thanksgiving turkey leftovers are just as likely to be turned into tacos as a casserole.

But local food traditions are under siege, not just by industrial approaches to food production, but also by global challenges such as climate change, and pressures created by a never-ending search for more oil. In New Orleans, these attacks took the form of the aftermath of Hurricane Katrina and the BP's Deepwater Horizon oil spill into the Gulf of Mexico.

"After Hurricane Katrina, New Orleans had to start over," muses Poppy. "We started from a spot where parts of the city had no restaurants, no grocery stores and no place to get fresh food. But I've witnessed an incredible rebirth. We now have Alice Water's Edible School Yard New Orleans, community gardens are sprouting up all over the place, and we have farmers markets again, like the Crescent City Farmers Market with over forty vendors. With Hurricane Katrina, we gained a new appreciation for everything, but especially our food, using delicious, authentic, local, fresh ingredients in our cooking. We have fresh food on the south shore now."

Perhaps no other city is as well-known and respected as a gastronomy center as New Orleans, itself a potpourri of cultures, flavors and tastes influenced by early French settlements, descendants from Africa and the flurry of international trade that passed through this bustling port city. But it's the Creole and Cajun cuisine that has earned its international notoriety.

"Cajun foods come from the country and are often hot and spicy with a predominance of pork and chicken," explains Poppy. "Creole cuisine, however, is largely based here in New Orleans, with our strong French roots, our busy port and thriving seafood industry. It's not hot or spicy, but rather full-flavored with the mixture of what my great-grandmother called 'seasonings,' those being bell peppers, celery and onions. Amazingly, in the 1830s, there were over four hundred vendors in New Orleans' French Market. Then, and now, New Orleans has such an incredible abundance." This abundance is what allows the city to rise above the many challenges it has faced over the years.

"I'd rather see a cotton patch goose on my plate than visit one in the zoo," smiles Poppy. She's quick to point out that we're talking about bringing back heritage breed animals and heirloom fruit and vegetables, saved from the brink of extinction through the work of non-profit organizations like Gary Nabhan's Renewing America's Food Traditions. She realizes that now, more than ever — especially after such catastrophic disasters as Hurricane Katrina or the BP oil spill — preserving our Earth's biodiversity demands that as many people as possible can come to have a taste for it, appreciate it and ultimately care enough to help preserve this biodiversity of flavors.

New Orleans Seafood Gumbo

*S*HE BEAT OUT the Food Network's Bobby Flay with this recipe. You might say it's all in the roux, a French term referring to a mix of oil or bacon grease and flour. "Instead of the caramel color of a roux in traditional French cooking, you'll want to cook it to a bittersweet chocolate color," advises Poppy Tooker.

INGREDIENTS

1   c. canola oil

1½ c. flour

5   gumbo crabs (or 1 lb. crab meat)

4   lbs. medium shrimp, with head and shell, if possible

1   c. onion, chopped (1 medium onion)

1   c. bell pepper, chopped (1 bell pepper)

3   stalks celery, chopped

2   lbs. okra, sliced in ¼-inch pieces

2   T. canola oil (for frying okra)

1½ c. fresh tomatoes, peeled, deseeded and diced (or 1 14-oz can crushed tomatoes)

½   gallon shrimp stock (prepared with heads, shells and veggie cuttings (except bell pepper)

1   clove garlic, minced

2   T. thyme

1   bay leaf

1   bunch green onions, chopped

½   t. salt

½   t. pepper

DIRECTIONS

❶ Peel shrimp and combine peels, onion skins and tops (except for peppers) in a stock pot. Cover with water and boil for 10 minutes. Strain and reserve.

❷ In a skillet, fry okra in very hot oil until lightly browned.

❸ Make a dark roux with the flour and oil. Add onions, stirring together until the roux darkens to a bittersweet chocolate brown. Add celery and bell pepper. Sauté for 5 minutes, then add the gumbo crabs, tomatoes, okra, herbs and the shrimp stock. Add garlic and salt and pepper to taste. Simmer 45 minutes or longer.

❹ Ten minutes before serving add shrimp and green onions.

❺ Serve on top of cooked rice.

YIELD: 12 servings.

Potato Soup

ONE IMAGE JUMPS TO MIND in describing this soup: a warm blanket. With hearty potatoes and a creamy base, this thick soup wraps your insides in cozy comfort. It's a meal in a bowl. The fall flavors pair nicely with some crusty bread. We like to use our autumn crop of Yukon Golds in this recipe, given their golden waxy flesh.

INGREDIENTS

½ c. celery, diced
½ c. carrot, diced
½ c. onion, diced
3 T. butter
2 T. flour
4 c. milk
3 c. vegetable stock
½ t. salt
½ t. seasoning salt
3 lbs. potatoes, peeled and cooked (6 medium potatoes)
1 t. paprika

DIRECTIONS

❶ In a large kettle, sauté the celery, carrot and onion in butter until tender.

❷ Stir in flour until smooth. Gradually add milk, cook and stir until thickened and bubbly.

❸ Add stock, salt and seasoning salt.

❹ Simmer for 10 minutes, stirring occasionally. Cube the potatoes and add to soup. Simmer for 20 more minutes.

❺ Purée in food processor in batches then return soup to pot.

❻ Serve immediately and garnish with a sprinkle of paprika on top.

YIELD: 8 servings.

We are the food we eat, the water we drink, the air we breathe. And reclaiming democratic control over our food and water and our ecological survival is the necessary project for our freedom.

VANDANA SHIVA, *EARTH DEMOCRACY*

Cream of Carrot Soup

*B*UGS BUNNY IS TO THE CARROT what Snow Miser is to Santa Claus, if Heat Miser doesn't lose his temper. (If you're too young or never owned a TV, Heat and Snow Miser play central roles in the 1974 holiday classic, *The Year Without a Santa Claus*). If carrots are great for improving eyesight — which they are — then feast on this soup for eagle eyes.

INGREDIENTS

- 1   lb. carrots, coarsely chopped (8 medium carrots)
- 2   c. potatoes, peeled and diced (2 medium potatoes)
- 1   c. onions, chopped (1 medium onion)
- 3   garlic cloves, minced
- ¼   c. butter (½ stick)
- ⅓   c. flour
- 2   t. salt
- 1   t. sugar
- 6   c. milk
- 1   c. half & half cream or evaporated milk
- 1   t. paprika

DIRECTIONS

❶ Bring a pot of water to a boil and add carrots and potatoes. Cook over medium heat for about 10 minutes until carrots and potatoes are tender. Drain, reserving cooking liquid.

❷ In a skillet over medium heat, sauté onions and garlic in butter until onions are translucent, approximately 5 minutes, then mix in flour, stirring for an additional 2 minutes.

❸ Place carrots, potatoes, onion mixture, salt and sugar in a food processor. Purée until smooth, adding reserved cooking liquid as needed for desired consistency.

❹ Pour into a large saucepan. Stir in milk and heat through over medium heat. Then add cream and heat through (but do not boil).

❺ Serve immediately and garnish with a sprinkle of paprika on top.

YIELD: 8 servings.

We learn from our gardens to deal with the most urgent question of the time: How much is enough?

WENDELL BERRY

Zucchini-Summer Squash Bisque

$\mathcal{W}$HEN OUR SUMMER squash and zucchini pile up on our kitchen counter and sit in five-gallon pails and fill the refrigerator, too, we know it's time to make soup. Rather than eating much of this soup in the summer, we tuck it away in the freezer. From December through April, we heat it up on our woodstove, add some cream (which doesn't freeze well) and savor it as the snowflakes fly.

INGREDIENTS

- 1   c. onion, chopped (1 medium onion)
- ½   c. butter (1 stick)
- 2½ c. zucchini, shredded
- 2½ c. vegetable or chicken stock
- 1   T. fresh basil (1 t. dried)
- ½   t. salt
- ¼   t. nutmeg
- 1   c. half & half cream
- ¼   c. fresh basil for garnish (optional)

DIRECTIONS

❶ In a large saucepan, sauté onion in butter until tender. Add zucchini and vegetable stock. Simmer, covered, for about 15 minutes. Add seasonings.

❷ Purée in food processor. The puréed base can be frozen at this point. Otherwise, return it to the sauce pan.

❸ Stir in cream and heat through.

❹ Serve with chopped fresh basil sprinkled on top.

YIELD: 4 servings.

Stirring squash soup.

Danish Potato Leek Soup

*I*N THE SAME WAY we let nature's abundance guide our cuisine and seasonal eating, we've learned to let go of cooking conventions. Not everything must be prepared on the stovetop or in the oven. Long before our solar Sun Oven, we had rediscovered the joys, aromas and super-energy-efficient approach to cooking on our woodstove, placed to one side of our kitchen, just like it used to be in the old days. Besides heating our farmhouse through the winter, the cooktop of the woodstove can be used to simmer sauces and soups, like this Danish Potato Leek Soup, to perfection.

INGREDIENTS

- 2   T. butter
- 12 c. leeks, cleaned and thinly sliced (4 large leeks)
- 1   T. fresh dill (1 t. dried)
- 3   lbs. potatoes, peeled and cubed (4 large potatoes)
- ½   t. salt
- 2   c. vegetable or chicken stock
- 2   c. milk
    sour cream

DIRECTIONS

❶ Melt butter in a large kettle over medium heat. Add leeks and dill; cook, stirring often, until leeks are soft, about 15 minutes.

❷ Add potatoes, salt and broth. Bring to a boil over high heat; cover, reduce heat and simmer for 30 to 40 minutes until potatoes are tender.

❸ Purée in batches in food processor. Return to pot and stir in milk.

❹ Cook over medium heat, stirring often, until soup is steaming. Add more salt to taste.

❺ For each serving, top with a dollop of sour cream.

YIELD: 6 servings.

Carpe Diem:
Seize and Savor the Potluck's Flavors

Remember that scene in *Dead Poets Society* when the English teacher John Keating, played by Robin Williams, jumps on the desk and shouts to his students: "Carpe diem. Seize the day, boys. Make your lives extraordinary"? By middle age, we finally grasped Mr. Keating's message. "Carpe diem" for us means "throw a potluck."

"Potluck" by definition means relishing the "luck of the pot," embracing the fact that you don't know exactly what will happen when you host this party. At this gathering where everyone contributes a food dish to share, you'll appreciate that simple sentiment: Savor the moment and celebrate life to its fullest because you know not what tomorrow may bring.

Think of a potluck as the antidote to redeem what ails modern society, delivered in a dish. A potluck stems from a rich history of sharing abundance in community, dating back to the Native American concept of a "potlatch," a communal event where the abundance and surplus produced by the community are shared freely. For many Native American tribes, the highest social status of any participant was based on who gave away — not who possessed — the most resources or material wealth. The antonym for potluck is hoard. By the late 1800s, potlatches were made illegal both in the US and Canada (but repealed in 1951). This attitude can slowly creep up without us even realizing what happened, like when we invest in a home security system rather than an extra set of dishes in anticipation of feeding a crowd.

Speaking of plates, we have quite the mismatched collection ready to go into potluck hosting mode, particularly during the summer months when the outdoors can readily accommodate the masses. We transform the old storage shed — now just an open roof over a concrete slab — into our "cantina," a party-perfect gathering spot complete with picnic tables, electric hook-up for blender drinks, a stage for impromptu music and twinkly icicle lights.

So channel your inner potluck Pied Piper to lure friends and family back to the potluck table. Here's how:

1. Activate Guests

Scatter the invite list beyond family and friends; appeal to those who may have never tasted a vine-ripened heirloom tomato. The local food theme

Musical event under the stars at the "Piazza" at a neighboring farm.

encompasses a wide range of people who would be great additions to the event — from area farmers to people who run businesses that prioritize local foods, like the owner of a restaurant known for its local fare.

2. Build a Bridge to Food Knowledge

Blend great food with a dash of education by creating a setting that engages and sparks conversation amongst your guests. We provide blank index cards and pens for our guests to write the name of their dish and share details on the ingredients that come from local sources, like "Pork brats from Jordandahl Farm in Argyle, Wisconsin" or "Cucumber salad from the gardens at Inn Serendipity." Consider using a map to visually connect guests with their local food sources. There's something about push-pins and post-its that grown-ups and kids alike respond to. Consider gifting some of your garden bounty

to those who came up short in theirs. Or send the person who brought the dish made with the greatest amount of local ingredients home with a bottle of your best cordial.

3. Mix with Music

Food and music make merry when mixed together. Cara Carper, a friend and local extension agent who has her pulse on the local food movement, discovered this when she and her husband, Dave, got married in her family's barn. The party rocked until dawn, with several guests never making it off the premises.

"Friends kept asking us when we were going to do that again," says Cara, realizing that food, friends and music bring people together in new ways. "The wedding was a one-time deal, but we kept the spirit and connections going with our biannual barn party, a big potluck with lots of music," she continues. "We wanted to create a venue at our barn party for local folks to share their talents. The barn stage is open to anyone. We even take out an ad in our local newspaper encouraging folks to come play. The rich music talent in our community always amazes me."

Take whatever happens with a potluck — whether hosted on a rooftop, on your patio or in a hog shed like ours — and go with the flow. One correction to carpe diem that we've learned to live with: sometimes the potlucks may never end. So grab a few tents for your potluck, just in case.

Tomato Dill Soup

HISTORIANS CLAIM THOMAS JEFFERSON introduced America to the tomato, as well as macaroni, French fries, ice cream and the waffle iron. Sure Thomas has some personal baggage, but at least he ate — and grew — his own vegetables at Monticello. He's known for passing out seeds to neighbors, families and even fellow politicians. So our Tomato Dill Soup is dedicated to Thomas and to any other politician willing to sow what she or he says.

INGREDIENTS

- 1   c. onion, chopped (1 medium onion)
- 1   clove garlic, minced
- 2   T. butter
- 4   c. fresh tomatoes, peeled & chopped (4 large tomatoes)
- 1   c. vegetable or chicken stock
- 1   T. fresh dill (1 t. dried)
- ¼   t. salt
- ½   c. mayonnaise
   sprigs of fresh dill or parsley to garnish

DIRECTIONS

1. In large saucepan, sauté onions and garlic in butter over medium heat for about 5 minutes.

2. Add tomatoes, broth, dill and salt. Cover the saucepan and simmer for 10 minutes.

3. Remove from heat and purée in food processor and return to saucepan.

4. Fold in mayonnaise.

5. Serve hot or cold, you decide. Reheat the soup gently if it's to be served hot, garnished with dill or parsley sprinkled on top. Cover and chill overnight if it's to be served cold.

YIELD: 6 servings.

COOKING TIP

Carving Up a Tomato

For many of our recipes, you can get away without peeling and seeding the tomatoes. For soups and sauces, however, it's best to remove the skins and seeds so you're left with the fruity flesh. Who wants chewy chunks of tomato skin in your soup? To peel a tomato, with a knife score an X on the bottom of each one, then toss them in a pot of boiling water for about 45 seconds until the skins loosen up. Remove tomatoes with a slotted spoon, then peel the skins off under cold running water. To remove the seeds, cut the tomato in half and scoop out the seeds with your fingers.

Becoming a Local Forager

Even the celebrity chefs are doing it these days, hiring foragers to hit the farmers markets for what's uber-fresh or unique, or heading to the rooftop gardens to cut the fresh herbs needed for their daily specials. Whole Foods Market now has foragers on their payroll.

But this isn't what we mean by becoming a local forager. Our definition involves actively searching for your food or provisions, but not just in your backyard kitchen garden. Becoming a local forager is to rediscover which wild foods are abundant where you live: deer, moose, native black walnuts or wild mushrooms in the forests; rabbits, Jerusalem artichokes or ring-necked pheasant on the prairie; or crawfish, bluegill or bass in a lake nearby. It's about responsibly savoring wild foods that have largely been eclipsed by

Chef frying up chanterelle mushrooms at the Wild Coast Restaurant at Treebones Resort, Big Sur, California.

more modern approaches to agriculture with annual row crops or livestock.

Wild foods tend to epitomize seasonal eating and can be defined by a season consisting of a matter of weeks — sometimes found only when certain weather conditions come together for an abundant harvest. Without a doubt, morel mushrooms are one such early spring delicacy that many landowners around us covet, their location kept secret to all but the closest of family relatives. On the West Coast, there's the flavorful chanterelle mushrooms.

Wild food foraging goes beyond hunting for nuts, berries and wild edibles. Perhaps it appeals to our more primal urge to eat closer to the land and dine on whole foods as nature intended. It's not just for the survivalist type, but also for those eager to return to a time and age where knowledge is not based on binary code. Wild foods distill genetic engineering to its essence: nature.

"Trying economic times are the great equalizer, and today people are hungry to take a journey outside the confines of cubicle life, to step off the grid, even if just once in a while, to get back in touch with their natural human roots," says Georgia Pellegrini, author of *Food Heroes* and *Girl Hunter*.

"There's always one focus when foraging for wild foods: know what you're eating," echoes Sam Thayer, born in Wausau, Wisconsin, where he first learned to gather wild food in vacant lots, backyards, city parks and at the edge of town. His approach to wild foods could just as easily define farmsteadtarian eating: mindful meals.

"I call it the 'banana test,' since we're very good at identifying the difference between a banana and an orange," continues Sam. Today, Sam's the Huck Finn of wild food foraging and author of *The Forager's Harvest*, an ideal companion book to carry into the woods when searching for a supper of fern fiddleheads or milkweed. "Once you become a good forager, you'll understand that wild foods are, in fact, as different as iceberg lettuce and romaine. I teach participants to question what the plants are before they put them in their mouth."

Wild foods defy our attempts to cultivate them. The closest thing might be shiitake mushrooms grown in an inoculated log in the woods. Wild food foraging harkens a return to the time of the hunter-gatherer, where intimate local knowledge and a deep understanding of animal behavior or ecology served the foragers well and kept them out of trouble, perhaps by selecting the edible mushrooms, not the poisonous ones. You'll need plenty of patience and perseverance; it takes time to find these wild delicacies.

If you can lose the Bambi sentimentality, or if you grew up hunting with your parents or family, then hunting deer or other wild game may seem as natural as putting a pole in the pond to see what's biting. Millions of Americans help keep the deer population in check while putting food on the table for their family all winter long.

"Hunting and gathering, when done ethically, is the last natural and instinctive interplay between humans, the land and animals," explains Georgia. "Hunting is also about conservation — a way to help sustain animal populations that have overrun their carrying capacity as we eliminate their habitat. Hunting is an act involving all of the senses. It is part of the natural cycle of life. Humans eat animals, animals eat animals and plants, plants feed from the dirt, and we turn to dirt. It's the last part that some people have a hard time with — where there is the flow of life there is also the flow of death, and they have to acknowledge their own mortality."

Where we live, just prior to Thanksgiving, it's "camouflage flu" season. Deer season. Many families count on culling of the deer population during deer season so they can stock their freezer with venison. With a state-issued hunting license for the season, armed and trained with a rifle or shotgun appropriate and legal for what you're hunting (varies greatly by state), and access to some woods or prairie depending on what you're looking to bag, you're good

to go. Have a plan, however, for "dressing" your harvest, either with fellow hunters to show you how — or learning about what's necessary before your skills bring you a kill.

In the city, foraging can take on a more unconventional approach, wild, but in a different sense. Freegans (freegan.info) — people who forage through garbage searching for food and other useful castoffs — push back at an economic system based on consumption and waste.

"Despite the media hype that would suggest otherwise, freeganism is not exclusively about Dumpster diving or reclaiming wasted food," explains Cindy Rosin, a Freegan and school teacher who lives in New York City. "Freegans can be gardeners or wild food foragers as well, not only Dumpster divers."

"We're bringing the social aspect and the love back into food gathering and preparation, and that can surround an elaborately prepared meal of organic local vegetables or a curbside binge on expired cookies," continues Cindy. "Freegans aren't just fringe-dwelling social dropouts — they're everyday people who are saying no to capitalism's abuses — saying there must be a better way if our planet is to survive. Reclaiming some small part of the 50 percent of our food supply that goes to waste is just one way for a conscientious person to refuse to be part of the problem."

Somewhere between *Girl Hunter* and Urban Forager, given the precipitous population decline in such cities like Detroit and the food revolution underway there and elsewhere, it may not be that far into the future where a pheasant season is possible between stretches of abandoned city lots and old warehouses. Meanwhile, on our farm, we're amazed how mulberry bushes push up through concrete so we can gorge on them come the Fourth of July. A premonition of what's to come: there are already parts of Detroit where you're more likely to cross paths with a pheasant than a person.

Winter Butternut Squash Bisque

*B*ISQUE SOUPS BLEND an ingredient dream team: nutritious and silky garden vegetable purée with a rich, heavy cream. For us, comfort food is about something that makes you feel better after you enjoy it. More healthy comfort food like this bisque soup gratifies, but without the guilt and bloating that may come from downing the comfort food peddled at a fast-food joint or processed food aisle at the supermarket. For those eager to cut a few calories and keep it lighter, substitute milk or evaporated milk for the heavy cream.

INGREDIENTS

¼ c. butter (½ stick)
1 c. onions, chopped (1 medium onion)
1 c. root vegetables (carrots, potatoes or rutabagas)
4 c. butternut squash, peeled and cubed
3 c. vegetable stock
¼ t. salt
½ t. nutmeg
½ c. half & half cream (or 1 c. evaporated milk)
½ t. paprika or 2 T. sour cream for garnish (optional)

DIRECTIONS

❶ In a large saucepan over medium heat, melt butter, then add in onions and cook until onions are tender.

❷ Mix the other fall root vegetables and squash into the pot. Pour in vegetable stock, salt and nutmeg. Bring to a boil over medium heat. Reduce heat and simmer until vegetables are tender.

❸ In a food processor, or using an immersion blender, purée the mixture until smooth. Return to pot and stir in the cream or evaporated milk. Heat through but do not boil.

❹ Serve with a sprinkle of paprika or a dollop of sour cream on top.

YIELD: 8 servings.

Let thy food be thy medicine
and let thy medicine be thy food.

HIPPOCRATES, 460–377 BCE

SIDES, SAUCES & SALADS

Cheese Roasted Asparagus

Roasted Asparagus in Balsamic Vinegar (vegan)

Oven-roasted Potatoes

Root Crop Kabobs (vegan)

Batter-dipped French Fries (vegan)

Swiss Rösti Potatoes

Roasted Root Vegetables (vegan)

Tomato Crouton Casserole

Roasted Fresh Tomato Sauce (vegan)

Slow-simmered Tomato Sauce (vegan)

Hollandaise Sauce

Sour Dill Cucumbers (vegan) (Todd and Jordan Champagne)

Spicy Kimchee (vegan) (Todd and Jordan Champagne)

Classic Sauerkraut (vegan) (Todd and Jordan Champagne)

Caesar Salad

Cucumber Salad

Creamy Spinach Salad

Strawberry Spinach Salad

Young Green Beans with Balsamic Vinegar

** see Liam's Favorites (page 219) for: Garden Fresh Salad

Nature's Ponzi Scheme

Garlic planters have thrived thanks to the largest Ponzi scheme ever conceived — more than Bernie Madoff's billions and perhaps more than the US Federal government's escapades with Social Security, issuing IOUs to Paul (into the future) to pay Peter now.

That's what happens when you plant a head of garlic, which usually consists of about 6 cloves. We harvest our garlic in June, curing them in our straw bale greenhouse. When it comes time to plant garlic late in the fall, we break apart the bulb and separate out each of the cloves: our seeds. By the second season, that head or bulb of garlic has produced 6 heads. By year three, as many as 36 bulbs (6 heads multi-plied by 6 cloves each). In year four, there are 214. You see where this is going. By year ten, more than 10,000 garlic bulbs. We've just created a vampire-free zone, without a doubt.

Unless we suffer a catastrophic crop failure, pretty uncommon for garlic crops, it's practically impossible to go bust — nature is hardwired to cover itself, reproductively speaking. For proof, try counting the blossoms on an apple or cherry tree in the spring. Some blossoms become apples or cherries, others don't (blame it on the bees, a late frost or some other weather calamity). The point here is that nature, more often than not, goes overboard on abundance. And if you tend your own orchard or garden, it doesn't take long to realize that the bushels of apples don't cost a penny. Just your time and some labor.

It's this fresh abundance that allows us to gorge on or process (for later use) from late May through early November in our northern climate. Fresh means selecting the freshest ingredients, fruits, vegetable or herbs found a hundred feet from our back door and not ones that have traveled for thousands of miles. In general, the more an ingredient arrives on your table resembling what it was in the field, the better its nutrient value and fiber content. The harder part is figuring out what is both fresh and ripe — there's nothing more disappointing than biting into an unripe apple or watermelon!

Some things are always tasty, regardless of size, like carrots. Baby carrots often featured at high-end restaurants are selected because they're more tender and flavorful. And the corollary, bigger is not always better for vegetables like zucchini (you can't enjoy the skin since it's too hard), cucumbers (they can get bitter or seedy) or beets (they get tough and woody).

For the rest of our fresh produce, however, we

Fresh garden salad greens.

consult friends, books, the Internet and seed catalogs to determine, for example, when the abundant muskmelons we grow are ready to eat. Is it color, smell or the magic touch or tap? We looked like ostriches, butts in the air and heads bobbing up and down, bending close to the ground in our attempts to catch a whiff of the sweet smell of sunshine from a ripe melon. We learned that our cultivar of melons, when ripe, should "slip" off the spot that they're connected to the vine with a gentle tug—a more reliable method. So for each of our fruits, vegetables and herbs, we learned the telltale signs of ripeness. For those who shop the farmers markets, receive a CSA box or ply the fresh produce aisles, this quest for fresh and ripe has been largely done for you—often masterfully.

So savor the best flavors and realize that the most nutritious foods you can eat are also the freshest, assuming you don't boil, steam or sauté them into mush. Depending on the vegetable or fruit, the minute they're harvested, their enzymes that help in their ripening also make them rot. When eating fresh, you're on the clock, even with the benefit of a refrigerator. Some foods, however, like garlic or potatoes, can be stored for months.

Since part of this chapter delves into salads, you'll notice the ingredient lists and recipes appear short. Nothing skipped, just quality ingredients added. We'd be ruining your meal if we'd suggest otherwise. Also worth noting, there's no iceberg lettuce, since there are far more nutritious and flavorful greens from which to choose. It's ironic that the crunchy iceberg is among the top three vegetables consumed by Americans. (The other two being but a variation on one, potatoes, in the form of either French fries or potato chips).

For anyone who snips some lettuce, pulls a radish or two and plucks a vine ripened tomato in order to toss up a salad, the fresh ingredients steal the show and demand simple recipes to spotlight and highlight what's already the rock star. When the garden and fresh flavors peak in abundance during the growing season—when salad greens jump 100 feet in five minutes from the garden to our plate—just a sprinkle of homemade salad dressing brings out their subtle flavors.

Liam Kivirist planting seeds.

Cheese Roasted Asparagus

*I*T'S UNLIKELY THAT we'll ever be able to save and freeze much of our asparagus—even with our numerous growing beds—since we can't help but eat it all as soon as it starts pushing up through the soil in early spring. Part of the problem after a winter largely without greens is that our bodies crave anything fresh and green come spring. Eating seasonally does have a few drawbacks (some might call them sacrifices), the least of which is that fresh lettuce, spinach, broccoli and small fruits rarely find their way onto our plates during the winter months. Absence, we agree, makes the heart grow fonder and, we'd maintain, the palate more eager. Instead of a potato side, try this recipe for dinner or breakfast.

INGREDIENTS

1   t. canola oil
1   lb. fresh asparagus, trimmed
2   T. green onion, chopped
2   T. celery, chopped
2   T. hard granular cheese, grated (Parmesan)
¼   c. bread crumbs
¼   c. butter, melted (½ stick)
¼   t. salt

DIRECTIONS

❶ Place asparagus in a lightly oiled 9 × 13-inch baking pan in one heavy layer.

❷ Mix remaining ingredients and spoon over asparagus.

❸ Bake at 375° for 45 minutes or until tender.

❹ Plate this dish on a white serving plate to bring out the vibrant green colors.

YIELD: Serves 4.

COOKING TIP

Say Cheese!

It's the mold that keeps on giving. We've learned to focus on using our local, high-quality European-style or artisanal cheeses. Artisanal cheeses contrast with the mass-produced (and bland) kind you find in the grocery store in many ways, the least of which are flavors, textures, varieties and distinctive types with defining characteristics, like a streak of blue in blue cheese or the creamy, tart bite of a chevre. Artisan cheesemakers make the cheese by hand, often by age-old methods, not machines or robots that churn out the industrial stuff. It's the process of ripening and aging the cheeses that results in the distinctive flavors, textures and, yes, aromas. With the diversity of cheese available and myriad ways to classify cheeses (texture, age, fat content and so on), for the purposes of this book we mention the type by names but the brand you may end up buying can differ depending on where you live. For example, this recipe calls for a hard granular cheese: a low-moisture cheese that tends to taste tangy, appear dense and have a granular texture, often just grated as a topping. While we may refer to it as Parmesan in this cookbook, we're not referring to a certain brand that's sold in a green can. Rather it's Parmigiano Reggiano, imported from Italy, or, in our case, a local version from Monroe's Emmi Roth Käse cheese factory called GranQueso.

Roasted Asparagus in Balsamic Vinegar

 O NAKED WITH THIS RECIPE. Just a splash of balsamic vinegar with some salt and olive oil is all that's needed to bring out the flavors of fresh asparagus.

INGREDIENTS

1   lb. fresh asparagus, trimmed
2   t. olive oil
½   t. salt
3   T. balsamic vinegar

DIRECTIONS

❶ Place the asparagus in a lightly oiled 9 × 13-inch baking pan.

❷ Sprinkle with oil and salt.

❸ Bake at 425° for 10 to 15 minutes or until lightly browned.

❹ Transfer to a heated serving plate to keep the asparagus hot, then drizzle with vinegar just before serving.

YIELD: 4 Servings.

 COOKING TIP **Retaining the Asparagus Crunch**
Keep fresh asparagus from going limp by placing them in an upright glass Mason jar in your refrigerator with cut ends submerged in a couple of inches of water.

Mason jar with asparagus popping out.

Oven-roasted Potatoes

*T*HE HECK WITH HASH BROWNS, the greasy-spoon diner speciality. This healthier alternative made with olive oil is a nice side for breakfast or great as a starch for dinner, too—just not on the same day.

INGREDIENTS

½ c. olive oil

¼ c. butter (½ stick), melted

2 t. beef bouillon paste (not stock)

1 t. thyme

1 t. marjoram

3 T. dried onion flakes

¼ t. celery seed

⅛ t. celery salt

2 lbs. potatoes, peeled & quartered (about 8 cups)

DIRECTIONS

❶ In a 9 × 13-inch baking pan, mix oil, melted butter, bouillon and herbs.

❷ Add potatoes and coat with mixture.

❸ Bake for about 30 minutes at 450°, until tender and golden brown. Turn potatoes occasionally while baking.

YIELD: 8 servings.

COOKING TIP

Better than Bouillon

We use Superior Touch Better than Bouillon organic beef base for this oven-roasted potatoes recipe. The fact that you can recognize the ingredients is a great start, plus it must be refrigerated after opened. It tastes great.

Root Crop Kabobs

So THE SUMMER IS SIZZLING ALONG. Perhaps your gardens are overloading you with more than you can handle, or the CSA box keeps showing up with a few mid-summer root crops that you don't regularly cook with, like turnips and rutabagas. Relax. This marinade recipe makes a big batch of about 24 c. of chopped veggies. Marinades are forgiving recipes; feel free to use other herbs you may have in the pantry or, better yet, fresh from the garden like dill or basil. Leftover kabob pieces taste great cold or reheated and served over rice.

MARINADE INGREDIENTS

- 1½ c. olive oil
- 2 T. garlic salt
- 2 T. dried oregano or about ⅓ c. fresh
- 2 T. dried thyme or about ⅓ c. fresh
- 2 T. sugar

KABOB INGREDIENTS

- 10 c. root crops, cubed into 1½-inch chunks (turnips, rutabagas, parsnips, beets)
- 6 c. summer squash or zucchini, cubed into 1½-inch chunks
- 5 c. onions, quartered
- 4 c. whole cherry or small tomatoes
- 16 wood kabob skewers

DIRECTIONS

❶ Steam root crops as recommended in cooking tip below.

❷ Place all marinade ingredients in a glass canning jar and gently shake until sugar dissolves.

❸ Place cut veggies and whole tomatoes in a large bowl and pour marinade over veggies. Gently stir to evenly coat veggies. Refrigerate several hours for veggies to absorb the marinade flavors, stirring about every 15 to 30 minutes.

❹ Soak wood skewers in water for about an hour before making kabobs (the skewers absorb water and are less likely to catch fire).

❺ Skewer marinated veggies on kabob sticks, about 5 veggie pieces per kabob. Grill approximately 5 minutes on each side until nicely brown.

❻ Serve over a bed of fresh lettuce greens for an added color punch.

YIELD: 16 kabobs.

COOKING TIP These kabobs can be made with just about any seasonally fresh veggie. Firmer root veggies like beets, rutabagas and turnips taste great in kabobs, just be sure to boil or steam them first (firm but tender, so you can puncture them with a fork) before putting them on the grill.

Batter-dipped French Fries

V Vegan

W̳E NEVER SAID WE DIDN'T EAT FRENCH FRIES, we just don't eat them every week. This is our version of America's favorite way to eat potatoes, except ours are organic, local and batter-dipped. We choose organic and grow organically for lots of reasons, the least of which are for the health of the eater, farmer and land. The USDA organic certification label is most essential when we cannot directly meet our grower or food producer. The certification process is both comprehensive and verified by someone not working for either the government or the grower. We rely on the Organic Consumers Association (organicconsumers.org) to keep us abreast of changes with organic foods.

INGREDIENTS

About 1½ pounds potatoes, peeled
1 c. flour
1 t. garlic salt
1 t. seasoning salt
1 t. salt
1 t. paprika
½ c. water or as needed
canola oil for frying
½ t. chili powder
½ t. salt

DIRECTIONS

❶ Slice potatoes into French fries and place in cold water for a couple of hours. The water removes some of the starch and will make your fries crispier.

❷ Heat oil in large skillet over medium-high heat or use a deep fryer.

❸ While the oil is heating, sift the flour, garlic salt, seasoning salt, (sea) salt and paprika into a large bowl. Gradually stir in enough water so that the batter can be drizzled from a spoon.

❹ Dip potato slices into the batter one at a time, and place in the hot oil so they are not touching at first. The fries must be placed into a deep fryer one at a time, or they will clump together. Fry until golden brown and crispy. Remove, and drain on paper towels.

❺ Serve immediately, sprinkled with seasoning salt and a dash of chili powder.

YIELD: 6 servings.

Cookery is not chemistry. It is an art.
It requires instinct and taste rather than exact measurements.

MARCEL BOULESTIN

Food Fight: Becoming a Victory Garden Grower

For us, patriotic is fresh spinach greens and carrots ready to harvest right outside our kitchen door — or a bushel of potatoes stored in our basement root cellar, stockpiled for the winter. It's powering our farm completely with homemade renewable energy.

As gardening and farmsteading patriots, we connect with that historic victory garden movement of the First and Second World Wars, connecting home-grown produce with homeland security. Today, there's a victory garden renaissance among enthusiastic growers like ourselves, revitalizing this patriotic call while also keenly aware of rising fuel and food prices.

Our 5.5 acres sits on a ridge with undulating hills falling away in every direction, filled with the big-three crops for our county: corn, soybeans and alfalfa. Most of what our neighboring farmers grow goes to feeding their dairy cows or a few pigs or sold as commodities. To help mitigate chemical and GMO (genetically modified organisms) drift onto our organic farm, we've added evergreens around the edges of our rectangular property every year since arriving more than a decade and a half ago. In the distance to the west are blinking and spinning sentinels, a recently erected wind farm that sends its renewable energy through the transmission wires into the Windy City, Chicago.

The farmhouse is a typical four-square, two-story wood-framed house with dormers facing north and south, surrounded by blue spruce and white pines we planted to serve as windbreaks and help to boost our home's energy efficiency. On the west side between two maples is a small pond, kept full with the downspout of one gutter; on the east side meanders our perennial flower beds that put on a kaleidoscopic display of color and foliage from April through November.

A white trellis, handcrafted by our neighbor Burnette Burkhalter, serves as the entrance through which one passes our flower beds into our three growing fields — our version of the Victory Gardens

Victory Garden WWII poster. Bright-colored posters produced for the government by artists from the Work Progress Administration (WPA) encouraged Americans to "Fight with Food."

that make up about a third of an acre. We've taken E. F. Schumacher's small is beautiful mantra to heart. Separating field one and two is a raspberry patch from which we make two harvests, the first in early summer and the second, late fall. There's also a tulip bed tucked in for an early spring show.

The 4-foot-wide raised beds in field two are book-ended with perennial flowers, an idea we borrowed after a visit the Center for Agroecology at the University of California Santa Cruz. The flowers aren't just for show; they mark the beds in early spring, attract bees throughout the summer and feed our souls in the same way that the food crops feed our bodies. The rest of the mounded raised beds in our gardens stretch about 50 feet long, separated by walking pathways in New Zealand clover to keep weed pressures in check.

As organic growers, we cycle through a 4-year rotation to confuse the bejiggers out of the insects, put a damper on possible fungus issues in the soil and avoid depleting soil fertility by growing the same plant in the same row over and over again. After our major mid-summer harvests of onions, garlic, potatoes and sweet peas, for example, we plant in a "green manure" cover crop of hairy vetch, sweet peas and winter rye — all killed off by our frigid winters — but only after it prevents our soil from eroding away. Instead of herbicides, we mulch like crazy, mostly with straw and newspaper, which also helps retain moisture and cut down on the need to use our drip irrigation system.

Several of our compost mounds are strategically placed at the edges of the gardens; slow heaps that turn into rich humus added back into our beds after about a year or so of decomposition. We also work in some of our neighbor's horse manure. Both help preserve moisture, boost the nutrient levels of our produce (as some research suggests) and increase our yields.

In the end, our version of Victory Gardens stand as testament to how we rekindled our urge to grow what we ate, selling some of our surplus to our guests, area restaurants or at farmers markets over the years. We now meet more than 70 percent of our food needs ourselves. Despite our un-agrarian upbringing in the suburbs, we managed to figure out how to retake control of our food supply. We've joined the millions of Americans who have picked up a hoe, purchased some seeds and got to work in their gardens — whether to save money, grow fresh, higher-quality ingredients or simply feel the satisfaction that comes from eating what you grow. It's not the survivalist instinct that has kicked in, but a pioneering, self-sufficiency one. There's nothing like growing your own salad rather than buying it in a bag or plastic box, all chopped up for us.

The last time the Victory Garden movement took root in the US was during World War II, when the government appealed to Americans to grow some of their own food, not just in rural areas, but in the city too, in backyards, rooftops or empty lots. Nearly 20 million Americans answered the call, becoming patriotic producers of the foods they consumed in their communities, in part, because commercially canned goods were rationed as a result of the war and there was limited fuel to transport food around the country. Gardening was no longer the providence of the poor or those who could not afford to feed themselves; rather, gardening emerged as a civic virtue, a responsibility to country and to community.

According to the USDA, more than 9 million tons of fresh vegetables and fruits were harvested from these gardens in 1943, an amount on par with the commercial production at that time and accounting for 40 percent of the produce consumed in America. Europeans, likewise, had their own gardening initiative, as they did previously during World War I. While many kitchen gardens declined or disappeared in the years following the war, in Europe gardening continued as a popular pastime in community gardens as well as kitchen gardens on small plots of land.

Our friend Rose Hayden-Smith, a garden historian with the University of California, understands the outcome of the Victory Garden movement better than most. She's a powerhouse with a passion for plants. Her heart and the focus of her academic work roots in Victory Gardens. But she's on a mission: how to rekindle that growing spirit.

"There are various reasons for today's revival of Victory Gardens," began Rose, as she took us on a walking tour of the historic University of California Faulkner Farm in Santa Paula, California, where she leads the educational programming at University of Californias Hansen Agricultural Center. "In addition to tough economic times, people are increasingly concerned about the health of our food system. They want to make a direct connection to where their food comes from. People are also looking for a return to community-based living, a time reminiscent of 1943 which was the peak of the Victory Garden movement when folks readily exchanged garden surplus and cultivated warm friendships with neighbors."

"Unfortunately, many people associated Victory Gardens with deprivation and hard times during the day," admits Rose, explaining the sudden disappearance of the gardens after the war. "They felt liberated to not need to garden anymore. The decades after World War II brought economic prosperity to America, and with that, the rise of processed and convenience food, leading our nation even further from home gardens and, one might add, healthy food. The obesity epidemic is no secret these days."

The troops are reorganizing. "While the doughboy and McDonald's clown may have managed to overtake the Victory Garden army of patriots a generation ago, we have noticed seeds of change sprouting," smiles Rose. "Today, Americans of all ages have enlisted to serve healthier meals to their families, prepared with fresh, affordable ingredients grown right out their back door. You could say that we've rediscovered the flavor of fresh."

Swiss Rösti Potatoes

For a Swiss twist to hash browns, try a local favorite in our hometown of Monroe, Wisconsin: Rösti (roe-esti) Potatoes. This recipe takes some flipping technique, and it's essential that you have a non-stick pan to avoid aggravation over the potato mixture that will otherwise stick to the pan. Use waxy-type potatoes (Yukon Gold) rather than the fluffy Russets if you can. In this recipe, we've replaced some of the butter with healthier olive oil and a little Swiss cheese to make it cheesier.

. . . . FARMSTEAD CHEF . . . .

INGREDIENTS

- 4 c. gold potatoes, peeled and shredded (4 medium potatoes or 1½ lbs.)
- ½ c. yellow onions, shredded
- ½ c. Swiss cheese, shredded
- 2 cloves garlic, minced
- ½ t. salt
- ½ t. pepper
- 3 T. olive oil
- 2 T. butter

DIRECTIONS

❶ Peel potatoes and shred in food processor or hand grater so that the potatoes resemble those needed for hash browns.

❷ Wash potatoes in cold water to remove excess starch, then place on dry, clean dishtowel. Press down on potatoes with the cloth to remove excess moisture.

❸ Sauté onions with garlic in olive oil in skillet over medium heat for 5 minutes or until translucent, stirring in garlic after about 3 minutes. Set aside.

❹ In a large bowl, mix potatoes, cheese, salt and pepper. Then mix in the onions and garlic.

❺ On stovetop, add 2 T. of oil and 1 T. butter to 12-inch skillet over medium heat. Then add the potato mixture using a spatula to level the potatoes evenly across the pan to create a round loaf about 1½-inch thick. Do not stir potato mixture. Cover the pan, cooking over medium heat for 6 to 8 minutes or until the bottom surface of the potatoes is golden brown. Add more oil as needed. Make sure the potato loaf mixture does not stick to the pan by running your spatula around the edges, then underneath the loaf. If you can slide around the potato loaf when lightly shaking the pan, you're in good shape. Remove cover and cook the potato loaf an additional 5 minutes, but watch to avoid burning the bottom of the potato loaf mixture.

❻ Prepare a flat baking sheet with a coat of canola oil. Remove skillet from stovetop. With protective hotpads, place the baking sheet over the skillet, then quickly flip over the skillet so that the partially cooked potato loaf drops onto the oiled baking sheet.

❼ Place skillet back on stovetop, adding 1 T. more of olive oil and butter. Slide the round potato mixture, uncooked side down, from the baking sheet onto the skillet. Don't miss the skillet or you'll have potatoes all over the counter — or the floor.

❽ Cook uncovered in the skillet for 6 to 8 minutes or until the bottom is golden brown. When completed, remove from skillet by slightly tilting, allowing the finished Swiss Rösti Potatoes to slide out onto a serving dish. Cut 4 pie-shaped wedges into the potatoes.

❾ Serve immediately family style on a large dish with 4 wedge cuts made, as if it were a pie. Or serve an individual slice with a sprinkle of a few nasturtium flowers or colorful bee balm petals.

YIELD: 4 servings.

COOKING TIP

After the shredded potatoes have been dried and are ready for cooking, mix in some cooked ground beef or sausage to make a meat-potato pizza (as an interesting side dish). Instead of ground beef or sausage, try adding carrots julienned and steamed or sautéed spinach for another vegetarian alternative.

Roasted Root Vegetables

OUR SPUDS GET BUMPED off the plate when our other root crops are ready. This recipe champions the overlooked rutabagas, turnips and parsnips. Who knew the taproot family of veggies (taproot, because they grow vertically downward, tapering in shape) pack more nutritional punch than the potato. Be sure to boil turnips and rutabagas first until they are tender-firm since they don't cook as fast as the other root crops like beets. Rutabagas and turnips remind us to rethink our food assumptions and to remember to sometimes choose the culinary path less traveled. They're not just for dinner, either. We serve these Roasted Root Vegetables for a flavorful twist in our morning fare.

INGREDIENTS

- 8 c. beets, turnips, rutabagas and potatoes, cleaned, peeled and chopped into bite-size pieces
- 2½ t. garlic salt
- 2 T. fresh oregano, finely chopped (2 t. dried)
- 1½ t. sugar
- 2 T. fresh thyme, finely chopped (2 t. dried)

DIRECTIONS

❶ Mix spices and oil in a glass jar and let set for about an hour or more.

❷ Boil turnips and rutabagas until they are tender-firm since they don't cook as fast as the other root crops like beets.

❸ Place veggies in a 9 × 13-inch baking pan. Drizzle spice and oil mixture over veggies and toss to coat.

❹ Bake at 425° for 20 to 25 minutes or until tender, stirring occasionally.

❺ Serve immediately as an alternative to a potato side dish.

YIELD: 6 servings.

Americans have a taste for food that's been seeded, fertilized, harvested, processed, and packaged in grossly energy-expensive ways and then shipped, often refrigerated, for so many miles it might as well be green cheese from the moon…. The global grocery store may turn out to be the last great losing proposition of our species.

BARBARA KINGSOLVER, IN *SMALL WONDER*

Tomato Crouton Casserole

W E TEND TO AVOID CASSEROLES, in general, because most cook the nutrients right out of the dish. As we discovered, there's no better — and quicker — way to get your "plumbing" working than eating a raw food diet for several meals. You can count on the fiber in the foods to get you going. But most of us, for lots of reasons, enjoy most of our foods cooked, at least a little bit, because it brings out the flavors. That's why we stand by this tomato casserole, with a crunch from the croutons and a buttery herb flavor infuses the tomatoes. We embrace the funky-shaped and ultra-flavorful heirloom varieties of vegetables and fruits, especially tomatoes. And this recipe puts their flavors and colors on display: reds, oranges and greens, with many other colors in between. It's a great way to work through some of the bigger tomatoes of your harvest, not fit to sell, share or eat plain perhaps due to a few blemishes, hornworm damage or pecks from the chickens. Cut away the imperfections and you're good to go. This recipe demands fresh tomatoes.

INGREDIENTS

1   t. canola oil

8   c. fresh tomatoes (8 medium tomatoes)

2   c. prepared croutons (see page 230)

½   c. butter, melted

1   t. salt

1   T. fresh basil, finely chopped (1 t. dried)

1   T. fresh thyme, finely chopped (1 t. dried)

¾   c. hard granular cheese, grated (Parmesan)

DIRECTIONS

❶ Cut tomatoes into wedges and arrange in a lightly oiled 9 × 13-inch baking pan. Top with bread croutons.

❷ Combine butter, salt, basil and thyme. Drizzle over bread and tomatoes.

❸ Bake at 350° for 20 minutes. Remove pan from oven and sprinkle cheese over tomatoes and bread croutons and bake in oven again for an additional 10 minutes or until tomatoes are tender.

❹ To serve, we often ladle a portion up alongside our Potato Latkes at breakfast, but this dish also makes a great side for lunch or dinner.

YIELD: 6 servings.

As for butter versus margarine, I trust cows more than chemists.

JOAN GUSSOW, ECOLOGICALLY MINDED NUTRITIONIST

Roasted Fresh Tomato Sauce

Canning tomato sauce the traditional way on the stove during the heat of the summer is better left for a different era; let's call it Plan A. Adding heat to a hot kitchen is the last thing we want to do in August, plus we've got so many irons in the fire and potlucks to go to, we just don't have the time. Our Plan B for tomatoes is implemented after Plan F: tray freezing the tomatoes whole in the freezer, and we put off making any sauce until we have time in the winter, usually on our woodstove. This Plan B oven-roasted tomato sauce is perfect for small batches to freeze and especially helpful if you're running low on freezer space. It can be a little runnier than canned sauce; to get rid of the excess liquid, we simmer the sauce in a Crock-Pot (or on the cooktop of our woodstove) in the winter.

INGREDIENTS

- 4 lbs. fresh tomatoes, skins peeled (about 8 medium tomatoes)
- 1 c. onions, chopped (1 medium onion)
- 9 cloves garlic, sliced
- ½ t. salt
- ¼ c. olive oil
- ½ t. salt
- ½ c. fresh basil, chopped (3 t. dried)

DIRECTIONS

❶ Cut tomatoes into quarters. Arrange tomatoes in a lightly oiled shallow roasting pan. Sprinkle on onions and garlic, drizzle with oil.

❷ Roast tomatoes at 300° for about an hour or until tomatoes are lightly browned and garlic is tender when pierced with a knife.

❸ Transfer in batches into food processor and process until smooth. Add salt and basil.

❹ Pour into freezer containers to freeze. Defrosted sauce can be used any way you use tomato sauce, like on pizza or pasta.

YIELD: 2 cups.

There are many of us who cannot but feel dismal about the future of various cultures. Often it is hard not to agree that we are becoming culinary nitwits, dependent upon fast foods and mass kitchens and megavitamins for our basically rotten nourishment.

M. F. K. Fisher

Slow-simmered Tomato Sauce

*T*HANKS TO THE FREEZER, we've found an appropriate use of technology that optimizes the efficiency of our summer harvest while providing a rich, thick tomato sauce for pasta or pizza. We freeze whole tomatoes at their peak ripeness in the summer, cellar our leeks and dry store our onions and garlic. Then in the middle of the winter we let the ingredients simmer away atop our woodstove for a July-like treat that warms the farmhouse with delicious aromas of simmering sauce. If there's a call for tomato sauce in the summer or early fall, a Crock-Pot serves as an energy-efficient standby.

INGREDIENTS

- 4 lbs. tomatoes, skins peeled (about 8 medium tomatoes)
- 3 c. onions, chopped (about 3 medium onions)
- 6 cloves garlic, minced
- ½ t. salt
- 2 T. fresh basil, finely chopped (2 t. dried)
- 2 T. fresh oregano, finely chopped (2 t. dried)

DIRECTIONS

❶ Defrost tomatoes that were frozen whole, peeling outside skin. Drain off as much water as possible. Sauté onions with garlic. When onions are soft, add tomatoes in chunks, stirring often to mix.

❷ Add herbs and seasonings, stirring often and allowing moisture to slowly simmer off.

❸ Cook this sauce down until it's thick for a flavorful pasta sauce.

YIELD: 3 cups.

Tomato sauce prepared atop the woodstove.

Hollandaise Sauce

*T*HIS RICH VELVETY SAUCE for eggs Benedict can be a fancy stand-in for pouring over lightly steamed broccoli or asparagus sides for a dinner meal. Maintain medium heat in a double boiler and whisk the sauce with easy circular stokes, avoiding overcooking (which will cause the sauce to separate). Because of the eggs, this is one sauce you'll want to enjoy right after it's prepared. Thanks to John, there's never any left over in our farmhouse.

INGREDIENTS

3   egg yolks
¼   c. water, simmering
2   t. lemon juice
¼   c. butter (½ stick)

DIRECTIONS

❶ Whisk egg yolks in a double boiler over low heat. Make sure water isn't too hot or eggs will curdle. Stir 1 minute.

❷ Add water, 1 T. at a time, whisking constantly. Stir 1 to 2 minutes until thick.

❸ Add lemon juice.

❹ Take off heat and stir in butter.

❺ Serve immediately.

YIELD: 1 cup.

You don't have to cook fancy or complicated masterpieces —
just good food from fresh ingredients.

JULIA CHILD

EATING LOCAL IN AN INVISIBLE WAY

**Todd and Jordan Champagne,
Happy Girl Kitchen,
Pacific Grove, California**

"This isn't boutique or gourmet food artistry," quips Todd Champagne, who with his wife Jordan started Happy Girl Kitchen Co. in 2002. "Vegetable fermentation is food security. It's a very easy way of putting real nutritional foods on our table every day, whether in the form of a dill pickle or sauerkraut."

We gathered on the porch of their home in Big Sur, California, as the sun climbed over the Santa Lucia Mountain Range, warming our bodies while we enjoyed a glass of their Kombucha, an effervescent non-alcoholic fermented tea made from sweetened black tea, cultured with a symbiotic colony of bacteria and yeasts that are believed to promote a more balanced and healthy digestive system.

As it turns out, there are more bacteria cells in our bodies than human cells by as much as nine to one, according to numerous studies, including those by Carolyn Bohach, a microbiologist from the University of Idaho. We're teeming with upwards of a thousand species of bacteria and micro-organisms, so small that they're practically invisible. Despite their size, some of these organisms produce chemicals that allow us to capture energy and nutrients from our food, while others help maintain our immune systems. So, eating certain fermented foods can improve our digestive health.

"If you lose access or choose not to use propane or electricity, how do you process your fresh fruit and vegetables?" asks Todd smiling, referring to a time when we weren't so addicted to fossil fuels to meet our every need. "Fermentation techniques often thrive at room temperatures. These ancient ways developed by our ancestors have both simple and durable recipes that have been passed along for generations."

"It goes way beyond fresh food storage, however," Jordan chimes in. "Fermenting vegetables actually increases the nutritional value of whatever it is that you're preserving, or it makes the raw food more easily digestible. For example, sauerkraut is more nutritious than fresh cabbage — higher in vitamin C and so forth. Plus there's all those beneficial bacterial that our bodies need to digest foods. Kraut has the same lactic acids as yogurt or kefir, both of which are often acceptable to those who are lactose intolerant."

As millions of Americans have rediscovered, fermentation is a great way to preserve the harvest and eat local year-round. At Happy Girl Kitchen, Todd and Jordan and their staff take fresh organic fruits and vegetables from farms, mostly located within 20 miles of their licensed commercial kitchen, and preserve the harvest one jar at a time. They are also

Happy Girl Kitchen Co. co-owners Jordan and Todd Champagne.

helping others can, too. Building a community of people who share their passion for food preservation, they offer workshops and deliveries of the local harvest in bulk quantities, enabling patrons to preserve the local harvest safely and affordably on their own. They're striving to do their part to maintain a strong local economy and food system that is more sustainable for all.

"Fermenting vegetables can be a great way to clean up your garden," jokes Todd. "Fermentation is a living process. You can watch the transformation of your raw ingredients colonized by tiny living things. Louis Pasteur, while marveling at microbial life, discovered 'pasteurization' when he used heat to kill those micro-organisms like bacteria, yeast and mold — themselves responsible for the array of unusual tastes many of us so enjoy and which cannot be faked, like blue cheese, miso, sourdough bread and sauerkraut. The taste of fermented foods can be influenced by the seasons and temperature, as well as by the ingredients. You could say, when making some fermented product, there are billions of chefs in the kitchen with you."

Happy Girl Kitchen Co. co-owner Jordan Champagne and daughter and staffer packing lemons in crocks.

Fermentation and food preservation are ancient in defining humanity's desire to preserve, aid health or imbue life with an intoxicating spirit, brew or wine. The Scots called whiskey in Gaelic "uisge beatha": water of life. Fermented foods, whether prepared in a traditional brine solution or distilled with yeast from malted barley, have long appealed to our more primal sense of health and well-being.

Nearly every human culture has its own traditional recipes for foods made using live cultures. The Germans have sauerkraut prepared from green or red cabbage, while the Korean version, kimchee, is made with cabbage but with quantities of other vegetables like carrots, radishes, garlic and onions. Sourdough breads use yeasts. Beer and wine acquire yeast-produced alcohols. Pickles made in the traditional way in a salt brine solution achieve their sourness from acid-producing bacteria, allowing the crunch of fresh cucumbers, perhaps flavored by adding dillweed or garlic — to be enjoyed months later.

"At Happy Girl Kitchen we're dedicated to preserving the harvest in a variety of ways," explains Jordan. And now, with Happy Girl Kitchen Café — part kitchen, part retail store and part café — they can invite customers into the lively 2,700-square-foot space to try more than 40 products made in their kitchen, including pickles, jams, marmalades, sauerkrauts, tomato goods and kombucha.

"Some folks simply enjoy stocking their pantry with freshly made and local versions of common condiments, like our country ketchup, says Todd. "They may then want to join others at one of our workshops and learn how to safely make their own. In this way our customers become participants because taste buds often inspire."

Happy Girl Kitchen's workshops cover both traditional fermentation and modern-day sterilization preservation processes. "We can cucumbers, for example, in two different ways," continues Jordan. "One way is vinegar pickling. We heat the jars filled with cukes and vinegar to kill the bacterial life and achieve an airtight vacuum seal, yielding a non-perishable 'canned' product. The other more traditional way is fermentation with the use of a salt brine that encourages live culture bacteria (rather than killing them) to over time 'sour' the cucumbers along with dill and garlic, with their production of lactic acid. These are the sour dills often sold from deli barrels."

"On a healthy farm, there is a commitment to diversity of life for the strength and stability of the overall system," adds Todd. "That's why at Happy Girl Kitchen we practice many different techniques of food preservation and the many alternative processes, because we all have different tastes. That's what makes potlucks so fun."

From their perspective, the widespread concern over the safety of eating or preparing canned foods is largely exaggerated. "Making pickled vegetables at home is so easy and safe," explains Jordan. "The key is proper acidity. True, when canning there's a potential to have botulism bacteria naturally present on the fruits and vegetables. It's a soil-borne bacteria. It's the proper acidity of your vinegar pickling brine, the natural acidity of the fruit or the addition of lemon juice or vinegar to tomato products that suppresses the growth of this harmful bacteria inside the heat-processed jars—in the anaerobic environment it needs to grow."

Like Padawan learners, we remain entranced by our lesson. "Because you can't see or smell a canned product contaminated with botulinum toxin, and because it can be lethal, it makes people nervous," shares Jordan. "But almost all fruit is naturally acidic enough to avoid this concern. The same is true for tomato varieties intended for canning as well as vegetables, so long as you add a vinegar brine which imparts safe high-acid levels to the finished pickles, typically under the pH of 4.6."

"It's the low-acid foods that are most susceptible," she continues as her daughter Jaya cuddles up at her side. "The bacterium *Clostridium botulinum* is merely a benign spore that's commonly found in soil. We actually eat small amounts of it all the time if we're eating fresh vegetables—like we should be. But when the *Clostridium botulinum* spores are trapped in an anaerobic environment like inside improperly acidified canned food, it creates a potentially lethal by-product. Knowledge always destroys fear, and that's why we're here."

Of all the food preservation techniques Todd and Jordan practice, it's working with microbial life, rather than against it, that they most enjoy. "We agree that buying fresh local ingredients in season is important," concludes Todd, "but we take it a step further with fermentation. By fermenting vegetables, dairy and grains, we foster the live cultures and promote cooperation with visible and invisible life that surrounds us. When we eat fermented foods, we eat this living biodiversity—the bacteria and other beneficial micro-organisms—these invisible members of our foodshed. When we do so, we're cultivating the local flora and fauna inside and outside our own bodies." Savoring fermented foods helps reconnect us to this invisible—and super-local—life that surrounds and is inside us—helping us maintain our health.

Sour Dill Cucumbers

*T*HESE ARE THE CLASSIC New York-style pickle which are naturally fermented in a sea-salt water brine. Through the years, this pickle continues to be the one that brings up the most childhood memories. Happy Girl Kitchen Co. has heard many stories at farmers markets when someone takes that first bite of a pickle…. "I remember in 1943 going to my first movie and sneaking in one of these nickel pickles to the theater!" Here's to creating your good memories. Pickling cucumbers are special varieties of cukes ideal for making pickles because they are shorter, often firmer and are harvested when young; they're commonly found at farmers markets.

INGREDIENTS

1 bunch of dill
4 grape leaves (optional for crunch)
4 t. pickling spices
4 lbs. pickling cucumbers
12 cloves garlic
¾ c. sea salt

DIRECTIONS

❶ Prepare the clean jars by adding in the dill, grape leaves and pickling spices on the bottom. Next, pack in the cucumbers and garlic trying to occupy as much of the space in the jar as possible.

❷ Mix the salt water solution of 5% salinity: 1 gallon of filtered water to ¾ c. of sea salt (do not use iodized salt as it will retard bacterial fermentation). One half-gallon batch is enough for these 4 quarts. Pour salt water over packed jar, making sure contents are submerged. The lid should be loose to allow air exchange.

❸ Place in 55 to 70° environment and out of direct sunlight. Let sit for 5 to 10 days, tasting occasionally, and refrigerate when desired sourness is achieved. (Skim mold that will form and float on the water surface but do not be afraid of it for it is a natural part of the fermenting process). Store in refrigerator. Best eaten within 2 months. Will keep safely for longer, but crunch and texture will fade.

YIELD: 4 quarts.

Spicy Kimchee

A KOREAN NATIONAL PASSION, kimchee is often eaten at every meal, including breakfast — estimates suggest that Koreans eat more than a quarter pound of kimchee every day. Chinese (napa) cabbage is the best to use, according to Happy Girl Kitchen Co., and this recipe usually includes radishes or turnips, scallions and other vegetables, with ginger, garlic and hot red chili peppers. The aromas created are enlivening themselves. Making Spicy Kimchee is very similar to making sauerkraut; however, it's usually eaten "younger" because it seems to ferment faster, often in 1 to 3 weeks.

INGREDIENTS

- 4 T. sea salt
- 4 c. water (non-chlorinated)
- 1 lb. Chinese (napa) cabbage (or bok choi), chopped
- 1 daikon radish or turnip, chopped
- 2 carrots, chopped
- 4 cloves garlic, chopped
- 3 T. fresh ginger root, grated
- 3 hot red chilies, dried
- 2 onions, scallions or leeks, chopped

DIRECTIONS

1. Mix a sea salt brine by dissolving 4 T. sea salt into 4 c. water.

2. Chop the cabbage into ½-inch slices. Since the Chinese cabbage is more delicate than the green cabbage, slice it initially chunkier than you imagine enjoying later, because it will shrink. Chop the carrots and radishes into ⅛-inch pieces. You can use a mandoline or food processor to slice them thinly.

3. Soak the vegetables in the brine for a few hours or overnight, until they are soft, with the help of a weight to submerge them.

4. Prepare the spices. Chop the garlic, grate the ginger, crush the chilies and slice the onions, then mix them together and set aside.

5. Drain the brine off the cabbage and save. Taste the vegetables and judge their saltiness; if they taste too salty, then rinse a bit. If you can't taste salt, then add a little bit at a time and mix in.

6. Combine the vegetables and spices.

7. Pack into a clean glass jar or vessel of choice, pouring over enough of the reserved brine to cover the mixture. Pack it tightly into the jar, pushing out air bubbles.

8. Weigh down the mixture with a smaller glass jar filled with the extra brine (which you might need later or eat on its own), a plastic bag filled with extra brine or just regularly push it down with your fingers every day.

9. Ferment in a warm place (not over 70°), like a kitchen counter, for about 1 week or until it's as sour as you like it.

10. Remove the weight, cap the jar tightly and store in your refrigerator. Best eaten within 2 months. Will keep safely for longer, but crunch and texture will fade.

YIELD: 1 quart.

Classic Sauerkraut

Sauerkraut is easy to make. Like at Happy Girl Kitchen Co., you just need to create the right conditions and the micro-organisms will do the rest. You'll be rewarded with crunchy, tangy golden kraut to enliven your winter. The fermentation process may take from 4 to 6 weeks.

INGREDIENTS

- 5 lbs. cabbage, chopped
- 3 T. sea salt
- 1 T. juniper berries (optional)
  suggested Spices: caraway seeds, celery seeds, garlic

OPTIONAL INGREDIENTS

- 1 lb. carrots or Brussels sprouts, chopped
- 1 lb. turnips or beets, chopped
- 1 lb. apples and/or raisins

DIRECTIONS

❶ Chop cabbage into a large bowl, coarse or fine, however you like it.

❷ Sprinkle on the sea salt now and then. Mix the cabbage and salt (and juniper berries) together to distribute the salt evenly. The salt pulls water out of the cabbage and creates a brine where the cabbage (and other vegetables) can ferment without rotting or softening. A note on salt: Use only non-iodized salt, such as sea salt, and non-chlorinated water, as these chemicals inhibit the growth of micro-organisms.

❸ Pack into clean vessel. Tightly push and pack the cabbage down using your hands or kitchen tool, forcing as much air out as possible and encouraging the cabbage to release its juices. A note on fermenting vessel: Many folks use earthenware crocks for making kraut since the wide mouth gives easy access for tamping and cleaning. Other suggested vessels are wide-mouth glass jars, non-reactive stainless steel pots or food-grade plastic buckets (which are all much lighter than crocks).

❹ Cover kraut with a plate or other lid that covers the surface snugly. Place a weight on the cover to help force the air out and keep the kraut pushed under the brine created. A glass jar filled with water or a plastic bag filled with salt brine all work well. Secure a breathable cloth over the container to keep debris out.

❺ Press down on the cabbage over the next few hours to force water out. It may take 24 hours for the brine to rise above the level of the chopped cabbage. Add a salt water solution as needed to cover the cabbage if after a day it remains high and dry. To make salt water solution, completely dissolve 1 T. sea salt into 1 c. of water.

6 Let fermentation happen! Put the vessel in a cool spot. Check on your kraut every day or two to skim off any surface scum which is just an aerobic phenomenon where the developing kraut has come into contact with air. Don't worry about it. The kraut below the surface is unaffected and fine. Rinse off your cover and weight to discourage mold from forming on the surface.

7 After 2 weeks, start tasting the kraut. It will be fully fermented in 2 to 4 weeks at 70 to 75°, or 5 to 6 weeks at 60°. The air bubbles you see rising to the surface, a result of our busy microbe buddies, will become slower and eventually cease once the kraut is fully fermented.

8 You can begin eating the young kraut anytime to enjoy the evolving flavor as it matures over several weeks. Remember to replace the clean weight on top, adding brine if necessary to keep it covered.

9 Store in refrigerator and start some more before it's gone. Pack the kraut tightly in jars and store covered in the fridge for several weeks (or longer). Eventually, the kraut softens and the flavor turns less bright. Rinse the crock and repack it with fresh salted cabbage and add some old kraut to get your new batch started with active cultures. Best eaten within 2 months. Will keep safely for longer, but crunch and texture will fade.

YIELD: 1 gallon.

Fermentation sign at Happy Girl Kitchen Co., Pacific Grove, California.

Caesar Salad

THE TABLESIDE SHOW of the preparation of a Caesar salad rivals that of a Japanese hibachi grill, where patrons sit and watch their meal being prepared in front of them. There's more than a show for the Caesar salad. When using these fresh ingredients, the tanginess and creaminess of the dressing that coats the leaves is paired with the crunch of the lettuce and croutons. For vegetarians, omit anchovies, Worcestershire sauce and eggs for a vinaigrette version.

INGREDIENTS

1   egg, coddled
1   garlic clove, minced
3   anchovies
1   c. olive oil
1   T. Dijon mustard
¼   c. red wine vinegar
2   t. Worcestershire sauce
½   fresh lemon
1   t. capers
1   head romaine lettuce, torn into 2-inch pieces
½   c. hard granular cheese, grated (Parmesan)
1   c. homemade croutons (see page 230)

DIRECTIONS

❶ Prepare a coddled egg by bringing water to boil in a small pot. Once boiling, add the egg for about 45 seconds, then remove the egg and set aside in a bowl to cool.

❷ With two forks, chop up and mix together the anchovies placed in a large wooden bowl lined with ¼ cup of the olive oil. Add garlic and continue to whisk with a fork — and if you want to be fancy about it — while also spinning the bowl.

❸ Into this "sauce" mixture, crack the coddled egg, whisking with the fork. Then add the Dijon mustard, red wine vinegar and Worcestershire sauce. Squeeze in lemon juice, continuing to whisk and spin the bowl if you're trying to impress a special friend, neighbors or the in-laws.

❹ The remaining olive oil should be added slowly while whisking until the dressing is smooth. You want the dressing to emulsify, or mix oil and vinegar into a smooth coating for the salad and croutons (that's where the coddled egg comes to the rescue).

❺ Add romaine lettuce (making sure most of the water has been removed after washing) and toss, sprinkling in capers and cheese and croutons. Serve immediately.

YIELD: 4 servings.

COOKING TIP · Coddled Egg to the Rescue

To help the oil and vinegar mix in the dressing, an emulsifier is needed: the coddled egg. By briefly cooking a fresh egg, coddling it, you're helping reduce a health risk associated with the uncooked egg, namely the danger of Salmonella. If in doubt, leave the egg out and rely on your whisking abilities to get the dressing smooth and creamy.

Cucumber Salad

*B*RING SALAD TO CENTER STAGE in the summer by building the rest of the meal around the garden-fresh crunch. Prep the cucumbers in the morning and leave them to marinate in the fridge and you'll have a salad ready for supper.

INGREDIENTS

- 2 medium cucumbers, sliced
- ½ t. salt
- 1 t. sugar
- 1 T. rice vinegar
- 1 T. fresh dill (1 t. dried)
- ½ c. sour cream
  fresh dill for garnish (optional)

DIRECTIONS

❶ Mix salt, sugar, vinegar and dill.

❷ Pour dressing over cucumbers. Chill for several hours.

❸ Pour off liquid. Add sour cream and serve with a few sprinkles of dill on top.

YIELD: 4 servings.

Creamy Spinach Salad

*C*ONSIDER THIS RECIPE the summer equivalent of creamed spinach in a salad form. The cottage cheese and sour cream give the salad a comfort food feel. Add a little horseradish if you like a dash of zing.

SALAD INGREDIENTS

- 8 c. fresh spinach, washed with stems removed and torn into small pieces (about ½ lb.)
- ½ c. small curd cottage cheese
- ¼ c. sour cream
- 1 c. chopped pecans

DRESSING INGREDIENTS

- ¼ c. sugar
- 1½ T. vinegar
- ¼ t. dry mustard
- ¼ t. salt
- 2 t. horseradish (optional)

DIRECTIONS

❶ Mix spinach, cottage cheese, sour cream and pecans in a large serving bowl.

❷ Mix dressing ingredients together in a small bowl, or gently shake it in a jar.

❸ Pour dressing over spinach mixture and serve immediately.

YIELD: 4 servings.

Strawberry Spinach Salad

$\mathcal{W}$E LIKE OUR STRAWBERRIES red on the outside—and inside. Not like those mega-mutations grown in California, often with the poison fumigant known as methyl bromide. Banned just about everywhere except in the US, in part, because it destroys the planet's ozone, this fumigant will likely be replaced by a new poison, methyl iodide. So we stick with our quarter-sized, organically grown, candy-like strawberries, gorging on them in June and freezing any extra. We choose only organic strawberries at a farmers market if we're on the road—and eat them only when they're in season. This salad could just as well be called the June Salad, since it's the only month we'll savor it on our farm. The dressing helps accent the sweetness of the fresh strawberries and spinach, with a nutty crunch from the chopped peanuts.

SALAD INGREDIENTS

- 8 c. fresh spinach, washed with stems removed and torn into small pieces
- 3 c. fresh strawberries, sliced

DRESSING INGREDIENTS

- ½ c. water
- 1 c. canola oil
- ½ c. salted peanuts
- ⅓ c. honey
- 3 T. apple cider vinegar

DIRECTIONS

❶ Mix spinach and strawberries in large salad bowl.

❷ Blend all dressing ingredients in blender. Pour to taste over salad.

YIELD: 4 large servings.

Young Green Beans with Balsamic Vinegar

*F*ORGET ABOUT THE soup-based casseroles to make green beans tasty. It's a timing thing. Rather than let your green bean plants become overloaded on the vine, pick them when they're young, tender and succulent. Don't worry, there will always be some you miss, for those casseroles.

INGREDIENTS

2   c. green beans, trimmed
1   T. balsamic vinegar
½   t. cumin
½   t. coriander
½   t. salt

DIRECTIONS

❶ Lightly steam green beans until tender, but still have a crunch. Test by seeing if a fork tip will easily penetrate the beans, but if you tried to cut sideways, it wouldn't.

❷ Place green beans in a serving bowl. Drizzle beans with balsamic vinegar and toss, mixing in sprinkled cumin, coriander and salt. They can be served immediately or refrigerated for later.

YIELD: 4 servings.

COOKING TIP — Balsamic Vinegar

The ultimate pantry staple, balsamic vinegar can liven up anything from salad greens to popcorn to vanilla ice cream (surprisingly good), without adding fat or empty calories. The Italian word "balsamico" means "balsam-like" in the sense of "restorative" or "curative." Quality and price range tremendously for balsamic vinegar, made from a reduced grape juice. Today you'll see a range made with a blend of artisan-made balsamic combined with boiled grapes or vinegar added. Ideally taste a few balsamic vinegars before spending a cent. Lower-cost commercial balsamic vinegars are typically aged three to five years and work great for salads, marinades or over vegetables. The more expensive versions are aged longer and, like premium olive oils, are what you want to use when the flavor is the focus, like over cheese or ice cream.

Farmer Liam's
STAND
Turnip $1/ea
Onions $1⁷⁵/lb. Beets $2/ea
Garlic $4⁷⁵/lb. Dill $1²⁵/oz.
Red Potatoes $1²⁵/lb. Basil $1⁵⁰/oz.

NIBBLES (APPETIZERS)

Warm Zucchini Dip

Swiss Fondue

Hearty Root Vegetable Dip (vegan)

California-style Guacamole (vegan) (Bryant Terry)

Asian Chicken Satay with Thai Peanut Sauce

Creamy Leek Pastries

Spinach-Cheese Bites

Bacon-wrapped Jicama

Hummus (vegan)

Dolmades (Stuffed Grape Leaves) (vegan)

Vegetarian Nori-wrapped Sushi (vegan)

Latvian Pirages

Vegetarian Tempura

Cucumber Slices with Feta Cheese Filling

Asian Egg Rolls

** see Liam's Favorites (page 211) for:

Tortilla Wraps

Spring Rolls

Small Bites, Big Change

"We're going to a tapas bar," we mentioned to Lisa's mom one day. What she and her husband of fifty-seven years heard was "topless bar." Stunned, they both gave us a once over. They knew we enjoyed taking soaks in hot springs, but this was something totally different.

To be fair, it's not the first time something like this happened. There was the time we were planning a trip to a tourism conference at the Kalahari Resort in the Wisconsin Dells. Of course, they heard "calamari resort." It's happened so often, we just laugh. Like the time when Lisa's mom, an excellent cook, came out of the kitchen, announcing she had a new "concussion" ready for us to try. Yes, she meant to say "concoction." She should have opened a restaurant; home cooking at her home is like fine dining, except you don't need to get dressed up; one of her meals even made "Mom's Best Meal" in *Taste of Home* magazine.

We love everything about eating tapas, the Spanish version of appetizers that can be enjoyed anytime. They can be cold or hot, savory, sour or sweet. At

Strawbales stacked in timber framing of granary.

a tapas restaurant, you might start with an order of a few different dishes, served with small plates for everyone around your table to try. If you're still hungry, order a few more. In most cases, you make a meal of the appetizers.

The closest thing around where we live is what the locals call "heavy hors d'oeuvres." We're not talking cheese slices or cut veggies with ranch dressing to dip into. Heavy hors d'oeuvres are what John's mom serves up for gallery show openings at the Monroe Art Center; she's surprised — and proud, rightly so — that the attendees enjoy her treats so much, like the bacon-wrapped chestnuts (see a variation on page 130) or chocolate biscotti (see a variation on page 183). Some of the gallery goers seem to be making a meal of the appetizers, just like they do in Spain. Sometimes, we do, too.

For most of us, appetizers represent a snack to whet our appetite. But appetites are no problem in this household. Our challenge is to avoid making a full meal of the appetizers before the main course is served. Here's where the portion control police need to step in, lock down the platter and remind us that starvation is not eminent and winter, well, winter isn't what it used to be back in the days of Ma and Pa Kettle, with the snow blowing in under the doorstop and the grain bin running low.

Which leads us to "nibble," a more descriptive word, reflecting both our eating style and our operating philosophy. Peck-ish, if you please. We tend to nibble not just at our food, but at the challenges of farm life or the occasional harsh realities of living on a warming planet. Resilience will be essential in our present era of extreme or peak everything. So the concept of nibbles resonates, from the serving platter to our daily work styles. Group some of our nibbles

together, and you have an awesome tapas meal…
write a page every day, and a half year later you have
a cookbook.

We often take our guests on a walking tour after
they've settled in at our bed & breakfast. The tour
ends at the dining room table or front porch, depending on the season. That's where we'll bring out
a plate of snacks, finger food that doesn't require sil-
verware. With an aroma of Spinach-Cheese Bites or
visual rainbow of fresh crisp vegetables surrounding
the hummus platter, some guests who might have
been on buzzing travel agendas instead pause, taste
and linger.

Perhaps this appeal of nibbling naturally stems
from our disposition to dabble, a yearning to try out
and experiment with new ideas. We have a knack for
nibbling; it keeps us sane. When situations bubble
over in complexity or to-do lists overflow onto a second page, we regroup, hold a "staff meeting" (of two)
or relax while wrapping some sushi or dolmades for
a break. We identify priorities for that day: what bite-
sized chunk can we accomplish during the next twelve
hours. By breaking things down, we can accomplish
the sum of the many parts, often in a fun way.

That's how we managed to get our own version
of a barn raising done, the deconstruction and re-
construction of what is now a straw bale greenhouse
heated mostly by the sun. What started as an idea
to save a historic old corn crib granary turned into
"straw bale summer," followed by "straw bale September." During the summer, a crew of three nibbled
away at removing a rotting copula and the outside
wooden skin of the building. By early September,
we framed in the spaces for the windows and doors
while adding the ten-collector solar thermal system
that would become the primary heat source for the

Completed strawbale greenhouse, in part, heated by the sun.

structure. With super-insulated R-43 walls, we knew
we wouldn't need much heat. Then came the stack-
ing, lathe and stucco work, covering up the two-story
structure.

By the time it was over, more than a thousand
bales were used. The walls had a wavy stucco appeal.
And new friendships made with a parade of volunteers, helpers and guests who wanted to throw some
mud and play in the straw. We even brewed our own
beer for the occasion to share; we called it Straw Bale
Stout (two would knock you off your feet and into a
chair). Over the years, some papayas and avocados
have reached for the sunlight while our son con-
structs elaborate cities of Legos below. It's been used
to start blackcurrants and flats of melon and basil. As
anyone who's ever built their own house or prepared
their own meals can attest, there's nothing more empowering than sticking with a project until it's done
the way you want. A lot of little steps will put you
atop the tallest mountain, given enough time. We're
the ones we're looking for to lead that change.

So when things overwhelm, think carrot stick,
not carrot cake. What can I nibble at today?

Warm Zucchini Dip

*F*RIENDS ASK US FOR THIS RECIPE. We gladly share. Then they call back when they read it, protesting that we forgot an ingredient. Zucchini serves apparently as the ultimate mystery ingredient in disguise. Everyone claims to taste something different in this recipe — the ingredient they claim we forgot — from noodles to soy sauce. We smile and confess: Nope, just good 'ol zucchini.

INGREDIENTS

2　c. fresh zucchini, shredded (or any summer squash)

1　t. salt

½　c. mayonnaise

½　c. plain yogurt

¼　c. hard granular cheese, grated (Parmesan)

¼　c. bell peppers, finely chopped

4　green onions, thinly sliced

1　garlic clove, minced

1　t. Worcestershire sauce

1.　t. canola oil

　　pita chips for dipping (see recipe page 64)

DIRECTIONS

❶ In a bowl, toss the zucchini and salt. Let stand for 1 hour.

❷ Drain and press out excess liquid.

❸ Mix in mayonnaise, yogurt, cheese, peppers, green onions, garlic and Worcestershire sauce. Stir until combined.

❹ Pour mixture into a lightly oiled 8-inch baking pan and bake at 375° for 15 to 20 minutes or until bubbly.

❺ Serve hot with pita chips for dipping.

YIELD: 8 appetizer servings.

If we figure out how to provide more of our food and energy close to home, the need for the kind of standing army that the founders deplored will begin to decrease — no more need to guard the five-thousand-mile-long straw through which we suck hydrocarbons from the Persian Gulf.

BILL MCKIBBEN, FROM *EAARTH*

Swiss Fondue

*I*N THE 1960S OR EARLY 1970S, every house in the burbs seemed to have a fondue pot. It made the family mealtime around the table fun. By the 1990s, gourmet fondue restaurants became the rage with their soft cushions and romantic candles, turning what was a frugal Swiss way to enjoy some old bread and some odds and ends of cheeses into a pricey affair. Our version of fondue showcases our locally made and award-winning Emmi Roth Käse Gruyère and Swiss cheeses. Yodeling is optional.

INGREDIENTS

- 4 garlic cloves, thinly sliced
- 2 c. dry white wine
- 4 c. aged Swiss cheese, shredded (1 lb.)
- 4 c. Gruyère cheese, shredded (1 lb.)
- 4 t. cornstarch
- 3 T. Kirschwasser (cherry brandy)
- 2 loaves crusty bread (like French baguettes), cut into cubes

DIRECTIONS

❶ Rub fondue pot thoroughly with garlic and discard garlic.

❷ Heat white wine in the fondue pot on the stove. When air bubbles begin to rise to surface (do not boil), add shredded cheeses very slowly, stirring constantly with a wooden spoon in a figure eight (not circles).

❸ When cheese melts and begins to bubble, mix Kirschwasser and cornstarch together separately, then add to cheese mixture, stirring well with the figure-eight pattern.

❹ Remove from stove and place on fondue burner in the center of the table. Adjust burner to keep fondue bubbling slightly.

❺ Spear a chunk of bread with fondue fork, dipping into fondue and coating bread. The stirring motion of each person's fondue fork helps maintain proper consistency of the cheese.

YIELD: 8 appetizer servings.

COOKING TIP The secret to a rich and creamy fondue is stirring in a figure eight; it keeps the cheese from getting stringy or globbing together.

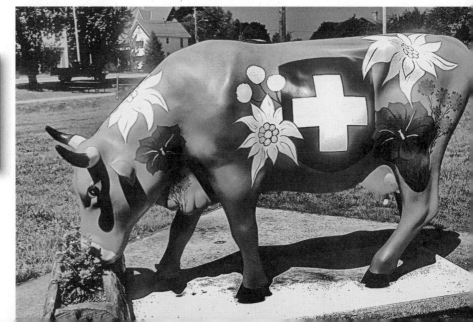

Swiss cow from New Glarus.

Hearty Root Vegetable Dip

V Vegan

CONSIDER THIS YOUR TURN-TO harvest recipe when you have a random collection of root crops that need some culinary love. This recipe readily uses a combination of shredded root vegetables; we like turnips, beets, potatoes, rutabagas and carrots, and also throw in an onion or even a leek. Traditionally a pâté is a mixture of meats blended into a spreadable paste. This recipe takes pâté where it typically doesn't go by using all vegetables. Shred the root vegetables together in the food processor; they will blend and the color of the dip will depend on the dominant vegetable. Be forewarned, red beets add a vibrant red. Nutritional yeast is a key ingredient. It's technically deactivated yeast (i.e., not the stuff you make bread with). Nutritional yeast is packed with protein and vitamins, especially those B-complex vitamins. We often use nutritional yeast wherever we might typically sprinkle Parmesan cheese, like over pasta, popcorn or a tossed salad.

INGREDIENTS

2   T. lemon juice
⅔   c. canola oil
1½   c. whole wheat flour
1   c. sunflower seeds
4   garlic cloves, minced
1½   c. nutritional yeast
¼   c. soy sauce
2   t. dried basil
1   t. dried thyme
1   t. dried sage
½   t. nutmeg
2   c. boiling water
6   c. root vegetables, shredded (try a combo of beets, turnips, rutabagas and potatoes)
6   dried bay leaves

DIRECTIONS

❶ In a large bowl, combine lemon juice, oil, flour, seeds, garlic, yeast and soy sauce and stir well. Add basil, thyme, sage, nutmeg and boiling water.

❷ Add vegetables; stir until well combined.

❸ Pour mixture into a lightly oiled 9 × 13-inch baking pan and place bay leaves on top.

❹ Bake at 350° for about 60 minutes or until firm and golden brown. Remove bay leaves.

❺ Serve warm or at room temperature with pita chips or hearty crackers. Do not serve the dip right out of the oven or when it's cold.

YIELD: 8 as an appetizer.

FEEDING THE MIND, HEART AND SOUL

Chef Bryant Terry,
Oakland, California

When we asked Bryant Terry what influenced him to adopt a vegan diet, he launches into the rap "Beef" from rapper KRS-One:

"Let us begin now with the cow
The way it gets to your plate and how
The cow doesn't grow fast enough for man
So through his greed he makes a faster plan
He has drugs to make the cow grow quicker
Through the stress the cow gets sicker..."

"Those words opened my mind as a teenager and empowered me to start shifting my thinking around food politics," explains Bryant, as we sit around his sun-drenched dining room table in his Oakland, California home, the creative base for his writing and culinary passions as a vegan chef. His edgy rapper voice is now silent, replaced by the warm, gentle tone of a man soon to be a first-time dad. Lisa first met Bryant through her work as a Food & Community Fellow.

"The term 'soul food' ushers stereotypes: fried chicken and all the comfort foods of the cuisine," admits Bryant. "Back home growing up in the South, these were special holiday treats, not everyday meals. Our daily family meals tended to center around healthy choices like lima beans, okra and collard greens, picked fresh from my grandparents' garden." Bryant is now on a one-man mission to redefine soul food; moving back to the healthier roots he remembers growing up in Tennessee, steeped in memories of his family that loved both their food and music heritage.

"My grandparents didn't see their garden as anything special, it was simply something you did that made common sense to bring healthy food to your table," Bryant reminisces. He admits he's fortunate that his grandparents' garden instilled in him a strong passion for food security through self-reliance. "Unfortunately, as a society we've lost that connection with home gardens. When we produce our own food, it's empowering. When we depend on someone else to provide all our food, it's a form of slavery." Like millions of Americans, he and his wife, Jidan, tore out the front lawn of their Oakland home and added two raised garden beds, inspiring some neighbors to follow their lead.

"I ate my fair share of Big Macs and Whoppers when I was younger. I know they are engineered in a way to be tasty and addictive," says Bryant. "But I now know food companies spend billions to convince us to eat these high-fat, high-salt, high-sugar and high-calorie, low-nutrient foods. Food is a springboard for folks, particularly young people, to start talking about these bigger issues." Reflecting on his own life, Bryant sees personal relationships with food and flavor as an ongoing journey, each chapter offering lessons — even those processed, sodium-drenched ones — we can relate to.

Vegan Chef Bryant Terry testing recipes in his kitchen.

"Before I heard those words of KRS-One and started reading books like *The Jungle* and Francis Moore Lappe's *Diet for a Small Planet*, I was your typical, fast-food eating teen," reflects Bryant as he offers us some of his vegan lemon cookies and a refreshing glass of lemonade, made from Meyer lemons he picked from his neighbor's tree. "I'm thankful for that processed-food experience because it gives me perspective for my work today."

But there's no finger-pointing, guilt-inducing preaching coming from this author. While he wrote the acclaimed cookbook, *Vegan Soul Kitchen*, he doesn't label himself a vegan. "Words trigger stereotypes, and that's not what I'm all about," he explains. "It's not my place to say that people should stop eating meat. That's a personal decision. But I am clear that we Americans definitely need to have more plant-based foods in our diet. I'm redefining soul food without artery-clogging fat and lots of sugar."

"Growing up, food integrated seamlessly with art, music and community," remembers Bryant. "My grandfather founded the Four Stars of Harmony, the first African American group to get on the radio in Tennessee, so there was always music in our house. My grandmother was singing African American work songs and spirituals while she cooked. Whenever she rolled out the dough for her fried pies, it was as if her spirituality through music was one of her ingredients." Bryant blends this musical element in his culinary work, offering "suggested soundtracks" for his recipes that draw on the influences of blues, jazz and hip-hop.

Art, food and gardens merge together in Bryant and Jidan's cozy dream home in the heart of Oakland, with regular farmers markets and a nearby park to play in with their yet-to-be-born child. But this home, like many of the elements of Bryant's creative life, stems from first creating a clear vision.

"It's called a 'vision board,'" explains Bryant, as we notice the colorful pencil drawing hanging on a wall. "We use this technique frequently as a way to visualize our goals." We study the drawing that details facets of their dream home, like being close to local shops, price range and even a visual of future family with the couple holding two kids. "We created this over a year before we found the home we're in now, a place that met our wish list and more. Look, our house even has a red door, just like Jidan drew," points out Bryant.

"We all have the potential to envision our future and then act to make it a reality, especially when it comes to food," Bryant inspires. "Everyone has an inner chef. You don't need to be some superstar to cook. Anyone can make food that's going to come out tasty."

The words of KRS-One still echo in our head as we share a farewell hug and high-five:

"Come on now man let's be for real,
You are what you eat is the way I feel."

California-style Guacamole

WITH MUSIC A STRONG inspirational force in Bryant's work, his recommended soundtrack for this dish is "Pinotepa" by Lila Downs from her *La Sandunga* album. As Bryant resides in the major leagues of musical hipness and we're still playing our 1980s cassette collection, we needed to look this one up. Reinventing traditional Mexican music with influences of everything from blues, jazz to even klezmer, Lila Downs tingles your soul and tastebuds at the same time. Bring on the guac!

INGREDIENTS

- 2 ripe Hass avocados, peeled and pitted
- 3 T. fresh cilantro, minced
- ½ c. red onion, diced
- 1 clove garlic, minced
- 1½ T. lime juice
- ¼ t. cayenne pepper
- ½ t. salt

DIRECTIONS

❶ In a medium serving bowl, combine the avocado and cilantro. Using the back of a spoon, mash the avocado until creamy but textured.

❷ Add the remaining ingredients and mix well.

❸ Serve with chips or pita chip for dipping. (See recipe page 64 for pita chips)

YIELD: 6 servings.

Bryant and Jidan Terry's vision map for their home in Oakland, California.

Asian Chicken Satay with Thai Peanut Sauce

*T*HERE'S NO SUCH THING as fried mysterious chicken parts in our household. Nuggets, some fast-food restaurants call them. If we're going to enjoy the mellow flavors of chicken — especially the pastured kind — then feast on this popular Thai dish that won't set your tongue on fire. The peanut sauce provides an exotic and creamy dip for the flavorful skewered chicken and is also tasty on rice.

CHICKEN SATAY INGREDIENTS

1   lb. chicken breasts
2   garlic cloves, minced
1   1-inch piece fresh ginger, minced
½   t. tumeric
½   t. cumin
2   T. brown sugar, firmly packed
½   c. chicken stock
3   T. fish sauce
3   t. soy sauce
18 wood kabob skewers

SATAY DIRECTIONS

❶ Cut chicken into ½-inch-wide strips and place in 9 × 13-inch baking pan.

❷ Combine remaining ingredients for marinade. Pour marinade over chicken strips. Cover and refrigerate for at least 2 hours, ideally overnight.

❸ Soak wood skewers in water for about an hour before making the kabobs (the skewers absorb water and are less likely to catch on fire). Thread chicken strips on skewers. Fill the first half of the kabob with skewered meat, leaving the lower half empty so you have a "handle" to easily pick up the satay.

❹ Grill chicken satay on a BBQ, basting with the leftover marinade. You can also broil the satay in your oven. Place the satay on a broiling pan and set the broiler to a medium heat (about 350°). Place satay close to heating element and turn meat every 5 minutes until cooked, while basting with the leftover marinade. Depending on the thickness of your meat, the satay should cook in about 8 to 12 minutes, but keep a close eye to avoid overcooking or drying it out.

❺ Serve with peanut sauce on a bed of lettuce greens.

YIELD: 6 appetizer servings.

PEANUT SAUCE INGREDIENTS

1 T. fish sauce

¼ c. rice vinegar

½ c. coconut milk

1 t. sesame oil

¼ t. red Thai curry paste

1 T. hoisin sauce

½ c. peanut butter

½ c. chicken stock

¼ c. half & half cream

¼ c. soy sauce

2 T. brown sugar, firmly packed

1 clove garlic, minced

1 T. lime juice

½ t. tumeric

⅛ c. chives or green onions, finely chopped

⅛ c. peanuts, crushed

PEANUT SAUCE DIRECTIONS

❶ Combine all ingredients except chives and peanuts, with a whisk in a small bowl, adding a little more coconut milk as needed to make a sauce.

❷ Pour into a small saucepan over medium heat until sauce starts to bubble. Remove from heat.

❸ Serve in a bowl, topped with a sprinkle of fresh crushed peanuts and finely chopped chives or green onions.

YIELD: 2 cups.

Health as the organic pioneers conceived it encompasses the whole system, not just you and me.... Health would have to take into account the environment, the quality of drinking water, the incidence of cancer among farming families, the pesticide-poisoning incidents suffered by farming families, the risks to infants and children, and perhaps even the pleasure and taste of well-grown food.

Samuel Fromartz, in Organic, Inc.

Creamy Leek Pastries

*A*N ELEGANT APPETIZER, these pastries showcase both our leeks and Gruyère and Swiss cheeses. The sweet richness of the leeks complements the creamy flavor of the cheese.

INGREDIENTS

6   c. leeks, cleaned and thinly sliced (2 large leeks)
½   c. butter (1 stick), divided
1   batch of pastry sheets (see page 231)
½   c. half & half cream
1   t. dried thyme
1   t. sugar
½   t. salt
1⅓ c. Gruyère or Swiss cheese, shredded
1   t. paprika

DIRECTIONS

❶ Melt 4 T. butter in a large skillet over medium heat. Add the leeks and sauté about 15 minutes or until very tender. Stop before the leeks get brown. Mix in the cream, thyme, sugar and salt, cooking over low heat until the cream is thick and coats the leeks, about 8 minutes. Scrape the mixture into a bowl and let cool to room temperature. Stir in the shredded cheese.

❷ Set the puff pastry sheets over a lightly floured work surface and roll sheet into a 10-inch by 10-inch square. With a 2-inch biscuit cutter (or a glass with about a 2-inch diameter), cut as many rounds as possible, about 20 per sheet. Make an indentation with your thumb in the center of each round, causing the sides to rise up a bit.

❸ Melt the remaining 4 T. of butter. With a pastry brush, lightly coat the edge of each round. Place the rounds on baking sheets.

❹ Bake the pastries at 400° for 10 minutes or until they start to rise and are golden brown. Remove from the oven.

❺ Place about 2 t. filling in the center of each round. Return to the oven and bake about 5 minutes more or until cheese completely melts.

❻ Serve warm with a sprinkle of paprika on top as garnish.

YIELD: 12 appetizer servings.

Spinach-Cheese Bites

A PLATTER OF PIPING HOT Spinach-Cheese Bites can "Friend Me" in a way no online social network can. Little bite-sized balls, these appetizers tempt people to gather, linger and "chat" in that good old retro way: in person. As the online connection world snowballs, it takes some spinach and cheese rolled together to remind us that we are each other's true social security, best felt when sharing snacks together.

INGREDIENTS

- 3 c. cooked and cooled spinach or Swiss chard (or a combination of both) finely chopped & tightly packed. Be sure to squeeze out as much water as you can. If using frozen spinach, this is about two 10-oz. packages.
- 3 c. bread crumbs
- 1 c. hard granular cheese, grated (Parmesan)
- 4 large eggs, lightly beaten
- ½ c. butter, softened (1 stick)
- ½ t. salt

DIRECTIONS

❶ Mix all ingredients in a large bowl until well-blended. We find it's easiest to mix using clean hands. Make sure the butter mixes in evenly.

❷ To prepare and serve immediately, roll level tablespoonfuls of the mixture into balls about the size of walnuts (about 40) and place on a lightly oiled cookie sheet. Bake at 350° for 10 minutes or until lightly browned and firm enough to pick up.

❸ Serve immediately.

YIELD: 10 as an appetizer.

COOKING TIP

These Spinach-Cheese Bites freeze exceptionally well. Roll level tablespoonfuls of the mixture into balls about the size of walnuts (about 40) and arrange them on a jelly roll pan or cookie sheet, close but not touching. Freeze until hard, then pack in freezer food storage bags. To serve frozen Spinach-Cheese Bites, remove the number of Bites you'd like from freezer bags and place the frozen balls on a lightly oiled cookie sheet; bake at 350° for 20 minutes or until lightly browned and firm enough to pick up.

Bacon-wrapped Jicama

*T*HERE WAS A TIME in Wisconsin where chestnuts fell not far from most homesteads. That's before the chestnut blight wiped out most of the trees by the 1950s, but not before people in the area created the delicious combo of chestnuts, bacon and a barbeque sauce, perfect for the winter holidays. With the chestnut trees gone, the food tradition is kept alive by substituting Chinese chestnuts or jicama, the softball-sized white vegetable that has a refreshing crunch and mild flavor. It's hard to go to a holiday gathering without these in a Crock-Pot or warmed serving tray.

INGREDIENTS

- 1 lb. jicama, cubed (1 medium jicama)
- 1 lb. bacon, ideally smoked
- ½ c. brown sugar, firmly packed
- 1 t. dry mustard
- 1½ c. ketchup
- 1 t. lemon juice

DIRECTIONS

1. Peel jicama and cut into ¾-inch cubes.

2. Wrap bacon around jicama, holding together with a wooden toothpick and trimming bacon strips as needed.

3. Place bacon-wrapped jicama in a baking dish. Bake at 350° for 30 minutes to cook off fat content. Remove from oven and place tightly together in a clean baking pan.

4. Combine brown sugar, dry mustard, ketchup and lemon juice. Pour over wrapped jicama.

5. Bake at 350° for an additional 20 minutes.

6. To serve, place jicama wraps on a serving platter. Extra sauce can be placed in a bowl to use as a dipping sauce.

   YIELD: 40 pieces.

COOKING TIP If you can't find jicama, two 8 oz. cans of whole Chinese water chestnuts can be used as a substitute. The Chinese chestnut is actually not a nut, but the edible corm from a marsh plant.

Eggs-cellent: Hens in the Henhouse

What's not to like about a gregarious hen following you around the garden or backyard, on the prowl for a grasshopper jumping to safety or a treat dropped to the ground for her to devour? Other than some clucking around, a small flock of three to five hens tend to keep pretty much to themselves, dutifully laying an egg a day for most of the year. It's another Ponzi scheme in the making if only the hens didn't molt (lose their feathers) during the winter months and focus their energy on keeping warm and feather replacement at the expense of egg production.

No need for a boisterous rooster, either, unless you're getting into the chicken-raising business that requires fertile eggs (happily accommodated by the rooster). Getting roosters, as we found out about by accident, results in early morning (and seemingly around the clock) crowing, not to mention some pretty rough behavior as they take charge of "their" flock.

For urban farmers, thousands of cities from Chicago to New York to LA allow their urban or suburban residents to have a few hens in their backyard, though not all municipal zoning offices are as supportive of chickens as they are with cats and dogs. To help urban chicken farmers, numerous communities have come about on the Internet to support others seeking to tend to their flock, including Backyard Chickens.com and UrbanChickens.net.

As a cook, the best part about having your own laying hens is the flavorful, nutrient-rich fresh eggs that start showing up in the hen house (or under random trees or bushes if your hens are truly free-ranging with roaming liberty of your property). They're pets with benefits besides the cuddle factor. Unlike the factory-farmed type—kept indoors, in small cages, medicated and often covered in their own wastes—hens you might get for your backyard or farmyard provide complete nourishment in each egg and have been found to be lower in cholesterol than the factory farm ones.

Be forewarned, the firm, nutrient-rich golden yolks will turn your quiche orange. The yolks themselves aren't runny like the store-bought ones where the hens see little or no sunlight and are usually fed an antibiotic feed. What nutrients? There's omega-3 fatty acids (certain fish are other great options) plus protein and a dozen minerals and vitamins like iron, zinc, vitamins A, D, E and B-12. And if you love deviled eggs, you'll be forced to let the eggs age a week or two, otherwise you'll be frustrated by how hard it is to peel the shells off a fresh hard-boiled one.

Happy chickens in an urban backyard chicken coop.

If you can take care of a guinea pig, you can care for a small flock of hens. For the best eggs, the hens need to have access to the outdoors and organic feed, a coop or shelter of some sort for protection from predators, to roost in and lay their eggs, plus access to fresh water (making sure it doesn't freeze during the winter in cold climates). It's the simplicity of this that makes having your own flock so appealing. That said, it was a neighbor's roaming dog that put the kibosh on our flock, an issue we couldn't resolve without escalating it (which we didn't).

There are thousands of chicken breeds, some prolific layers while others look like clowns. There are also breeds that are best for eating, so-called broilers. (It's a separate, more involved and macabre topic we'll leave for you to explore on your own or can read about in Deborah Niemann's book, *Homegrown and Handmade*, if you're ready to explore processing your chickens at home.)

We started out with leghorns, but quickly progressed to Araucanas that lay the multicolored eggs as well as brown eggs from Rhode Island Reds and Barred Plymouth Rocks — delivered to us as two-day-old pullets (imagine small, fuzzy bright yellow Tweety Bird) in a small cardboard box by the United State Postal Office from the McMurray Hatchery. Just for the record, shell colors have absolutely nothing to do with the quality or nutrition of the eggs; it's just a genetic thing, like the color of our skin.

And for you kitchen gardeners, the chickens are like having roving rototillers, a chemical-free insect pest removal service and, of course, a super source for nitrogen fertilizer — just make sure you compost their poop before putting in your garden beds due to its concentrated levels. Permaculture designers tend to love chickens and you will too.

If you get a diverse flock, you might get white, brown, light blue and even pink colored eggs. By letting them free-range outside, inside a pen area or roaming without constraint, they'll eat just about everything during the warm season months. True omnivores; if they can get it in their beak, they'll eat it.

If you're renting an apartment or living in a condo where having a henhouse is out of the question, for the best tasting, most nutritious eggs, go for the organic, free-range, cage-free and local kind — ideally from farmers you know and trust. Like so many marketing terms these days, there's little substance behind the cage-free, all-natural, free-range antibiotic-free labels, so organic remains the best choice if knowing your farmer is not possible.

Urban chickens in Del Mar, California.

Hummus

WHILE THIS RECIPE will get you started, you may wish to "season to taste." Hummus pairs well with both warm pita bread and the pita chips (see page 64). We buy the dried chickpeas and the tahini paste at an ethnic grocery store or bulk bins at our food cooperative. If you like your hummus less creamy, omit the baking soda from the process. If you're pressed for time, two 15-ounce cans of beans can also be used and skip the boiling step, but we prefer the taste with dried beans.

INGREDIENTS

- 1½ c. dry chickpeas
- 1 t. baking soda
- 2 cloves garlic, minced
- 4 T. lemon juice
- 2 T. tahini paste (ground sesame seeds)
- 2½ t. salt
- ½ t. cumin
- ¼ t. paprika
- ¾ c. olive oil

DIRECTIONS

❶ Mix chickpeas and baking soda and cover with water in a large pot. Soak overnight.

❷ Drain water and rinse chickpeas, then put into a pot with water and bring to a boil. Simmer for 45 minutes or until beans are soft.

❸ Drain water. Put the beans, garlic, lemon juice, tahini, salt, cumin, paprika and olive oil in a food processor. Blend until smooth. If the hummus is too thick, add more olive oil or water. Season to taste.

❹ Serve in a bowl, topped with a little paparika for garnish. Hummus can be refrigerated in a closed container for several days.

YIELD: 10 appetizer servings.

Spilling the Beans on Beans

Beans rank high in complex carbohydrates, fiber, iron and folic acid. Eating beans with grains together, like hummus and pita chips, makes a complete protein with full amino acid benefits. One cup of uncooked beans yields 2 to 3 cups cooked beans. It's best to soak the beans before cooking for 8 to 12 hours to soften the skin so beans cook faster; it also improves their digestibility, since some of the gas-causing enzymes in the beans are released into the water.

Dolmades (Stuffed Grape Leaves)

DON'T BE SCARED OFF by the fact that it looks like you're eating something wrapped in a leaf. You are. After your first bite, we're pretty confident that we'll have you hooked on the salty-sweet-crunch of these. Many dolmades have lamb in them. Ours don't. White rice works fine, or consider the healthier alternative, brown rice.

INGREDIENTS

- 3 c. onion, chopped (3 medium onions)
- 4 c. cooked rice
- 1 c. pine nuts (or cashews)
- 1½ c. water, divided
- 1 c. dried currants (or raisins)
- 1 t. cinnamon
- 3 bay leaves
- ½ t. salt
- 3 T. fresh mint (not necessary, but if you happen to make this during summer mint abundance, do add it in)
- 1 large jar (16 oz.) grape leaves, rinsed and patted dry
- 1 T. lemon juice

DIRECTIONS

❶ Sauté onions in olive oil about 5 minutes or until soft. Stir in rice and pine nuts and sauté 3 minutes more.

❷ Add currants, cinnamon and bay leaves and 1 c. water. Reduce heat to low and simmer 15 minutes. Stir in mint and salt.

❸ Cut tough stems off grape leaves. Line a large pot with about 4 leaves.

❹ Place one grape leaf smooth side down on a work surface and set a tablespoon of filling near base of stem end of leaf. Fold end and sides over filling and roll toward point of leaf.

❺ Set seam side down in pot. Repeat with remaining leaves and filling, packing tightly together and layering on top of each other.

❻ Mix lemon juice with remaining 1 c. water and pour over leaves. Cover with 3 grape leaves and invert a heatproof plate on top. Cover with pot lid and bring to a boil over medium heat. Reduce heat to low and simmer for 45 minutes. Remove from heat and let stand about 2 hours or until liquid is absorbed.

❼ Serve at room temperature or warm.

YIELD: About 100 small rolls, depending on leaf size.

Maybe a person's time would be as well spent raising food as raising money to buy food.

FRANK A. CLARK

Vegetarian Nori-wrapped Sushi

Vegan

*H*ISTORICALLY, SUSHI EVOLVED as a utilitarian food as far back as 300 BCE when fermented rice was wrapped around fish as a form of food preservation. Today, sushi reminds us of the contradictions of our modern world. Inherently, sushi isn't just food — it's art. Layers of nori, a super-nutritious, dried seaweed, plus fish, rice and vegetables make an amazing visual display when creatively rolled. Sadly, some of these works of edible wonder are grabbed in the takeout line as fast food, eaten alone. Instead, join us in the sushi art renaissance and bring back reasons to "play" with your food while layering your vegetables. Make an edible kaleidoscope and linger to share and eat the results. This veggie sushi travels well, though it's best eaten within the first five hours since the rice may dry out and harden.

INGREDIENTS

- 2   c. cooked sushi rice, cooled
- ½   c. carrots, julienned (⅛-inch-thick matchsticks)
- ½   c. sugar snap sweet peas
- ½   c. lettuce, shredded
- ½   c. spinach, shredded
- 4   sheets nori
- ¼   c. soy sauce (for dipping)

DIRECTIONS

❶ Cook rice and cool.

❷ Place nori on a flat surface. Arrange approximately ½ c. rice and ½ c. vegetables on long edge of nori. Use carrots, sugar snap peas, lettuce, spinach or any combination you'd like.

❸ Gently roll nori, starting with the rice/veggie side.

❹ Using a serrated knife, slice nori into 1-inch pieces. Slicing on a diagonal makes attractive pieces.

YIELD: 6 servings as appetizer.

COOKING TIP | **De-stringing Sugar Snap Sweet Peas**
Because many market growers or backyard gardeners like heirloom varieties of sugar snap peas, to prevent the string of the sugar snap from getting stuck in your teeth, make sure to snap the plant-connected end off and yank up the string that runs up the seam.

Vegetarian sushi with fresh veggies, served as an appetizer at Inn Serendipity.

Latvian Pirages

THESE PIRAGES (pier-rogz) come from Lisa's Baltic roots. It's a traditional bread roll made on birthdays and holidays that tastes best warmed up in the oven. The bacon filling is rolled inside the bread dough. Sometimes during the baking process, the seal cracks and a little bacon pops out; in the Latvian tradition, these special pirages are "smiling" at you. Think of that next time the jelly drips out of the PB&J or soup drips down your chin: the mess is actually because of its joyful ingredients.

FILLING INGREDIENTS

2   lbs. bacon (thick-cut), diced very fine
1   c. onions, chopped (1 large onion)
¼   t. nutmeg
½   t. salt
¼   t. pepper

DOUGH INGREDIENTS

2   t. sugar
4½ t. dry active yeast (two .25 oz. packages)
½   c. warm water
7   c. or more flour
2   c. whole milk
¼   c. butter
2   t. salt
¼   c. sugar
½   c. vegetable oil
3   eggs, lightly beaten, divided
½   c. sour cream
½   t. sugar
½   c. water

DIRECTIONS

❶ For filling, sauté onion and bacon together on medium heat until cooked through. Add nutmeg, salt and pepper and set aside to cool.

❷ In a small bowl, mix sugar and yeast with warm water. Set aside in a warm place for 10 minutes. Yeast should bubble up to double the size.

❸ Meanwhile, scald milk, (heat until small bubbles form but do not boil), and put it in a large mixing bowl. Add butter to milk and stir to let butter melt. Add salt, sugar and oil and stir.

❹ Separately, mix two eggs with sour cream. When milk is cooled to lukewarm, add egg mixture.

❺ Add yeast mixture and two cups of flour. Beat thoroughly with wooden spoon or electric mixer. Add another cup of flour and continue beating.

❻ Remove beaters and continue kneading by hand or with a dough hook. Add almost all of the rest of the flour. The dough will be quite stiff but still sticky. Beat with dough hook or knead by hand until dough is shiny and doesn't stick to your hands, about 6 to 8 minutes.

❼ When the dough is ready, slap the dough down on the counter a few times.

❽ Place ball in a lightly oiled bowl. Sprinkle some flour on the dough and cover with a clean towel. Place in a warm spot to rise, about 1½ hours, or until doubled.

❾ Punch dough down and divide into 4 equal pieces. Roll each piece into a long strand about 20 inches long. With a knife, cut each strand piece into even pieces about 1 inch long.

❿ With your hands, roll and flatten each piece into a patty. Place 1 t. of filling in the middle. Fold edges up and pinch seems together. Place rolls on a lightly oiled cookie sheet with the pinched seams under. Bend rolls slightly into a crescent shape, cover with towel and let rise again until doubled, about 25 minutes.

⓫ Before putting into the oven, brush tops with lightly beaten remaining egg and stab with fork to release steam. Bake at 400^6 for about 12 to 15 minutes until golden light brown. Brush with sugar water (½ t. sugar mixed with ½ c. hot water). Cool on rack.

YIELD: 7 dozen appetizers.

Lisa's last name, "Kivirist," is rooted in stone imagery. Translated from Estonian, it means a stone marker like you'd see on a wild trail.

Organic Eating on a Dime

Our notion of "savoring the good life" comes with a price tag, but not in the conventional sense. Eating seasonal, organic, local and farmsteadtarian doesn't have to mean emptying your bank account. For health reasons alone, organic food is a steal of a deal when you weigh the costs of medical treatment or care later in life. Why gamble with your health by eating foods containing chemical residues that have been found to be possibly dangerous to your health? The US is the only place on the planet where we spend less on food than on medical costs.

When it comes to eating, we all have different living situations, tastes and preferences. Our choices are varied and personal. Empowering folks with tangible tools to eat better and more frugally impacts our food systems, our health and the environment. Here are few strategies we've used with great success.

Eat lower on the food chain more often

By eating lower on the food chain, we end up focusing on foods higher in nutrients and lower in inputs and costs. By incorporating more things like beans, tofu and whole grains, we increase nutritional value at a much lower cost than meat proteins, both to the environment and our bank account. Growing fruits and vegetables requires a lot less land, water and fossil fuels. For a single calorie of beef, 25 calories of fossil fuels are needed. For 1 calorie of a fruit or vegetable, it's often only 2 calories or less of fuel required. We applaud those who have opted for meatless Mondays. We eat a meat dish about once or twice a month on average.

Eat high on quality and use less

Just a bit of high-quality flavor goes a long way. An organic, locally grown option may cost more in comparison to its industrially produced cousin across the aisle, but you don't need to use as much of it in volume. We brew Fair Trade Sumatra coffee from Equal Exchange for our morning perk-up. Because our brew is so flavorful, we can get away using less of it every time we make it.

Stock up the pantry

Ingredients should be about quality and taste, not convenience. Save money, time and fossil fuel — not to mention upping nutritional value — by dining chez you. Keeping an organized, stocked pantry goes a long way to creating a more self-reliant household. So take our Farmstead Pantry Checklist (see page 224) to the store for nearly every pantry staple you'll need for any recipe found in this book. Your home is the most convenient convenience store.

Buy in bulk

Purchase the basics that you use regularly in bulk from a local food-buying club or food cooperative. At bulk prices, organic items like flour and sugar are often competitive in price to the non-organic kind. Most families of two to four people can stock up with 50-pound bags twice a year to meet their cooking needs. Flour, sugar, rice or other grains and beans should be stored well-sealed in heavy-duty food grade plastic bins.

Eat up

The corollary to "buy in bulk": make sure you use it. Every winter we "eat through" our pantry, finishing off grains, rice, canned food and other oddities we accumulated over the year rather than letting it rot or go past its expiration date. We also make sure we savor the garden produce stored from the past summer. Frozen zucchini is not red wine, friends. It doesn't get better with time. This annual process saves us more than a $1,000 a year. According to some studies, the average American household wastes approximately 15 percent of food purchased annually, or 474 pounds, costing them about $590.

Substitute ingredients if you can

Think out of your recipe box and experiment with substitutions using items you already have on hand or that are in your pantry. No buttermilk? Use 1 c. of any kind of milk, remove 1 T. milk and add 1 T. vinegar or lemon juice. Let it stand 5 minutes until it curdles. Many of our recipes provide choices for vegetables or fruits to be added as well as options for fresh or dried spices.

Prioritize your purchases

When working with limited fresh food budgets, focus on buying organic what the Environmental Working Group dubs the "dirty fifteen" — those fruits or vegetables with the highest pesticide absorption: peaches, blueberries, spinach, apples, bell peppers, celery, nectarines, strawberries, cherries, kale, lettuce, grapes (imported), carrots, pears and potatoes. Since the list sometimes changes, you can download a tip card at foodnews.org/walletguide.php or learn more at beyondpesticides.org. That said, most of us can afford to eat nearly all of our food grown organically. It's a matter of revisiting our priorities, with our health at the top. You may have to come to terms with the reality that keeping the chemicals, GMOs and preservatives out of our food may trump one or two restaurant meals a month or a daily coffee shop fix.

Vegetable Tempura

*G*RANTED, SUMMER HEAT plus 400° of bubbling oil don't create a comfortable environment for kitchen projects. Don't punt, just pull out the patio chair and take the fryer outside (we often use a turkey fryer set-up). We're not talking about frying Twinkies, but many summer vegetables make great candidates for tempura, like broccoli, summer squash and our favorite, beets. John is our resident summer fry-daddy; he makes mega batches of tempura on a picnic table set-up next to the greenhouse, pulling electric line out via an extension cord. He'll still "complain" about the heat, but he's really just angling for Lisa to bring him out a frozen mochaccino (page 207). An easy price to pay for heaps of these crunchy, lightly battered jewels.

BATTER INGREDIENTS

- 1 egg
- ⅔ c. water
- ½ c. flour
- ½ c. cornstarch
- 1 t. baking soda
- 1 t. baking powder
- 1 t. sugar
- ½ t. salt

VEGETABLES AND OIL

- 1 c. summer squash, cut into ½-inch slices
- 1 c. onions, quartered and layers separated
- 1 c. beets, cut into ½-inch slices
- 1 c. broccoli, cut into 2-inch florets
- 4 c. canola oil for frying (or more, depending on size of fryer)

DIRECTIONS

❶ Beat egg and blend in water.

❷ Mix flour, cornstarch, baking soda, baking powder, sugar, salt. Lightly stir into egg mixture. Batter will be lumpy.

❸ Dip vegetables into batter and deep-fry until golden brown. Drain on paper towels placed on top of newspaper.

❹ Serve immediately with a sprinkle of seasoning salt and honey mustard or ranch dressing (see recipe page 229) dip sauces.

YIELD: 8 servings as appetizer.

John Ivanko with Indiana food writer Marshall King preparing tempura for an Inn Serendipity potluck.

Cucumber Slices with Feta Cheese Filling

*W*HEN YOU HAVE CUCUMBERS coming out of your ears, what should you do? Dressed up a wee bit, cucumbers can look spectacular on a plate. Try this recipe featuring a medley of flavors that tease your palate with sweet, sour and salty tastes, depending on what hits what part of your tongue. Adapted from *Country Living: The Farm Chicks in the Kitchen* by Teri Edwards and Serena Thompson, this recipe provides a stunning, but simple, way to share cucumbers.

INGREDIENTS

2   cucumbers
½   c. rice vinegar
2   T. honey
½   c. sour cream
¼   c. mayonnaise
½   c. feta cheese, crumbled
      (½ lb.)
½   c. chives, chopped
1   T. fresh dill (1 t. dried)
      about 24 fresh basil leaves
      (optional)

DIRECTIONS

❶ Cut ends off cucumber and cut into ½-inch slices. Scoop out and remove a little pulp from the center of each slice to make a "cup" (be careful not to dig through to the other side).

❷ Mix together the rice vinegar and honey. Place cucumbers in a bowl and drizzle with vinegar dressing. Cover and refrigerate for 1 hour.

❸ Mix together the sour cream, mayonnaise, feta cheese, chives and dill.

❹ Shake marinade off cucumbers and fill each with about 1 hearty teaspoon of the filling. Garnish with a fresh basil leaf on top.

YIELD: 6 servings as an appetizer.

Asian Egg Rolls

*A*SIAN EGG ROLLS ARE OUR FAVORITE way to clear out the freezer in the early spring, using up random veggies before the fresh spring harvest starts. A way to cross-pollinate global cuisine with American garden fare, egg rolls exemplify how we farmstead chefs blend cultural influences and make them our own. There's a built-in community component to egg roll making, like sushi rolling, since we've learned that they taste best fresh and crisp out of the fryer. We like to make these when Liam's buddies sleep over. Making egg rolls feels like a party, and kids eat multiple servings of vegetables.

INGREDIENTS

- 6 c. vegetables, sliced (try pea pods, broccoli, carrots or zucchini)
- ½ jicama, peeled and cut into ¼-inch cubes
- ½ c. water
- 2 T. cornstarch
- 1 t. soy sauce
- 4 t. oyster or fish sauce
- 1 package egg roll wrappers (15 wraps, 8-inch squares)

DIRECTIONS

❶ Stir-fry vegetables until crisp-tender, about 8 minutes. Add jicama at end to preserve its crunch. Remove cooked vegetables from pan but keep pan hot.

❷ Combine water, cornstarch, soy sauce and oyster or fish sauce. Pour into pan and stir over medium heat until thick (will look like a gravy).

❸ Add cooked vegetables and coat with sauce. Remove from heat and let cool before rolling egg rolls.

❹ To wrap, place the egg roll wrapper out in front of you. Place approximately 1 heaping tablespoon of the cooked filling in the middle of the wrapper. Using your finger, spread a little water along the edge of each side of the wrapper. Flip the side in front of you up first, followed by the side on the left and then right. Roll up and seal by running a wet finger along the edge.

❺ To fry, slide each egg roll into the oil one at a time. Deep-fry until golden brown, usually about 8 to 10 minutes. Drain on paper towels.

YIELD: 24 egg rolls.

MAIN DISHES

Crispy Eggplant Parmesan

Quick Pizza

Deep-dish Pizza

Fried Green Tomato & Basil Sandwich

Zucchini "Meatballs" (vegan)

Maple Syrup Marinated Wild Salmon (Phil and Judy Welty)

Casablanca Couscous (vegan)

Beet Burgers

Basil Pesto with Handmade Linguine

Spanakopita (Spinach Pie)

Stuffed Roti with Chickpea Filling

Italian Sausage Risotto (Beth and Jody Osmund)

Sloppy Joes (vegan)

Potato Pierogis

Grecian Leek Pasta

Grilled Shish-kabob Souvlaki (lamb) with Tzatziki Sauce

Walnut Burger

Herb-infused Ribs (pork)

Indonesian Asparagus and Pasta

** see Liam's Favorites (page 214) for:

Macaroni & Cheese

A Declaration of Food Interdependence

America's founding fathers signed the Declaration of Independence on July 4, 1776, affirming the rights to life, liberty and the pursuit of happiness. It set in motion the formation of a more perfect Union, founded upon the principles rooted in the land, in democracy and freedom.

Thomas Jefferson, perhaps more than any other founder, recognized the importance of agriculture in the nourishment of what has become our great nation today. While he had many detractors and skeptics, he advocated for the small family farmers — and a limited Federal government. From crop rotation to contour plowing, Jefferson appreciated the young nation's interdependency on the land and the fruits it provided. He is in fact responsible for the eggplant, broccoli and Brussels sprouts we eat today, having introduced them himself to American soils. He also recognized the finiteness of the continent, and called for stewardship and care.

At the time of the American Revolution, much of the population grew at least some of their own food. We were a largely agrarian nation, with inklings of the industrial greatness that would arrive in the 20th century, albeit at a dire cost to both ecological systems and fellow humankind, impacts we're still trying to ascertain. While the US abolished slavery about a century after the Revolution, much of our agricultural system still depends on exploited migrant labor, and often by illegal immigrants.

After the robber barons came the multinational corporations. Food production became the purview of a shrinking crop of increasingly large-scale farms, often operating as corporations themselves. Federal policies, especially through the Farm Bill, masked the true cost of food with producer subsidies and a highway system to move it around.

By the end of the 20th century, these corporations and their lobbying interests took powerful positions that helped write the very laws that regulated their business. Since the majority of politicians serve urban or suburban constituents having little interest in farming issues, one might wonder why they would even approve the Federal Farm Bill. What many people don't know is that as much as 50 percent of the Farm Bill funding goes toward the Supplemental Nutrition Assistance Program (SNAP), formerly called Food Stamp Program, as well as school lunch and other nutritional programs. In 2010, over 40 million Americans depended on the SNAP. So in America, you could say eating is a political act, too.

Meanwhile, independence and freedom for the American people related to food and drink became largely defined by the number of food choices and the ability to earn money to pay someone else to grow or produce what we ate. We the eaters have become dependent upon the industrial food system to provide for our survival. If you live in a low-income

Lisa Kivirist raising a carrot to farmstead independence and interdependence. Without the wind and sun, our farm would not run or grow food.

part of a city, like Detroit, there may not even be a supermarket to serve you. Yet in a well-to-do suburb, there might be warehouses of food. And, because it's a food system dependent on cheap, abundant oil, so too, is our next meal.

But those of us who shop at farmers markets or grow some food in our gardens know that independence and happiness have much more to do with relationships and friendships than with the size of our bank account. Trust is what holds these relationships together, forged from a respect for each other and the land, and the importance of food and community in our daily lives. Both are essential to our prosperity.

Food is a currency that defines healthy communities. The Transition Town movement where citizens come together to build community resilience is based on the same foundations of our founding fathers, that of collaboration, democracy and sharing. These citizen-led initiatives address many facets of resiliency like energy, transportation or housing, achieving greater local self-reliance and stronger local economy. Instead of hording stocks, bonds or land, food caches or knowledge, transition initiatives (transitionus.org) are helping rebuild our basic skills sets, like how to can tomatoes or grow basil. The local food system seems to be a common starting point for many of these communities once awareness of the issues has attracted enough interest among residents.

There are numerous examples throughout this book of ways to reconnect with real food, if not grown on your rooftop, then by purchasing directly from the growers or producers and largely sidestepping corporate America. From farmers markets to small-scale artisanal cheesemakers, from family or cooperatively run dairies to local beekeepers, scratch the surface in any community and there's a growing number of opportunities to buy real food directly from real people.

A declaration of American interdependence — among farmers and diners, city slickers and country folk, people and the land — may hold out the greatest promise and hope for tomorrow, as energy costs soar ever higher and climate change makes it snow in Mexico, flood in Australia and leads to massive forest fires in China. Soon, we may all be eating more farmsteadtarian, not by choice but circumstance. We're in it together now on our common home: Earth.

All politics are local, it's said. So, too, might it be for most of our food and drink. A great thing, we think. While this cookbook includes a smattering of recipes requiring ingredients found outside the Midwest, there's plenty that don't. It's not that we're hardcore apple junkies, for example, with our collection of apple creations. Rather, we just have them by the bushel by the second week in September.

We eat what grows in abundance where we live. The fun part is rediscovering what grows where you live and figuring out what variations in this cookbook will work well for your locale. Got blueberries? Replace them where it calls for fresh raspberries. If your CSA box provides more sweet potatoes than you can eat baked, try replacing them in our potato latke recipe (we did and they're scrumptious). Of course, give the recipe substitution a try before serving it to a house full of guests.

We like to celebrate interdependency day every day with a nod in thanks to the yeoman farmer who made it possible. After all, without these farmers — perhaps yourself included — we wouldn't be around for very long. So let these main dishes celebrate independence and the interdependence of the foods found on our plates.

Crispy Eggplant Parmesan

*J*OHN WILL NEVER FORGET the year without a harvest of eggplant. Lisa, however, is desperately trying to. We didn't lose the eggplant to drought, flea beetles or kids trampling the plants. One day, while weeding, Lisa lost her focus and ended up pulling out both the weeds and the healthiest eggplants we ever grew. She started weeding the eggplant row and got so into the clearing-out zone that she became a human goat, pulling out everything. For a second she proudly looked back at the row when she finished, clear of everything, then realized what happened. It's now a running joke, as we do savor this eggplant dish each summer, and remember the legendary human goat. So try to keep the big picture in mind; stay focused on the task at hand, and never throw the eggplant out with the burdock.

INGREDIENTS

- 1 medium eggplant (about 1 lb.)
- 2 eggs
- 2 T. milk
- ½ c. hard granular cheese, grated (Parmesan)
- ½ c. wheat germ
- 1 t. dried basil (dried coats better than fresh, which tends to clump)
- 2 c. tomato sauce (see page 102)
- 1 c. feta cheese, finely crumbled (1 lb.)

DIRECTIONS

❶ Slice the eggplant into ½-inch slices, leaving the skins on. Lightly salt eggplant slices and place on a baking sheet. Let stand for 10 minutes. Water will bead on eggplant; pat dry.

❷ In a small shallow bowl, combine the eggs and milk.

❸ In another small shallow bowl, combine the cheese, wheat germ and basil.

❹ Dip the eggplant slices first in the egg and milk mixture, then into wheat germ mixture, turning to coat both sides. Place the coated slices in a single layer on a lightly oiled baking sheet.

❺ Bake at 400° for 20 minutes or until the eggplant is a crisp golden brown on the outside and tender in the inside.

❻ While eggplant is baking, heat tomato sauce.

❼ To serve, place several eggplant slices on each plate. Spoon tomato sauce over eggplant and sprinkle with feta cheese.

YIELD: 4 servings.

Quick Pizza

*I*T'S A QUICK AND EASY PIZZA since the crispy crust is not yeast-based so it doesn't need to rise. What makes this pizza exceptional are the ingredients: the fresh vegetables, homemade sauce and quality cheeses and fresh crust, all made by hand.

INGREDIENTS

2   c. flour
½   c. whole wheat flour
1½ t. baking powder
½   t. salt
¼   c. butter (½ stick)
1   c. milk
2   c. tomato sauce (see page 102)
    pizza toppings of choice
½   t. canola oil

DIRECTIONS

❶ Place the two flours, baking powder and salt into the food processor and pulse until mixed. Drop in the butter pieces and pulse until large crumbs form.

❷ With the motor running, pour in the milk and process just until a clump of dough forms.

❸ Scrape the dough onto a lightly floured surface. Form 4 balls. Roll out each ball with a lightly floured rolling pin into an 8-inch circle.

❹ Place two circles on a lightly oiled baking sheet. Top with the toppings of your choice and bake at 450° for 12 to 15 minutes or until golden on top and bottom. Peek underneath the crust to make sure it's golden brown.

❺ Serve immediately. If there are any leftovers, they're best re-heated in the oven to maintain the crispiness of the crust.

YIELD: 4 pizzas.

Pizza coming out from a hot stone in a convection oven.

Deep-dish Pizza

*I*S ALL ADDICTION BAD? What if the obsession stems from pizza? That's how we felt during our urban jaunts to Chicago where, of course, some classic deep-dish pizza needed to be on the menu. But back on the farmstead, alas, we had the option of either going cold turkey on deep-dish pizza or tackle a recipe for that essential pizza ingredient: the crust. Here's our adaptation of the pizza at Lou Malnati's, a Chicago landmark. The secret is in the cornmeal.

DOUGH INGREDIENTS

1½ c. warm water

2¼ t. dry active yeast (one .25 oz. package)

1 t. sugar

4 c. flour, divided

¼ c. olive oil

¼ c. cornmeal

1 T. salt

TOPPINGS INGREDIENTS

4 c. cheese (mozzarella, havarti)

2 c. tomato sauce (see page 102)

2 c. onion, chopped

2 c. bell peppers, sliced

4 c. spinach, shredded

DIRECTIONS

❶ In a large bowl of an electric mixer, mix warm water, yeast and sugar. Let stand for 5 minutes.

❷ Mix in 3 c. flour, olive oil and cornmeal. Use dough hook of mixer on low speed until smooth. Add remaining flour in ¼ c. increments. Mix in thoroughly before adding next flour addition. May need a little more or less flour to reach dough consistency. Mix 3 minutes more. Dough should feel slightly sticky but not stick to hands.

❸ Remove dough from mixer. Form into a ball and place in bowl lightly oiled with olive oil. Spread a little olive oil lightly on top of dough. Cover with plastic wrap and refrigerate overnight.

❹ Let dough stand at room temperature approximately 2 hours before rolling out.

❺ Sauté onions and peppers in skillet over medium heat for about 6 minutes or until tender. Add spinach until wilted.

❻ Roll dough to ½-inch thickness and place on lightly oiled pizza pan. Top with tomato sauce, cheese and toppings. Bake at 400° for 35 minutes or until crust is brown and cheese is lightly browned and bubbly.

❼ Serve immediately. If there are any leftovers, they're best reheated in the oven to maintain the crispiness of the crust.

YIELD: 8 servings.

Fried Green Tomato & Basil Sandwich

*T*HIS HEARTY VEGGIE SANDWICH captures the peak of garden freshness. We go through a summer phase where we eat this every day for a week. Enjoy it while the garden lasts. We use the Artisan Bread recipe on page 62 or splurge on a crusty sourdough bread at our favorite local bakery. The sandwich is crispy on the outside and juicy inside, filled with aromatic basil.

INGREDIENTS

- 2 medium green tomatoes
- 2 T. cornmeal
- ½ t. salt
- 2 c. melting cheese, shredded (try mozzarella, havarti or smoked Gouda)
- 1 c. fresh basil leaves, packed
- 8 slices crusty bread
- ¼ c. butter (½ stick), softened
- 4 T. mayonnaise
- ¼ c. canola oil

DIRECTIONS

❶ Slice tomatoes into half-inch slices.

❷ Combine cornmeal and salt in small bowl. Dip the tomato slices into the mixture and coat both sides.

❸ Heat oil in frying pan over medium-high heat (do not let it smoke) to coat bottom of pan. Fry the tomato slices until they are tender and golden brown on each side, about 3 minutes per side. Set the fried tomatoes aside to allow them to cool slightly.

❹ Butter each outside side of each slice of bread.

❺ Spread approximately ½ T. mayonnaise on each inside slice of bread. Top with fried tomatoes, approximately 6 basil leaves and ½ c. shredded cheese.

❻ After forming sandwiches (buttered sides on the outside), return to pan over medium heat until cheese melts and bread turns a golden, crispy brown.

❼ Carefully slide sandwiches from pan and place on a plate, cutting sandwich in half. Serve immediately, garnished with a pickle wedge.

YIELD: 4 sandwiches.

COOKING TIP — A Frost Alert Meal

Tomatoes and basil will not likely make it though a frost, so before the first frost of autumn, harvest everything. Then grill up some Fried Green Tomato & Basil Sandwiches.

Zucchini "Meatballs"

OKAY, SO THEY ARE NOT REALLY MEATBALLS. More like a dressed-up fritter. But the hearty texture makes these a protein-packed (thanks to the chickpea flour) topping for spaghetti or even cut in half for pizza toppings. We're always on the lookout for new ways to use zucchini, and these freeze particularly well, so it's a good way to process the squash for winter comfort food.

INGREDIENTS

- 3 medium zucchini, thinly sliced
- ½ t. salt
- ¼ c. onions, finely chopped
- ½ t. ground ginger
- 2 T. fresh cilantro (2 t. dried)
- ½ c. chickpea flour

DIRECTIONS

❶ Sprinkle zucchini with salt. Set aside for ½ hour. Squeeze excess liquid from zucchini.

❷ Chop zucchini, add onion, ginger, cilantro and chickpea flour. Mix well and form into 16 balls.

❸ Fry over medium heat until golden, about 10 minutes, then remove and set on paper napkins to drain off excess oil.

❹ Serve as you would meatballs with spaghetti and sauce. These are also delicious as fritter-style appetizers with a ranch dip sauce.

YIELD: 16 meatballs.

COOKING TIP Break out of the white flour box. What a sheltered life we led before, when recipes revolved around the processed white flour. By definition, "flour" is a powdery foodstuff made by grinding and sifting the meal of a grain. While grinding wheat to make white flour is most common, lots of things can be ground and sifted such as rice, corn and chickpeas. A staple in Indian cuisine, chickpea flour has a high level of protein and no gluten.

BACK TO THE LAND:
MAPLE TREES AND MENTORING

Phil and Judy Welty,
Welty's Sugar Bush,
Browntown, Wisconsin

It was called the Welty's Sugar Bush, owned and operated by Phil and Judy Welty from 1968 to 1975. Nestled along a hillside, the mostly wooded thirty-five acres that made up the Welty's Sugar Bush included hundreds of sugar maples. The trees produced more than 10,000 gallons of sap each spring, siphoned off by more than 1,000 taps. When they first started, Phil and Judy hauled 5-gallon buckets of sap by hand and heated the evaporator in their 300-square-foot sugar shack with wood. They produced about 300 gallons of syrup in a good year.

"School kids came out regularly during the week for a tour and a taste," smiles Phil. Like many food entrepreneurs, he and his wife were eager to share their knowledge and introduce kids to real food, harvested and processed locally. "Then we had to gear up for when the kids brought their parents out the following weekend for our syrup and popular maple sugar candy." The amber-colored syrup seemed ample reward for the hard work during the maple syrup-making season from late February through early April in Wisconsin.

As it turns out, real maple syrup is one of the most valuable liquid commodities around, going for about $75 per gallon these days. When it opened, Phil and Judy's maple syrup operation was the only one in the area. So naturally, their nature-based enterprise boomed on land they rented from the landowner. People could taste the rich flavors and quality, easily beating out the imitations and chemically flavored syrups sold at the store.

Their wild foods venture was so lucrative that their profits ended up becoming the down payment for the property. They eventually built their log cabin homestead, including an expansive kitchen garden, solar thermal system for domestic hot water and a small wind turbine to generate electricity. The decision to build their log cabin, along with their decision to launch a new renewable energy enterprise during the first American energy crisis and OPEC oil embargo years, led them to wind down their Sugar Bush operation. The future was solar and self-reliance, and they started Solar Use Now of Wisconsin, operated from their homestead.

"My grandfather's pride and joy was his Victory Garden," says Phil, explaining how they both became interested in small-scale farming, foraging for wild foods and homesteading. "We ate off his Victory Garden."

Phil and Judy Welty's homestead with wind turbine and solar thermal system.

"And off what we found along the roadside," adds Judy. "Back then, it provided an abundance of wild foods like asparagus, ground cherries, mushrooms, raspberries, blackberries and wild grapes. It just about sustained us for the whole year, since we canned and preserved everything we harvested or foraged."

Our first meeting with Phil and Judy, years later, after we had begun the work of transforming our farmstead into a more self-reliant homestead, was not by chance. They drove up our driveway, looking to ask us about the solar thermal system we had recently installed on our roof. Since they had installed more than thirty such systems in the 1970s, they were curious as to why a young couple from Chicago would think to put such a system on their roof (after all, oil was only about $18/barrel in 1997).

And so sparked a friendship and mentorship that became pivotal to the success of our largely fossil-fuel-free homestead today, since Phil and Judy eagerly shared their knowledge of everything from canning tomatoes to renewing our understanding of how the sun moved across the sky through the seasons. We often sought counsel from these two sages, wise in the ways of practical homesteading skills.

While we may have become friends through our relationship with renewable energy and homesteading skills, it was through food that we became family. They had us over for Judy's pizza nights, and we joined their family for their annual fondue party to usher in the New Year—a slow food experience if there ever was one—a meal cooked one bite at a time.

The year 2006 was a special year for us. We celebrated the return to the road of a plug-in, all-electric CitiCar, completely rewired and restored by Phil. Now, our trips to the bank for our business are made possible by this electric car. Only about 2,600 of these CitiCars were made by the Sebring-Vanguard Company from 1974 to 1976, the embargo years that foreshadowed the second energy crisis of the late 2000s, when oil ran as much as $148/barrel in 2008.

We celebrated this birthday occasion like many Americans do, with a cake—a triple-decker cake carefully sculpted in the wedge shape of the CitiCar. Pieces of the CitiCar cake were shared with every Solar Tour visitor—along with numerous test drives navigated by Phil—bringing a tasty connection to both our transportation and the abundant and local fuel choice for the car: a .5 kW solar electric system placed next to our garage.

CitiCar cake shared with visitors to the National Solar Tour at Inn Serendipity.

Maple Syrup Marinated Wild Salmon

*T*HIS RECIPE IS INSPIRED by Welty's Sugar Bush and a desire to eat sustainably caught fish. We avoid farmed salmon that's usually raised in floating feedlots, opting instead for Alaskan wild-caught salmon. Like the rest of our fish and seafood, we look for certification by the Marine Stewardship Council (msc.org). Our quick reference is the sustainable Seafood Watch pocket guide or card by region of the country from Monterey Bay Aquarium (montereybayaquarium.org) or Environmental Defense Fund (edf.org). Unfortunately, nearly all commercial Atlantic salmon is now farmed. For wild Alaskan salmon, several kinds might be considered: chinook or king salmon, with a rich, buttery red flesh and the highest oil content; sockeye or red salmon, with a rich flavor and deep red flesh; coho or silver salmon, with a lower oil content and a less firm texture than the other two. This salmon goes great with Oven-roasted Potatoes (page 92) and our Caesar Salad (page 112).

INGREDIENTS

2   lbs. boneless wild Alaskan salmon, fillets

2   T. maple syrup

½   c. orange juice, freshly squeezed

½   c. bourbon

½   c. soy sauce

2   cloves garlic, minced

2   t. fresh ginger, grated

1   T. brown sugar

3   T. canola oil

3   T. green onions, finely chopped

¼   t. salt

¼   t. pepper

½   fresh lemon, thinly sliced (optional)

½   medium yellow onion, sliced into ¼-inch slices (optional)

DIRECTIONS

❶ Combine maple syrup, orange juice, bourbon, soy sauce, minced garlic, grated ginger root, brown sugar and oil in bowl. Sprinkle salt and mash and blend mixture with fork to release flavors.

❷ Place salmon fillets skin-side up, in a glass cake pan. Pour marinade mixture over salmon fillets and let sit covered in the refrigerator for 8 hours.

❸ To broil in the oven, pour ½ c. marinade on a foil-lined jelly roll pan. Place the fish skin side down on the foil and pour about 1 c. marinade on top of the fish. Add sliced lemon and onions on top of fish. Broil fish at medium heat (450°) for about 15 minutes, watching carefully to avoid overcooking. Baste occasionally with remaining marinade.

❹ For outdoor grilling, heat grill to medium heat, then cook individual salmon fillets on grill with skin side down. Depending on the thickness of the fillets, cook for 15 to 20 minutes, checking frequently to avoid overcooking. When bottom side is done, turn fillets over and grill the top side for 5 additional minutes.

YIELD: 4 servings.

None of us are teachers; we are all students, learning from each other's experience.

MARK BOYLE, *THE MONEYLESS MAN*

Casablanca Couscous

*J*UST SAY THE WORD "CASABLANCA" and you start feeling exotic, sexy and channeling Bogart. Imagine what happens when you make a whole meal on that theme, inspired by the western city in Morocco. With hints of curry and raisins, the sauce juxtaposes savory and sweet. We like to continue the North African theme and serve it over couscous, but you can just as easily use rice, another whole grain or just eat it plain. "Cook it again, Sam."

INGREDIENTS

- 1 lb. tofu, cubed
- 1 c. onion, chopped (about 1 medium)
- 1 c. carrots, peeled & sliced
- ½ c. chopped walnuts
- 2 c. cooked chickpeas (one 16 oz. can, drained)
- 2 c. tomato sauce (see page 102)
- ½ c. raisins
- 1½ c. water
- 2 t. curry powder
- 1 t. paprika
- 1 t. salt
- 1 c. couscous
- 2 T. olive oil

DIRECTIONS

❶ In large pan, brown tofu, onion, carrots, nuts.

❷ Add chickpeas, tomato sauce, raisins, water, curry, paprika and salt. Bring to a boil. Cover and simmer for 40 minutes.

❸ Separately, boil 1½ c. water with 2 T. oil. Add couscous, stir, cover, reduce heat and simmer for 5 minutes.

❹ Serve vegetables over steaming couscous.

YIELD: 4 servings.

COOKING TIP Couscous is among one of the healthiest grain-based products with a much higher vitamin punch than pasta. It isn't a grain itself, but made from moistening semolina wheat into tiny balls and then coating them with finely ground wheat flour. Most couscous you'll find in the store has been pre-steamed and dried. It cooks up fluffy and is ready to eat in minutes.

Beet Burgers

*W*E USED TO THINK the nicest B&B compliment came when folks chose to stay here on their honeymoon. But Ben and Alissa topped that last summer. Not only were they returning guests who came back for their honeymoon, they served our beet burger recipe at their wedding reception. These burgers take time to make so we like to make a triple batch and freeze some of the extra patties. They taste surprisingly good cold and the deep red color of the beets give a hearty burger feel. We once served them to Lisa's carnivore dad. Maybe it was an English-as-a-second-language thing, or perhaps we talked too fast, but he still thinks he ate "beef" burgers.

INGREDIENTS

4	c. beets, grated (4 medium beets)
1	c. onion, chopped (1 medium onion)
1	c. cooked long grain brown rice
1	c. sunflower seeds
½	c. sesame seeds
2	eggs, lightly beaten
2	T. soy sauce
1	c. cheddar cheese, grated
3	T. flour
¼	c. canola oil

DIRECTIONS

❶ Mix all ingredients well in a large bowl. We find it easiest to do this with clean hands.

❷ Form into patties and place on lightly oiled baking sheets. Bake at 350° for about 45 minutes. After about 40 minutes, flip patties for the last 5 minutes of baking. Cooked patties should be browned and firm. You may need to use a spatula to get patty off baking sheet.

❸ Serve these burgers just like you would a hamburger, with lettuce, tomato, cheese and condiments inside a bun. We like ours with barbeque sauce. John loves them cold, like pizza, the next day.

YIELD: approximately 12 burger patties.

 Rice Advice
Brown rice is less processed and therefore a healthier rice option. For different flavors or textures, try basmati or jasmine rice, or a local wild rice if you're lucky to live somewhere it's readily available.

Basil Pesto with Handmade Linguine

WE MAKE LARGE BATCHES of pesto during our peak basil season and freeze it for wintertime enjoyment. Another of our "ingredients to taste" recipes, this simple recipe packs a powerful punch when it comes to flavor.

PESTO INGREDIENTS

- 6 c. fresh basil leaves, washed and firmly packed
- ½ c. pine nuts, walnuts or pecans
- ½ c. hard granular cheese, grated (Parmesan)
- 2 cloves garlic, minced
- ½ t. salt, or to taste
- 2 T. olive oil

LINGUINE INGREDIENTS

- 2 c. flour
- ½ t. salt
- 2 eggs
- 2 T. water

PESTO DIRECTIONS

❶ In a food processor, combine basil, nuts, cheese, garlic and salt. Blend or process with several on-off turns of food processor or until a paste forms, stopping the machine several times and scraping sides to completely blend all ingredients.

❷ With the machine running slowly, gradually add the oil and process until the consistency of soft butter.

❸ Serve immediately on a bed of fresh linguine, garnished with shavings of Parmesan cheese or sprinkle of chopped basil. Leftover pesto can be stored in the refrigerator for several days, but make sure you splash some lemon juice over the top of an airtight container to prevent it from browning when it comes in contact with air.

YIELDS: 6 servings.

Making pasta is easy and fun. Start with linguini, then try ravioli.

LINGUINE DIRECTIONS

❶ Combine flour and salt in a mixer. Add eggs one at a time. Slowly add water a teaspoon at a time until you have a smooth, pliable dough. Don't worry if there are a few lumps.

❷ Place dough on a lightly floured sheet of plastic wrap and cover the ball tightly and let sit for about 15 minutes.

❸ Break off about a ½ c. piece and run through a pasta roller in a hand-crank pasta making machine, starting with the number 1 setting and continuing to roll at different levels until you reach the desired thickness.

❹ Roll through the pasta cutter on the linguini setting or other noodle width you desire. Dust noodles lightly with flour and hang on a noodle drying rack (or a creative equivalent like a clean drying rack for towels). We like to cook and eat the noodles right away, but you can dry them fully (usually overnight) for later use.

❺ To cook, add noodles to boiling water and cook 1 to 2 minutes until done. Be careful not to overcook them or you'll end up with a hard glob of cooked dough.

YIELDS: 1 pound of pasta (approximately 4 servings).

COOKING TIP **Just Freeze It**
Basil freezes really well. Immediately after you've processed the pesto, transfer to a freezer storage container and fill to the fill line, but not to the top. Add a splash of lemon juice to cover the top of the pesto and then tightly close the lid and place into the freezer.

Spanakopita (Spinach Pie)

*Y*OUR KIDS DON'T HAVE to be Popeye to eat spinach — and love it. Among our son's favorite "special meals," the Greek spanakopita is appealing to young and old alike because of its buttery phyllo dough crunch, rich egg-spinach-dill-feta filling and its saltiness.

INGREDIENTS

5 c. fresh spinach (about 2 lbs.)

1 c. onions, finely chopped (1 medium onion)

¼ c. olive oil

1 c. feta cheese, finely crumbled (1 lb.)

4 eggs, lightly beaten

3 T. fresh dill (3 t. dried)

½ lb. phyllo pastry dough sheets (defrosted)

½ c. butter, melted (1 stick)

DIRECTIONS

❶ Wash fresh spinach, pat dry and chop fine.

❷ Sauté onion in olive oil until soft and slightly browned. Add spinach and simmer to remove excess moisture.

❸ In a medium bowl, crumble cheese and mix in eggs and dill. Combine with spinach mixture and stir until well-blended.

❹ Line a 9 × 13-inch baking pan with one sheet of phyllo. Brush sheet with butter. Lay another sheet on top and brush with butter. Repeat until pan is layered with 10 sheets of buttered phyllo. Keep the phyllo sheets covered with a damp cloth as you work to prevent them from drying out. Pour in spinach-cheese mixture. Top with 8 more buttered sheets of phyllo.

❺ Bake at 350° for about 45 minutes, or until top is golden brown.

❻ Let sit for 15 minutes before cutting. Serve warm, perhaps with a side cucumber or Caesar salad.

YIELD: 8 servings.

Nothing will benefit human health and increase the chances for survival of life on Earth as much as the evolution to a vegetarian diet.

ALBERT EINSTEIN

Stuffed Roti with Chickpea Filling

*R*OTI IS A CARIBBEAN SANDWICH stuffed with curried veggies, potatoes and chickpeas. Another of our "travel sandwiches" since they make hearty, healthy road food when there's nothing but fast food in sight off the Interstate. We heat them piping hot, then wrap them in foil to keep the roti warm "to go." The roti are nicely complemented by a dipping sauce, like our ranch dressing (see page 229).

ROTI DOUGH INGREDIENTS

4   c. flour
2   t. baking powder
1   t. salt
¼   c. vegetable oil
1   c. water

FILLING INGREDIENTS

½   c. onion or chives, chopped
    (1 small onion)
1   clove garlic, minced
1   t. curry powder
½   t. ground cumin
¼   t. salt
2   c. potatoes, peeled and cubed
¾   c. water
1   c. cooked chickpeas (½ a 10 oz.
    can)
1   T. butter

DIRECTIONS

❶ To make the dough, combine the flour, baking powder and salt in a mixing bowl. Gradually add the oil and water to the bowl, mixing and kneading the dough as you go. The dough should not be so wet that it sticks to your fingers, but should hold together when pressed into a ball. Form a ball and set the dough aside (covered) for about 15 minutes.

❷ To make the filling, sauté the onion and garlic in a skillet for 4 to 5 minutes over medium heat. Add the curry, cumin and salt and cook 1 minute more.

❸ Add the potato and water and cook for about 15 minutes, until the potatoes are tender.

❹ Add the chickpeas and cook for another 5 to 10 minutes, until the filling is chunky and thick. Set the filling aside.

❺ Divide the dough into 4 to 6 equal-sized balls. Flatten each ball and roll out into thin 8-inch squares, trying to roll the dough as thin as you can. Fill the middle of each square with about ½ c. of the filling. Wrap the dough around the mixture, burrito style, and seal the filling inside.

❻ To cook the roti, heat the butter in an electric fry pan or skillet over high heat until it sizzles. Reduce the heat to medium and, using a large spatula, place a filled roti in the pan. Cook for 3 to 4 minutes, until the crust is a golden brown. Turn with a wide spatula and continue cooking. Repeat the process with the remaining roti.

YIELD: 4 servings.

MEET YOUR MEAT MAKER

**Beth and Jody Osmund,
Cedar Valley Sustainable Farm,
Ottawa, Illinois**

Lisa met Beth Osmund on a bus headed to a reception at the USDA office building in DC one balmy spring evening, an admittedly unusual setting for two Midwest farm chicks to cross paths. Surrounded by concrete and politicians, these two female-farmer-food-activists met at the National Women in Agriculture Conference, both of them trying to bring the sustainable message to a gathering dominated by voices from chemical agriculture.

The connections between Lisa and Beth started flying on that bus. Lisa shared her vegetable growing mission, and Beth explained her family farm's

approach to raising meat with a mantra of land stewardship and care for animal welfare. We might raise different things on our farms, but we share a passion for sustainability. And a side of greens pairs nicely with Italian Sausage Risotto, as we learned. Both Chicago transplants to rural areas, we also home-schooled our kids. Our homesteads are a couple of hours apart.

"The farm and learning and life in general all blend for our family," says Beth. "Together we can play a role in improving our environment through providing healthy, sustainable food options for families, and we want our kids to understand this process hands-on. We see everything as connected."

Beth and her husband, Jody, along with their young children, moved back to Jody's family farm in 2003 to start Cedar Valley Sustainable Farm. What began as a vegetable CSA evolved into the first meat CSA to serve Chicago. They've grown and are now feeding over 300 families in the Chicagoland area with monthly deliveries of poultry, pork, beef and eggs, items they raise on the farm or produce in partnership with neighbors.

"Transparency is the most important ingredient in creating a sustainable food system," explains Beth, a woman who epitomizes the new generation of women on the farm who eat what they raise and can explain why, too. "Know your farmer and, importantly, know what your farmer knows. Any producer should be able to talk knowledgably about what they are raising, from beef to beets, and should be open to invite you to the farm to experience things for yourself."

Beth realizes bringing up the topic of "meat" when discussing sustainability can result in a tsunami of opinions and perspectives. "We look at meat on a continuum," outlines Beth. "On one hand you have CAFOs (confined animal feeding operations), promoting cheap food with animals knee-deep in excrement. On the other end you might have animals processed onsite by the butcher who raised them. We are food activists by the choices we make, by where we place our food dollars and priorities on that spectrum. We're trying to help folks have more options on the sustainability side of the equation."

The Osmunds define their sustainably raised meat in ways that respect their animals' natural instincts, while leaving the land in better shape than they found it. They price their product to reflect a true, fair cost of what it takes to run their business with no government subsidies or corporate skimming, while providing a livable wage for their family and the other farmers they work with. Their animals have access to the outdoors; some are raised exclusively on grass, while most have diets supplemented or finished with grain, producing meat aligned with the taste preferences of their customers.

Beth takes pride in her encyclopedic knowledge of their meat. Ask her if their grain is organic and you'll get a short answer — no — followed by a transparent explanation as to why: "If we bought organic grain, it would add both cost but, importantly, require being trucked in over three states. It would be organic but soaked in petroleum since it had to travel so far," comments Beth. "Instead we buy local grain from a farmer three miles down the road who doesn't use GMO seed, keeping more money in our local economy and foreign oil out. Adding some corn to our cows' diets creates the intramuscular fat that creates the fatty taste Americans like."

It's the flavor, along with their philosophy, that keeps their customers satisfied and their business growing. "Happy animals make true happy meals," Beth adds. "When animals are raised in the natural setting where they have access to the outdoors and are well-cared for, it shows up as flavor on the plate. We intimately know our herd and flocks and connect those dots for our customers, creating a connection with animals that can never happen in a supermarket."

If you're not raising your own meat or don't have a place like Cedar Valley offering regular deliveries, your easiest and most economical option would be to buy a quarter or half of a cow or pig direct from a farmer in your area. "You'll need a freezer to store the meat," advises Beth. "The amount you need depends on your family size and cooking habits. Start with a quarter of a cow or half pig and see how long that lasts."

We invited Beth and her tribe to our farm for our annual Reunion festivities that summer, when we gather friends and garden goodness against a backdrop of summer fun, like water balloon skirmishes of kids ganging up on parents. Beth came with an enthusiastic full cargo load, bringing the family tent, husband Jody and kids Richard, Duncan and Jack — along with enough brats to feed the crowd in attendance.

It says a lot about a person if they are willing to drive hours with their family to a place they've never been to sleep outside among people they don't know based on an hour-long bus conversation one of them had with a then-stranger. Maybe a love of farming and food can be the next Match.com to bring people together; simply knowing someone else who shares

your values of food, family and sustainability can serve to build trust and faith, instead of the walls and barriers we see too much of today. We use this "food filter" often as it serves us well to connect with kindred spirits.

"My kids are carnivores born and bred," smiles Beth. "But I do not want our food to be faceless. Too many people today are used to eating chicken with no face or connection to the land. My boys will grow up with an intimate experience of the farm and family business, and hopefully a deeper understanding and appreciation for the natural world that surrounds us."

By adding in the Osmund boys to our Reunion that July, the kids outnumbered adults. Their brats, grilled over an open fire in the woods behind our farm, satisfied all. How often do you get the chance to eat something that comes full circle, both raised and grilled by the same hands?

Italian Sausage Risotto

*B*ETH CONTRIBUTED THIS RECIPE for the classic Italian dish of rice and broth cooked to a creamy consistency. Arborio rice is a short grain, firm and chewy, named after the town where it is grown in Italy. Beth came to visit one cold December weekend, bringing all the ingredients and cooking it up on our woodstove. Talk about winter comfort food.

INGREDIENTS

- 1 lb. Italian pork sausage
- 1 c. onions, finely chopped (1 medium onion)
- 1 T. butter
- 1¼ c. arborio rice
- ½ c. red wine
- 3 c. chicken stock, hot
- ⅓ c. grated Parmesan cheese (plus extra to serve)
- ½ t. salt
- ¼ t. pepper

DIRECTIONS

❶ Fry sausage in a large skillet, breaking it up into small pieces as it cooks. When it is lightly browned in about 8 minutes, remove from pan.

❷ In the same pan, melt the butter, add the onion and cook over medium heat until onions soften. Add the rice and toss until well coated in butter, stirring constantly.

❸ Add the wine and stir until it is absorbed. Add the sausage and stir through.

❹ Add the stock and bring back to a boil. Reduce the heat to very low, cover and cook 15 to 20 minutes until the broth is absorbed and the rice is tender, stirring occasionally.

❺ Remove from heat. Stir in cheese, add salt and pepper to taste and serve on a plate with extra Parmesan cheese sprinkled on top.

YIELD: 4 servings.

You become responsible, forever, for what you have tamed.

ANTOINE DE SAINT-EXUPÉRY, *THE LITTLE PRINCE*

Sloppy Joes

V
Vegan

*L*IFE CAN BE MESSY. From tracking garden mud into the house to sticky spousal miscommunication, things don't always fit into tidy compartments. These sloppy joes celebrate that fact and can't hide the lentil-based filling likely to escape from the bun. The flavor of this dish intensifies with time; leftovers are encouraged. The tomato sauce has a sweet tang to it; we have friends who use it for ketchup.

INGREDIENTS

2 c. water

½ t. salt

1 c. brown lentils, well-rinsed

1 T. olive oil

1 onion, chopped

2 c. chopped tomatoes or tomato sauce

2 cloves garlic, minced

3 T. tomato paste (use more ketchup if you don't have paste)

½ c. ketchup

1 t. dried mustard

2 t. chili powder

3 T. molasses

½ t. Worcestershire sauce (omit for vegan)

½ t. salt

¼ t. pepper

potato rolls (page 59), hamburger buns or rice

DIRECTIONS

❶ Bring water to a boil and add salt. Add lentils; boil over medium heat for 20 minutes or until tender, stirring occasionally.

❷ While lentils are cooking, heat oil in skillet. Sauté onions over medium heat until translucent. Add tomatoes and garlic, then sauté for 5 minutes.

❸ Add tomato paste, ketchup, mustard, chili powder, molasses, Worcestershire sauce (omit if vegan) and salt. Simmer the stew for 5 to 10 minutes.

❹ When lentils are tender, drain and reserve cooking liquid. Add lentils to tomato sauce. To obtain desired consistency of a traditional sloppy joe, add additional cooking liquid. Stir and heat thoroughly.

❺ Serve hot over open-faced potato rolls, hamburger buns or rice.

YIELD: 4 servings.

Potato Pierogis

W E LOVE ATTENDING street fairs or community festivals in big cities, especially if they're in places called Little Italy, Ukrainian Village or Greektown. We always go for the pierogis at Polish festivals. No big surprise, given Lisa's Baltic roots and John's Slovakian heritage. Among the church-sponsored food tents featuring makeshift food stalls, we bask in the dining experience of made-to-order freshness and, of course, traditional ethnic recipes that may have originated in the homeland many generations ago. Every winter we enjoy this recipe based on the popular Central and Eastern European dumpling filled with potatoes, garlic, cheese and onion.

FILLING INGREDIENTS

2½ lbs. potatoes, peeled & cubed (about 5 medium)
¼ c. butter (½ stick)
1 onion, chopped or 2 small leeks, cleaned & sliced
2 garlic cloves, minced
1½ t. seasoning salt
1 lb. cheddar cheese, shredded

DOUGH INGREDIENTS

6 c. flour
1 t. salt
3 eggs, lightly beaten
1½ c. water

DIRECTIONS

❶ Boil potatoes until tender but still firm, about 15 minutes. Drain potatoes and mash in large bowl.

❷ Separately, sauté onion or leeks and garlic in butter until tender. Mix onion mixture with mashed potatoes and add cheese and salt. Mix until thoroughly combined.

❸ For dough, combine flour and salt in large bowl. Mix in eggs and water. Turn onto a floured surface and knead for 5 minutes or until smooth, adding more water as needed.

❹ Roll out dough to ⅛-inch thickness. Cut into 5-inch circles, using a bowl as a guide.

Place about 3 T. of filling in center, fold over and press edges with the fork tines for an attractive seal.

❺ Place pierogis, a few at a time, into a large pot of boiling water and cook for about 6 minutes until they float to the top. Drain on a clean towel. At this point you can place on baking sheet and freeze for future use.

❻ To serve immediately, fry in butter until both sides are golden brown. Add a dollop of sour cream on top with a sprinkle of finely chopped chives.

YIELD: About 20 pierogi.

COOKING TIP This recipe makes a hearty-sized batch so you can keep the freezer pierogi-stocked when you need a quick, easy supper or side dish.

Grecian Leek Pasta

SOMETIMES WE NEED a magic ball of thread to guide our route to some feat which lies ahead of us, perhaps like that offered to Theseus, vanquisher of the Minotaur on the island of Crete. Not only did Theseus kill the Minotaur, led to it through a complex labyrinth by the magic ball of thread he was given, but he was clever enough to unwind the spool so as to find his way back out of the labyrinth after the ordeal was over. Our understanding of our food system and our relationship to the land, the farmers and our daily bread is the magic ball of thread that helps us navigate wiser food choices. This pasta celebrates the Mediterranean diet, with its olives and feta cheese, to nourish you on your food journey through the labyrinth of decisions you'll face.

INGREDIENTS

1 package (10 to 12 oz.) whole wheat pasta (or make your own linguini, page 156)

5 garlic cloves, minced

6 c. leeks, cleaned and thinly sliced (2 large leeks)

2 t. fennel seed

1 T. olive oil

½ c. water

3 c. chopped tomatoes or 2 c. tomato sauce (see page 102)

½ c. kalamata olives, chopped

1 T. fresh oregano (1 t. dried)

½ t. salt

½ c. feta cheese, finely crumbled (½ lb.)

DIRECTIONS

❶ Cook pasta according to directions and set aside.

❷ Sauté garlic, leeks and fennel seed in oil in large skillet until leeks are soft, about 10 minutes. If mixture starts to stick to the pan, add a little water.

❸ Stir in tomatoes, olives, oregano and salt. Simmer uncovered until sauce thickens, about 20 minutes.

❹ Remove from heat. Add feta cheese.

❺ Combine with pasta and serve, garnished with parsley.

YIELD: Serves 5.

Whether it's baking their own bread, infusing their own oils, starting a compost pile, growing potatoes in a garbage bag, or learning how to make a really good pie. I think these are some of the most satisfying things a human can do in the frenetic pace of modern times and they are demanding more of it.

GEORGIA PELLEGRINI, AUTHOR OF *FOOD HEROES* AND *GIRL HUNTER*

Grilled Shish-kabob Souvlaki (lamb) with Tzatziki Sauce

*H*ERE'S A RECIPE to satisfy the primal urge to grill the perfect equation: meat plus fire. These lamb kabobs drink up the smoky fire and radiant heat and the grilling mellows out the rich flavor of the lamb. With the higher fat content of the lamb, you'll find it easier to keep the kabobs juicy and moist, a perfect inaugural dish if you're a novice grill master. Skip the round of ouzo until you've got the grilling done.

INGREDIENTS

2   freshly squeezed lemons (or ½ c. lemon juice)
1   c. olive oil
2   c. dry red wine
½   c. fresh oregano (3 T. dried)
2   t. seasoning salt
2   pounds of lamb, cut into 1-inch cubes
2   medium onions, cut into 1½-inch chunks (for skewering)
2   green or red bell peppers, cut into 1½-inch chunks (for skewering)

TZATZIKI SAUCE INGREDIENTS

1   c. sour cream
2   T. fresh dill, finely chopped (2 t. dried)
1   c. cucumber, shredded
1   clove garlic, minced
¼   t. salt

DIRECTIONS

❶ In a large bowl, mix lemon juice, olive oil, wine, oregano and seasoning salt to create marinade. Place the vegetables and lamb in two separate medium-sized bowls. Pour half the marinade in each bowl to fully cover vegetables and lamb, and stir to coat with marinade. Refrigerate at least 4 hours or ideally overnight, stirring occasionally.

❷ Soak wood skewers in water for an hour prior to skewering (skewers absorb water and are less likely to catch fire). Thread lamb, onion and pepper slices, alternating their order, on skewers.

TZATZIKI SAUCE DIRECTIONS

❶ Mix all ingredients. Chill in refrigerator for 1 hour.

❸ To grill outdoors, preheat grill to medium heat, then add kebabs and cook for approximately 7 minutes, turning skewers over every couple of minutes for even cooking on all sides. Baste kabobs with remaining marinade. Kabobs can also be broiled in an oven at a medium broiling temperature (500°). Cook for approximately 7 minutes and baste with remaining marinade.

❹ Serve in pita bread (see page 64) with grated lettuce, chopped tomatoes and tzatziki sauce (or Hummus, see page 133).

   YIELD: 4 servings.

❷ Mix again, then serve as needed. Mixture will last about three days refrigerated.

   YIELD: 4 servings.

The greatness of a nation and its moral progress can be judged by the way its animals are treated.

MAHATMA GANDHI

Walnut Burger

W E'RE NUTS OVER THESE vegetarian burgers. Different than most veggie burgers, there's practically no soy anything in it (nothing, if you skip the Worcestershire sauce), unlike those found in the frozen food section of the grocery store. Since tasting the Wisconsin-original signature Walnut Burger at the historic Trempealeau Hotel in Trempealeau, we worked to come up with our own version of their coveted — and top-secret — recipe. Nutritionally, studies have shown that walnuts are a great source of antioxidants and omega-3 fatty acids. These burgers also provide plenty of calcium and protein with the cheese and eggs. But it's the flavor and taste that have turned hamburger lovers a bit nutty.

INGREDIENTS

1 onion, finely chopped (about 1 medium)

3 cloves garlic, minced

¾ c. walnuts, finely chopped

¼ c. almonds, finely chopped

1 c. bread crumbs (see crouton recipe on page 230 for tips on making your own bread crumbs)

½ c. wheat germ

3 T. nutritional yeast

½ t. sage

½ t. thyme

½ t. pepper

1 t. cumin

1 t. coriander

1 t. salt

½ c. cheddar cheese, grated

½ c. mozzarella cheese, grated

¼ c. Parmesan cheese, grated

4 T. canola oil

1 T. Worcestershire sauce

2 eggs, beaten

2 c. brown rice, cooked and cooled

DIRECTIONS

❶ In a skillet, sauté the onion and garlic over medium heat, until onions are translucent.

❷ In a food processor, combine walnuts, almonds, bread crumbs, wheat germ, yeast, sage, thyme, pepper, cumin, coriander and salt; process until finely ground. Add cheeses and mix together. Then add 1 T. oil, Worcestershire sauce, sautéed onion and garlic; pulse until coarsely mixed. Add cooked rice.

❸ Whisk egg and add egg to blended mixture in food processor and blend to mix.

❹ Divide mixture into 6 equal-size parts; roll into balls, and flatten with the palm of your hand into ¾-inch-thick patties.

❺ Heat remaining 3 tablespoons oil in a large non-stick skillet. Over medium heat, fry 8 to 10 minutes for each side until burgers are browned on both sides and crisp.

❻ Serve as you would a hamburger, perhaps with lettuce, tomato and condiments in a bun. We like our Ranch Dressing instead of ketchup or mustard, since it complements the rich nutty flavors of the burger.

YIELD: 8 patties.

COOKING TIP

What's in a Worcestershire Sauce?

Flavor. A Worcestershire sauce offers a way to add a "meaty" umami taste to a dish. It's made from fermented anchovies with tamarind, garlic, soy sauce and other spices. We stick with the Lea and Perrins brand made in England because it avoids the high-fructose corn syrup found in brands made in the US.

Herb-infused Ribs (pork)

*T*HE SUBTLE CACOPHONY of herbs catapult this rib recipe to the top of our list. We recommend pork spareribs that are flatter and contain more fat which keeps the meat tender.

MARINADE INGREDIENTS

2 freshly squeezed lemons (or ½ c. lemon juice)
1 c. red wine vinegar
1 c. canola oil
1 T. salt
1 T. onion salt
1 T. celery salt
1 T. dried majoram (or 2 T. fresh)
1 T. dried oregano (or 2 T. fresh)
1 T. dried thyme (or 2 T. fresh)
1 T. dried basil (or 2 T. fresh)
3 T. soy sauce
3 T. Worcestershire sauce
5 cloves garlic, minced
4 lbs. pork spareribs

DIRECTIONS

❶ Combine all marinade ingredients in large pot.

❷ Add pork ribs to the pot with marinade and refrigerate overnight.

❸ To cook, place pot on stove and simmer on medium heat for 30 minutes.

❹ Remove ribs from pot, then grill on medium heat for about 15 minutes, flipping once to evenly cook both sides. Ribs can also be broiled in the oven on medium heat (450°) for about 15 minutes, basting every 5 minutes with the remaining marinade. Watch carefully because ribs can burn or dry out quickly when broiling.

❺ To serve, place on large platter, cutting each rib for individual servings.

YIELD: 4 servings.

COOKING TIP

Spices can be challenging when trying to cook with local ingredients. Turmeric and saffron add distinct flavors to a dish yet come at the cost of plenty of food miles. Here's our take: Spices fly on cheap seats. They're light in weight, and proportionately speaking, they go a long way. A little paprika goes further in making a meal than imported tomato sauce from Italy. Because we buy relatively small quantities and try to buy organic and Fair Trade certified spices, we can sprinkle curry with confidence, knowing that the people and the land that produced it are being paid fairly and cared for. We use spices from Frontier, an Iowa-based co-op and the spice industry leader in sustainable sourcing. You'll find Frontier products in bulk aisles at natural food stores and co-ops.

Indonesian Asparagus and Pasta

For many of us, one of our earliest memories of a homemade meal is a peanut butter and jelly sandwich. As evidence, the average American kid eats a 125-foot-high tower of peanut butter and jelly sandwiches by the time they graduate high school. We like a good old PB&J every now and then. But when we buy organic peanut butter by the five-pound jar at our natural foods co-op, most of it gets cooked into dishes, adding both flavor and a protein punch. The peanut butter combined with soy sauce give this pasta dish an Asian flair. Paired with the asparagus and chives, it adds a different twist to spring flavors.

INGREDIENTS

- ½ c. chicken or vegetable stock
- 2 T. soy sauce
- 1 T. peanut butter
- 2 T. onion, minced
- 1 T. lemon juice
- 1 t. brown sugar, packed
- 1 lb. fresh asparagus, cut into 1-inch pieces
- 6 oz. pasta (or make your own linguini, page 156)
- ½ c. green onions or chives, chopped

DIRECTIONS

❶ Cook pasta according to directions and set aside.

❷ In a small saucepan, combine the broth, soy sauce, peanut butter, onion, lemon juice and brown sugar. Stir constantly and bring to a boil. Remove from heat and keep warm.

❸ At the same time, in a large skillet, sauté asparagus in olive oil for about 8 minutes. Add green onions and sauté for about 3 minutes until crisp-tender.

❹ Drain pasta and toss with vegetables and sauce before serving in large bowl.

YIELD: 4 servings.

Peas Support Willy Street Co-op

CAKES, PIES & SWEETS

Amish Fry Pies

Strawberry Dessert Pizza

Apple Crisp

Carrot Cake

Creamy Apple Pie

Grandma Sue's Pie Crust

Pear Crumb Pie

Rhubarb Cream Bars

Mocha Biscotti

Peppermint Biscotti

Shaker Lemon Pie (Nancy Vail & Jered Lawson)

Pumpkin Mousse Cheesecake

Whipped Cream

Maraschino Cherries

Caramel Sauce for Caramel Apple Buffet

Strawberry-Rhubarb Streusel Pie

Chocolate Zucchini Roll

Artisanal Eating, Cooking and Living

Like most kids, he calls it the way he sees it. Our son Liam is one tough critic, of food, film or books. Receiving six stars out of ten, with ten being the best, puts you in his top 1 percentile. When it comes to our farmstead cuisine, he offers no slack, no breaks on account that we're family. Unlike the rest of the Kivirist clan, however, he also possesses the rare ability to take a pass on dessert if his belly is full, so the desserts have to be good, really good, to pass his muster. As for Lisa and her mom, desserts could be a whole new food group.

When brainstorming names for this cookbook, Liam kept tossing out titles related to the concept of happiness. Food is happiness in his book, and it means more than heading to bed with a full belly. Food satisfies in ways beyond the sugar high we might enjoy — it nourishes our bodies, our senses and, if savored with others, offers the conviviality of a shared meal.

Desserts, though, represent the exclamation point of happiness — if not also indulgence. It's a sweet treat, a finale to a relished meal, usually accompanied by a grin, chuckle or, for the technically inclined, a tweet. For small children, such sweets may result in bursts of energy that can turn borderline crazy.

We found starting our own family business more akin to a dessert than any other course. Finding your passion and creating a business around it, as we write about in *ECOpreneuring*, is the ultimate sweet spot for a happy, meaningful and fulfilling life. The enterprise may generate lots of profits, or just enough to allow us to plow them back into the business to make our business better, perhaps by powering it with renewable energy or providing the time necessary to care for the soil.

Too many corporations try to solve our problems with stuff and services. Now we're having trouble living without all these things, yet we feel overstuffed. Before we started our own business, we had jobs. We worked for someone else, helping make their company richer and toiling away for their board of directors' dreams, not ours. We were stuck in the earn-and-spend mode that demanded a job with paychecks we signed over to buy just about everything we needed, like food, water and a roof over our heads. The harder we worked, the less we got ahead, since our expenses grew faster. Sure there were a few promotions and pay raises, but not anything like those received at the top of the corporate chain. It didn't take us long to discover that the theory of trickle-down economics was a farce for all but a select few.

Perhaps by providence, we found ourselves drawn to farmers markets or farmstands when we traveled, impressed by the authenticity of the products, the flavors of the foods the farmers grew and the sense of community shared. These cheesemakers, butchers, farmers and bakers, along with beekeepers, orchardists and wild food foragers, cherish their artisanal approach to production — an approach that's intensely personal. If they had a label for what they sold, the face on it is their own. These artisans were unified by their time-honored craft and the products that they made by hand and in small batches. What artisans make is real: fresh vegetables, cheese, fiber for clothing we wear and the dining room table we sit around every day.

It's such a contrast to bankers, for example. Bankers make billions just moving around representations of money on their computers, but produce nothing at all. They're loaning and trading representative currencies they don't even own. After years in the garden and surrounded by the abundance of nature, we've come to the conclusion that money does grow on trees — in the form of apples or pears. It's in the soil too; we call it our black gold. The artisanal cheeses our county's farmers and cheesemakers produce is known as "Green County gold." Some people may call us peasants (or hobby farmers), but we're hardly poor — or hobbyists. We're rich in a different sense of the word, rich with friends, health, food and happiness.

Now at the helm of our own business, the extrinsic motivations, like paychecks or vacation days — what kept us at our old jobs — melt away. Making the world a better place through our enterprise is whipped into the icing on the cake. Like reaching a mountain summit, desserts are the peak. We use only real butter, cream cheese and fresh, seasonal fruits for ingredients. High in calories, true, but our resident critic, Liam, approves.

A hundred years ago, integrated family-run businesses were the norm, from farm-based enterprises like ours to retail shops on the square in downtown Monroe where shopkeeper families lived in apartments above the storefront. Everyone shared all the ups and downs, small and large. Communities were likewise woven together in an intricate web of interrelationships among locally owned enterprises — just like a healthy, diverse ecosystem. Thanks to globalization, economies of scale and merger-mania, much of this cohesion has been sacrificed to greed, leading to a decline in family-supporting employment opportunities and the loss of civic involvement.

In our own way, we've worked to recreate such integration, crafting a new blend of entrepreneurship incorporating homesteading traditions with 21st-century technology, striving to operate in ways that enhance, restore or conserve the natural world on which we depend. Like many of our endeavors, it's made possible through our mentorship under and support from our neighbors affectionately known as "Uncle Phil" and "Aunt Judy," and partnerships with non-profit organizations like the Midwest Renewable Energy Association and the Midwest Organic and Sustainable Education Service.

As for desserts, everything about pie calls for an artisanal approach, least of which is the pie crust recipe that's passed down generation to generation and made by hand. From fresh fruit fillings or a dollop of whipped cream on top, there really is nothing more American than apple pie.

So go ahead and be an artist of life and get cooking in the kitchen — if not also in an enterprise of your own creation. Remember, homemade pie, by definition, can only be made from scratch at home. So laugh when you see it next time advertised at a restaurant or, better yet, in the frozen section at a supermarket.

Artisan goat cheese maker Diana Kalscheur Murphy of Dreamfarm in Cross Plains, WI.

Amish Fry Pies

*T*HERE'S SOMETHING WHOLESOME about the Amish: their pastoral ways, rejection of most modern technology, unwavering embrace of community, self-reliant work ethic. It's ironic, then, that Amish cooking—while drawing on lots of fruits, vegetables and mostly pastured meat products—is high in fats and protein, a diet believed to be less healthy than the lower-fat and cholesterol diet championed by nutritionists today. Many Amish meals are based on recipes passed down through generations after arriving in America more than 250 years ago. So what's the key to the general good health of the Amish? Intense physical activity by men and women alike, thanks to the farming community they live in. Our Inn Serendipity woods cabin place is nestled in the heart of Wisconsin's Amish country. Amish buggies clatter down the unpaved roads, and many of the Yoders send us a postcard every fall, before hunting season, to get permission to hunt on our land. Hillsboro, the nearest town, serves as a hub for Amish shopping needs, including a small Saturday morning farmers market with several Amish vendors. That's where we discovered Amish Fry Pies. Despite our preference for butter, this fry pie recipe demands a high-quality margarine since it holds up to the high temperature of the frying oil. You can substitute other fruit pie fillings for the apple, such as blueberry or cherry.

FILLING INGREDIENTS

9   c. apples, peeled, sliced and chopped
1   c. brown sugar, firmly packed
1   t. cinnamon
1   t. nutmeg

DOUGH INGREDIENTS

9   c. cake flour
2   T. sugar
1   T. salt
3   c. margarine (6 sticks)
2   c. water
4   T. canola oil for frying

DIRECTIONS

❶ For the filling, sauté apples with brown sugar, cinnamon and nutmeg until apples are tender. Set aside.

❷ In a large mixing bowl, combine flour, sugar and salt.

❸ Cut in shortening until pieces are the size of small peas.

❹ Add water a little at a time until the flour mixture is moistened.

❺ Form into 4 balls. Divide each ball into 10 pieces and roll each piece into a circle.

❻ Top one side of circle with filling and fold circle in half. Crimp edges to seal.

❼ If you don't have a need for 40 fry pies immediately, tray freeze them at this point.

❽ Heat oil over medium heat; do not let smoke. Fry a few pieces at a time, turning once, for about 10 minutes or until golden brown. Cool on wire rack.

GLAZE INGREDIENTS

2   pounds powdered sugar
    (about 7 ½ c.)

⅛   c. cornstarch

⅛   c. powdered milk

1   t. vanilla extract

½   c. warm water (more if
    needed)

❾ Meanwhile, in large mixing bowl, combine all glaze ingredients until smooth. While pies are warm, dip them completely into the glaze. Allow pies to drip on wire racks until cool.

❿ Serve on a large platter. Later in the day, after you've enjoyed every bite, make sure you plant a field, paint a room, clean the garage or volunteer to clean up the bleachers after your kid's baseball game.

YIELD: 40 fry pies.

COOKING TIP

Make Your Own Cake Flour

No need to purchase cake flour—you can make your own with pantry staples. Use the following equivalent to make one cup of cake flour: For every 1 cup of flour, replace 2 T. flour with 2 T. cornstarch. The strength of the gluten is broken down in the cake flour, making the resulting baked good more tender and delicate in texture.

Amish farmland in Vernon County, Wisconsin, not far from our cabin place.

Strawberry Dessert Pizza

*T*HINK OUT OF THE PIZZA BOX, or the shortcake mold. For years, every June we went through a frustrating round of trying to make strawberry shortcake, and every year it came out the same: Too dry for our liking. It tasted like strawberries on a big cotton ball. But it's such a popular, traditional strawberry dessert, right? This cycle went on for a couple years until we saw a "fruit pizza" in a bakery shop, delivering inspiration for a new strawberry dessert vision. But why wait for dessert, it's pizza right?

CRUST INGREDIENTS

6 T. butter, softened (¾ stick)

½ c. sugar

1 egg

½ t. vanilla extract

½ t. almond extract

1¼ c. flour

½ t. baking powder

½ t. salt

FILLING INGREDIENTS

1 package cream cheese, softened (8 oz.)

½ c. powdered sugar

2 c. fresh strawberries, sliced

1 c. sugar

¼ c. cornstarch

2 c. crushed strawberries (with juice)

DIRECTIONS

❶ In a mixing bowl, cream butter and sugar until fluffy. Beat in egg, vanilla and almond extracts.

❷ Mix flour, baking powder and salt. Gradually add flour mixture to creamed mixture and blend well. Cover and refrigerate for 1 hour.

❸ On a floured surface, roll dough into a 12-inch circle. Transfer to a lightly oiled 12-inch pizza pan. Build up edges slightly.

❹ Bake at 350° for about 18 to 22 minutes, or until lightly browned. Cool completely.

❺ In a mixing bowl, beat cream cheese and confectioner's sugar until well-blended. Spread over crust. Arrange sliced strawberries on top.

❻ In a saucepan, combine sugar, cornstarch and crushed berries until well-blended. Bring to a boil over medium heat and stir for about 3 minutes or until thickened. Cool until warm to touch. Spoon over strawberries. Refrigerate until serving.

YIELD: 12 servings.

Apple Crisp

*W*E'RE LETTING THE APPLE out of the bag: Liam won't eat this apple crisp, or apple pie for that matter. This might sound strange; he's a great eater and likes fresh apples, unique dishes — even veggie sushi or spinach. Why this disconnect? Apparently he's burned out. By the time he was six, we've made so many fresh apple crisps and pies that he needed a few years off. Who knew you could have such an early seasonal eating crisis? No worries here, though; we're amused and pleased. If we managed to serve too much of a seasonal food that our child turns down a sweet, we're doing okay. The bottom line, more crisp for us and our guests. He still counts raw apples among his favorite snacks.

INGREDIENTS

1   t. canola oil
4   c. apples, sliced
¾   c. brown sugar, firmly packed
½   c. flour
½   c. oats
1   t. cinnamon
1   t. nutmeg
⅓   c. butter (5⅓ T.), softened

DIRECTIONS

❶ Arrange apples in lightly oiled 8-inch square baking pan.

❷ Mix sugar, flour, oats, cinnamon and nutmeg.

❸ Cut in butter and spread topping over apples.

❹ Bake at 375° for 30 minutes or until topping is golden brown.

❺ Serve warm. For added indulgence, plop a dollop of whipped cream or vanilla ice cream onto each serving, sprinkled with a pinch of cinnamon.

YIELD: 4 servings.

How many apples fell on Newton's head before he took the hint?
Nature is always hinting at us. It hints over and over again.
And suddenly we take the hint.

ROBERT FROST

Carrot Cake

*C*AKE, IN OUR OPINION, needs to be moist or it isn't worth eating. This carrot cake fits the bill. Don't let the long list of ingredients intimidate you; most of them are spices flavoring the cake. The rich cream cheese frosting puts it over the top.

CAKE INGREDIENTS

1½ c. whole wheat flour

⅔ c. flour

2 t. baking soda

2 t. cinnamon

½ t. salt

½ t. nutmeg

¼ t. ginger

1 c. sugar

1 c. brown sugar, firmly packed

1 c. buttermilk

¾ c. canola oil

4 eggs, lightly beaten

2 t. vanilla

2 c. carrots, shredded

8 oz. crushed pineapple, drained (½ can)

1 c. chopped nuts (walnuts or pecans work well)

1 c. coconut

½ c. raisins

FROSTING INGREDIENTS

½ c. butter, softened (1 stick)

½ package cream cheese, softened (about 4 oz.)

4 c. powdered sugar

1 t. vanilla extract

2 to 3 T milk

CAKE DIRECTIONS

❶ Combine flours, baking soda, cinnamon, salt, nutmeg and ginger.

❷ In a large bowl, combine sugars, buttermilk, oil, eggs and vanilla.

❸ Add flour mixture to sugar mixture and stir in carrots, pineapple, nuts, coconut and raisins until well-blended.

❹ Pour into three lightly oiled 9-inch round pans and bake at 350° for 30 minutes or until cakes test done. Can also be baked in a 9 × 13-inch baking pan; bake for 35 to 40 minutes or until cake tests done.

❺ Cool 10 minutes in pan before removing and cool fully before frosting.

FROSTING DIRECTIONS

❶ In a mixing bowl, cream butter and cream cheese. Gradually beat in powdered sugar and vanilla. Add enough milk to achieve good spreading consistency. Note: Cake frosting will be soft when you apply it. After refrigeration it will firm up.

❷ If you need a dish for a picnic, make cupcakes instead. Pour the batter into lightly oiled muffin tins and bake at 350° but start checking after 20 minutes to see if they are done.

YIELD: 12 servings.

COOKING TIP The buttermilk adds a needed dash of sour flavor to the cake, but most of us don't have a quart of buttermilk lying around—Lisa's dad is the only person we know who actually drinks and enjoys buttermilk. An easy substitute is to pour one tablespoon lemon juice into a one-cup container. Fill to the one-cup marker with milk and let sit five minutes before using (it will curdle and look a little gross but adds that needed zing to the cake batter).

Creamy Apple Pie

THIS PIE IS AFFECTIONATELY NICKNAMED "Joy Pie" in our house, because the recipe came from Joy Rohde. The Rohde family farmed this land we now live on for over a hundred years. It's the kind of pie that makes you happy, joyful. It's one of our favorites because the filling is so simple to make and comes out perfectly creamy; no ice cream needed. Let this pie cool to room temperature before cutting since the filling will tend to slip out.

INGREDIENTS

- 1 unbaked single crust pie shell (9-inch) (see page 180)
- 8 c. apples, peeled and sliced
- 1 c. sugar
- ¼ c. flour
- 1½ t. vanilla extract
- ⅓ c. milk
- ½ t. salt
- ½ t. cinnamon
- ¼ c. butter (½ stick)

DIRECTIONS

❶ Lay apples in the pie crust.

❷ Make a "syrup" (no cooking needed) by mixing the sugar, flour and vanilla. Add the milk and salt, then stir well. Sprinkle apples with cinnamon and dot with butter.

❸ Pour syrup mixture over apples and bake 1 hour at 350° or until apples are tender.

YIELD: 8 servings.

Grandma Sue's Pie Crust

*J*OHN'S MOM, SUE, reigns as champion pie baker in the family. "I just love pie," says Sue. While you'll encounter many variations on pie baking from various families, we're loyal to ours.

SINGLE PIE INGREDIENTS (ONE 9- OR 10-INCH)

1½ c. flour
½ t. salt
½ c. butter (1 stick)
4 to 5 T. cold water

DOUBLE CRUST PIE INGREDIENTS (ONE 9- OR 10-INCH)

2 c. flour
1 t. salt
⅔ c. butter (about 1¼ sticks)
5 to 7 T. cold water

DIRECTIONS

❶ Mix together flour and salt.

❷ Cut in butter with a pastry blender or two butter knives until pieces are the size of small peas. To make pastry extra tender and flaky, divide shortening in half. Cut in first half until mixture looks like corn meal. Then cut in remaining half until like small peas.

❸ Sprinkle 1 T. of the water over part of the flour-shortening mixture. Gently toss with fork; push to one side of bowl. Sprinkle next tablespoon of water over dry part; mix lightly. Mix gently until all is moistened.

❹ Gather up with fingers; form into a ball. For two-crust pie, divide dough for upper and lower crust. Form each in ball.

❺ On lightly floured surface, flatten ball slightly and roll to ⅛-inch thick. If edges split, pinch together. Always roll spoke-fashion, going from center to edge of dough. Use light strokes.

TO BAKE SINGLE PIE CRUST

❶ Transfer pastry to pie plate. Fit loosely onto bottom and sides. Trim ½ to 1 inch beyond edge. Fold under and flute.

❷ If baked pie shell is needed, prick bottom and sides well with fork—to prevent puffing as shell bakes. Bake in 450° oven until pastry is golden, 10 to 20 minutes.

❸ If filling and crust are to be baked together, do not prick pastry. Pour in filling; bake as directed in the pie recipe.

Pear Crumb Pie

APPARENTLY THE NEGLECTED ugly stepsister in the pie world, pear pie hasn't made any top pie flavor list. Even Baker's Square makes four different kinds of apple pie but shuns the pear. What a shame! Paired with a streusel crust, pears bake up nicely with a more complex, grainy flavor than their fall apple counterpart. Better yet, savor a slice with a dram of Pear Liquor (page 205).

INGREDIENTS

1 single unbaked pie shell (9-inch) (see page 180)

FILLING INGREDIENTS

½ c. brown sugar, firmly packed
2 T. cornstarch
½ t. cinnamon
¼ t. ginger
½ t. salt
¼ t. nutmeg
6 c. pears, peeled and thinly sliced (about 6 large pears; 3 lbs.)
1 T. lemon juice

TOPPING INGREDIENTS

⅔ c. flour
⅓ c. brown sugar, firmly packed
⅓ c. butter (5⅓ T.)

DIRECTIONS

❶ Combine filling ingredients; spoon into pie crust.

❷ Bake at 400° for 25 minutes.

❸ For topping, combine flour and brown sugar. Cut in butter until crumbly. Sprinkle over filling. Bake 40 minutes longer.

❹ Cover edges with foil during the last 15 minutes to prevent over-browning if necessary.

❺ Serve with a dram of Pear Cordial (see page 205).

YIELD: 8 servings.

Go out on a limb. That's where the fruit is.

WILL ROGERS

Rhubarb Cream Bars

YOU DON'T WANT TO MARRY RHUBARB, just date her. Actually, we learned what we really want is an intense, heavy, lustful spring fling and then move on, dumping her for the seductive strawberry of summer. Before you think we're getting kinky with our produce, let us explain. For years every spring, we'd freeze lots of rhubarb. Our early gardening season energy propels us into the Energizer Bunny of food processing, and we're slicing and packing up rhubarb with visions of winter pies to come. Only come winter and we find we're not craving her tart, sassy flavor. When we defrost the rhubarb, it gets mushy and watery, not the perky memory we have of her in spring. So we gave up on anything long-term and revel instead in the seasonal affair, indulging in sweet treats like these Rhubarb Cream Bars in the spring and then parting ways: Same time, next year.

CRUST INGREDIENTS

2 c. flour
¾ c. powdered sugar
1 c. butter (2 sticks)
1 t. canola oil

FILLING INGREDIENTS

4 eggs, lightly beaten
½ t. salt
½ c. flour
2 c. sugar
4 c. rhubarb, diced

DIRECTIONS

❶ Combine flour and powdered sugar. Cut in butter until crumbly.

❷ Press into bottom of lightly oiled 9 × 13-inch baking pan.

❸ Bake at 350° for about 15 minutes or until lightly browned.

❹ While crust is baking, make filling. Blend eggs, salt, flour and sugar until smooth. Fold in rhubarb.

❺ Spread over hot crust.

❻ Lower heat to 325° and bake 40 to 45 minutes or until filling is lightly browned. Cool completely and then cut into bars.

YIELD: 18 servings.

Laughter is the best seasoning there is. It's the spice of life.

UNKNOWN

Mocha Biscotti

NOTHING LIKE CRUNCHY COOKIES with our coffee. Nothing like a little coffee in your cookie. This mocha biscotti serves up both.

INGREDIENTS

- 2 c. flour
- 1 c. sugar
- 1 t. baking powder
- ½ t. baking soda
- Pinch salt
- 3 eggs
- 1 t. vanilla extract
- 4 T. cocoa powder
- 2 t. instant coffee powder
- 1 T. canola oil
- 4 t. water
- ½ t. almond extract

DIRECTIONS

❶ Stir together flour, sugar, baking powder, baking soda and salt.

❷ Whisk together eggs and vanilla. Add to the dry ingredients. Mix just until smooth.

❸ In a small bowl, combine cocoa, coffee, oil and water. Divide the dough in half (dough will be sticky). To one half, add the cocoa mixture. To the other half, add the almond extract.

❹ Place half of the almond dough on a well-floured surface. Pat dough into a 4-inch-by-8-inch rectangle. Top with half the cocoa mixtures. Roll up into a cylinder to form a 14-inch log. Repeat with remaining dough.

❺ Place the logs on a lightly oiled baking sheet. Bake at 325° for about 20 to 25 minutes, or until firm to the touch.

❻ Transfer logs immediately to a rack to cool. Reduce oven temperature to 300°. Cut the logs on an angle into ½-inch-thick slices. Stand the slices upright on the baking sheet (make sure there is some space between the slices so they will dry out) and bake for 40 minutes. Let cool before storing.

YIELD: Approximately 3 dozen biscotti.

COOKING TIP: These crunchy cookies ship particularly well for food gifts as long as they're packed carefully.

Peppermint Biscotti

ONE WINTER WE REALIZED we had accumulated a big plastic bag filled with various candy canes and peppermint candies. We hate to to throw things out — yet we realized we'd never eat the candies. So we developed this "re-purposing" recipe to transform those candy canes and mints into something new and improved. We now have a holiday cookie tradition where friends collect and send us their leftover candy canes to transform into these cookies.

INGREDIENTS

¾ c. butter, softened (1½ sticks)
¾ c. sugar
3 eggs
2 t. peppermint extract
3¼ c. flour
1 t. baking powder
¼ t. salt
1½ c. crushed peppermint candy, divided
white chocolate bark for frosting

DIRECTIONS

❶ In a large mixing bowl, cream butter and sugar.

❷ Add eggs, one at a time, beating well after each addition. Beat in extract.

❸ Separately, mix flour, baking powder and salt. Stir in 1 c. peppermint candy.

❹ Gradually add flour/candy mixture to creamed mixture, beating until blended (dough will be stiff).

❺ Divide dough in half. On a baking sheet, roll each portion into a 12-inch-by-2½-inch rectangle.

❻ Bake at 350° for 25 to 30 minutes or until golden brown. Carefully remove to wire rack. Cool 15 minutes. On cutting board, cut at an angle into ½-inch slices.

❼ Place cut side down on baking sheets. Bake 12 to 15 minutes until firm.

❽ For frosting, melt chocolate. Drizzle chocolate over cookie in a swirled design.

YIELD: 3 dozen biscotti.

Changing the Future of Food, Slice by Slice

Nancy Vail & Jered Lawson,
Pie Ranch,
Pescadero, California

Just say the word "pie" and folks start to smile. Who can resist a tempting slice of pie, particularly one juicy with fresh fruits of the season? Pie filled with strawberries, juicy red. Rhubarb pie topped with buttery streusel crumble. Lemon pie, tangy and tart with a dash of sweetness. Blackberry pie, rich with the dark berries of summer. How about pumpkin pie, serving up fall flavors topped with whipped cream? You're drooling. We are too. But most of us just eat the pie, smack our lips and move on. Not Nancy Vail and Jered Lawson, who founded Pie Ranch. They see pie as a means to open doors and minds and inspire young people to care about our food system.

As we walk their land at sunset, golden light bounces off their early spring crops as our kids play hide and seek amongst the Meyer lemon trees. Goats bleat and barn doors squeak as we examine the new wood oven and outdoor kitchen. This land, which happens to be a pie-shaped plot, exudes an aura of possibility and hope.

"It's about education and social change here at Pie Ranch," explains Nancy. "Community is the key ingredient in everything we do. By providing opportunities to come to the farm and share in the process of raising healthy, fresh food in a way that stewards our landscape, people walk away thinking differently about where their food comes from and start making more mindful choices."

Most organic farmers we know see themselves as activists, not just food producers. But Nancy and Jered believe pie can truly change the world. The non-profit Pie Ranch is 27 acres in two "slices." The upper slice is owned by Jered and Nancy and leased to the non-profit. The lower slice is now owned by the non-profit with the help of many individual supporters. Pie Ranch entices us with pie but quickly moves deeper, connecting the dots of food and farming, particularly with youth in the San Francisco area who may never have been out of the city before.

"Pies are the lure we use to hook people on the benefits of cooking from scratch," says Jered. "If we want to see young people reimagine their role in the system and not just be passive consumers of fast food, then it helps if they have a taste of what it could be, and what it could look like, from seed to table." Jered and Nancy, along with their staff and community partners, raise all the key ingredients that go into pie, enabling visitors to experience the whole cycle of pie-making, from grinding the wheat to gathering eggs to harvesting a host of garden goodies for the filling.

"There's nothing like watching a kid eat their first berry picked from the plant, warm with the morning sun. At first this might be quite a strange and out-of-the-box experience, but once they taste the berry they're hooked," adds Jered. "When young people go through such a food experience and truly

Jered and Nancy Lawson at Pie Ranch, Pescadero, CA.

taste the flavor and farm freshness, both their lives and eating habits could change forever."

Pie Ranch's new wood oven and outdoor kitchen addition highlight another ingredient Nancy and Jered view as vital: building community around a shared meal. A collaborative effort from the start, many Pie Ranch hands contributed to this wood-fired brick oven project that now stands the size of a small shed and can crank to temperatures over 1,000 degrees.

"The wood oven is the antithesis of the fast-food drive-through; this is slow food at its finest," explains Jered. "We're still experimenting with the potential of this oven and the variety of foods it can make. The oven takes a good day of firing to fully heat the wall through, enabling us to start preparing quick, flash-baked foods like pizza, and then move onto breads,

winter squash, roasted root vegetable dishes, and as the temperature drops, we can put on pies and pots of beans, and finish it off with a batch of goat milk yogurt." An outdoor kitchen complements the oven, providing key kitchen elements including a sink and work top. But talk about culinary inspiration: instead of staring at walls, you're engulfed by farm beauty. Kind of like cooking inside a Monet painting.

"The common denominator here is everyone does something to prepare for a meal," Jered details. "From rolling dough to washing dishes, there's a family-like bond that naturally erupts when people come together to prepare food and then share it together. If we can keep the whole process outdoors, from harvesting to cooking to eating, it takes the experience to a whole new level."

In addition to the young people coming to farm for educational experiences, Pie Ranch also helps support and encourages the next generation of farmers with hands-on training. Apprentices reside on-farm for the full growing season, sharing in all aspects of sustainable agriculture production and food justice education. We shared a meal at Pie Ranch with this season's new crop of apprentices who enthusiastically brought fresh pies to the potluck meal.

"Oops, it's a little soupy," new apprentice Jenny Trotter says with a grin as she cuts the rhubarb strawberry pie, juices flowing into the pan. "But no worries. Call it cobbler style pie," she adds as we eagerly line up for our scoop. Jenny may be new to Pie Ranch, but she's already nailed Nancy and Jered's core lesson: In any shape or form, pie brings people together and celebrates farm-fresh ingredients, even if they're a bit soupy.

"We think of Pie Ranch as a place for "pie-in-the-sky" visionary thinking, a means to create meaning and measurable change," sums up Nancy. "Enjoyable and thoughtful engagement with good food can bring individuals, families and institutions — from children to school boards — together to create a more healthful and just society. We provide the inspirational slice to get things started."

Shaker Lemon Pie

*P*RACTICALLY A YEAR-ROUND FRUIT in California, Meyer lemons bring a juicy zing to this pie that form an unusual partnership with a sweet sugar base. You can use any type of lemon in this recipe, just remember the juiciest, less acidic and sweetest lemons are those with thinner yellow skins, like the Meyer lemons. "Zesting" a lemon means removing only the colored part of the skin with a vegetable peeler or grater. The most intense lemon flavor lies in the zest because of the heavy oil concentration there. Start the filling for this pie the day before you bake it; the longer you let the lemons hang out with the sugar, the stronger the lemon flavor.

INGREDIENTS

   One 9-inch double pie crust
   (see page 231)
2 large lemons
2 c. sugar
¼ t. salt
4 eggs
¼ c. butter, melted (½ stick)
3 T. flour

DIRECTIONS

❶ Grate the zest from the 2 lemons, then slice the lemons paper-thin (i.e., as thin as you possibly can) and remove seeds. Combine the zest and the lemon slices in a bowl with the sugar and salt. Cover and let sit at room temperature for 4 to 24 hours (ideally 24), stirring occasionally. You'll notice the liquid releasing from the lemons and making a sugary paste.

❷ Prepare the piecrust and line a 9-inch pie pan with half the dough.

❸ To finish the filling, whisk the 4 eggs in a large bowl until frothy. Whisk in the melted butter and flour. Stir in the lemon mixture and pour into bottom of crust. Cover with vented top crust or a lattice.

❹ Bake at 425° for 30 minutes. Reduce temperature to 350° and bake another 20 to 30 minutes or until knife inserted into center comes out clean and the top crust is a golden brown. Let pie cool completely before serving. Store in refrigerator but bring to room temperature before serving.

YIELD: 1 pie.

The thing about education is that you can learn why your actions have positive or negative effects. The thing about ignorance is that you can do the same harmful thing over and over again, guilt-free, slowly killing yourself while reacting and blaming others.

JILL BLEVINS

Pumpkin Mousse Cheesecake

*P*UMPKIN AND MOUSSE seem like dance partners from different dessert planets. Drop a pumpkin on your toe and it will hurt. A mousse, by its culinary definition, whips air bubbles into something to make it light and fluffy. Try this recipe and you'll never return to that flat and heavy traditional pumpkin pie again.

INGREDIENTS

1   graham cracker crust (see page 226 for recipe), pressed into springform pan

1   c. whipped cream (see page 189 for recipe), for topping

CREAM CHEESE LAYER INGREDIENTS

1   package cream cheese, softened (8 oz.)

2   eggs

¾   c. sugar

PUMPKIN LAYER INGREDIENTS

3   eggs, separated

2   c. cooked pumpkin purée

½   c. sugar

½   c. milk

1   t. cinnamon

1   t. nutmeg

¼   c. sugar

¼   t. salt

DIRECTIONS

❶ Prepare graham cracker crust.

❷ Start with the cream cheese layer. In a mixing bowl, beat cream cheese until fluffy. Beat in sugar and eggs, one at a time, until well-blended.

❸ Spread cream cheese mixture over crust and bake at 350° for about 25 to 30 minutes or until firm. Cool completely.

❹ For pumpkin layer, separate the 3 eggs. In a saucepan, mix egg yolks with pumpkin and cook over medium heat until thickened. To that pumpkin mixture, add ½ c. sugar, milk, cinnamon, nutmeg and salt. Turn off heat and let sit on burner for 5 minutes. Remove from heat and cool completely.

❺ In a large bowl, beat egg whites until stiff. Add remaining ¼ c. sugar and beat until well-blended. Fold egg whites into pumpkin mixture and pour this pumpkin layer over the cream cheese layer. Bake at 350° for 15 minutes or until set.

❻ Cool completely and chill overnight before serving. Serve with a dollop of whipped cream on top.

YIELD: 12 servings.

Whipped Cream

*T*ALK ABOUT MISLEADING ADVERTISING. "Whipped cream" that is sprayed from an aerosol can or filling those non-dairy plastic tubs are neither whipped in the traditional sense, nor made with heavy cream. So make your own real whipped cream, just for the taste of it. Save some money, too. You'll be paying double the price for the store-bought stuff with mostly air and water.

INGREDIENTS

1   c. heavy cream (1 pint; milk fat of 35 to 40%)

DIRECTIONS

❶ Pour heavy cream into an electric mixer, start at a low speed until the cream gets foamy and then speed things up. You can also mix by hand using a whisk. Whisking by hand should take about 4 minutes.

❷ Serve immediately on top of apple pie, apple crisp or anything that needs a luscious real dairy topping.

YIELD: 2 cups whipped cream.

Growing food in urban or suburban gardens is becoming widespread. House pets can help keep raccoons and woodchucks at bay.

Maraschino Cherries (not for the kids)

FORGET EVERYTHING YOU REMEMBER about the red-dye-laced, high-fructose corn syrup cherry adorning sundaes. Meet the real maraschino. This recipe reaches back generations to the marasca cherry in Croatia. For hundred of years, folks made a ruby red cherry liquor by preserving the whole fruit and dubbed it "maraschino cherries." You can still find the rather expensive marasca liquor, but a cheaper cherry liqueur will work fine in this recipe. Not for children, the cherries keep their tart appeal and make a delicious grown-up treat drizzled over ice cream. We've seen different variations on whether or not to keep the pits inside the cherries. We like keeping the pit as the cherry retains its shape and doesn't get mushy.

INGREDIENTS

1 lb. sour cherries (pits intact)
3 c. cherry liqueur

DIRECTIONS

❶ Place the cherries in a Mason jar or other glass container with a lid. Pour the liqueur over the cherries. The goal is to add enough liqueur to immerse the cherries, but they will bob to the top of the liquid anyway.

❷ Refrigerate for at least 2 weeks. Gently swirl the container every 2 to 3 days to immerse the cherries in the liqueur. Store in refrigerator for up to 6 months.

YIELD: 4 cups of cherries.

COOKING TIP

Whipped Cream or Butter

Be careful not to overwhip your whipped cream. If the cream starts to stiffen and appears grainy, stop immediately or you'll end up with a bowl full of butter. Not that a bowl of butter is bad; it's just not the best topping for Pumpkin Mousse Cheesecake or a bowl of ice cream.

Caramel Sauce for Caramel Apple Buffet

E VER SINCE LIAM ENTERED the Halloween trick-or-treating age range, the aftermath is like a powder keg of sugar waiting to blow. He's all about volume, and our community embraces the festivities (you'll see lots of adults dressed up handing out candy), so it's in good fun. But even we couldn't go through the volume of candy; when you're getting bored with mini Milky Ways, you know you have issues. But we found the ultimate antidote: the Caramel Apple Buffet. If you've ever grazed on a salad bar or been tempted by a sundae bar with all the fixings for your two scoops of ice cream, then you can imagine the scene with the assortment of leftover candy arranged in bowls. Just chop up or crush the candy, slice up some apples and make the caramel sauce below — then dunk and dip. We rationalize this also covers the "creative re-purposing" category, so indulge and enjoy.

INGREDIENTS

½   c. sugar

½   c. brown sugar, firmly packed

2   T. flour

1   c. heavy whipping cream

¼   c. butter (½ stick), cubed

2   t. vanilla

DIRECTIONS

❶ In a saucepan, whisk together sugar, brown sugar, flour and whipping cream over medium heat. Bring to a boil and boil for 3 minutes.

❷ Remove from heat, mix in butter and vanilla.

❸ Let cool completely. Pour into a clean, sterile jar (we like to use glass canning jars) and store covered in the refrigerator. Best heated before serving.

YIELD: 1½ cups.

Caramel apple bar.

Strawberry-Rhubarb Streusel Pie

*T*HE CONCEPT OF STRENGTH through diversity adds value—and flavor—in the kitchen. For example, take pie. Let's say we make two pies: one strawberry and the other rhubarb. Both tasty in their own right, but if you combine the two fruits, we'd argue the resulting flavor tastes even better. The strawberry's sweetness softens the tart twang from the rhubarb, and the pie exudes a deeper, more complex essence. Same theory applies in life, gardening, relationships. One ingredient is good, but multiple perspectives plus a little streusel and whipped cream on top—now that's magic.

CRUST INGREDIENTS

1   c. flour
2   T. powdered sugar
⅓ c. butter (5⅓ T.)
1   t. canola oil

FILLING INGREDIENTS

2   eggs, separated
1   c. sugar
3   T. flour
½ t. salt
1½ c. fresh rhubarb, chopped
1½ c. fresh strawberries, sliced

STREUSEL TOPPING INGREDIENTS

¼ c. flour
¼ c. whole oats
¼ c. brown sugar, firmly packed
2   T. butter

DIRECTIONS

❶ For crust, mix together flour and powdered sugar in a large bowl. Cut in butter until mixture is crumbly. Press into a lightly oiled 9-inch pie pan.

❷ For filling, beat egg whites until stiff peaks form. Separately, beat egg yolks and mix in sugar, flour and salt.

❸ Fold rhubarb and strawberries into egg yolk mixture. Fold in the beaten egg whites. Pour into unbaked crust.

❹ For streusel, mix flour, oats and brown sugar. Cut in butter until mixture is crumbly. Sprinkle over pie filling.

❺ Bake at 425° for 10 minutes. Reduce heat to 250° and bake for approximately 30 more minutes until set.

YIELD: Serves 8.

Chocolate Zucchini Roll

TALK ABOUT A REINVENTION: this rolled cake dresses up the butt of all garden jokes (zucchini) into an elegant dessert. The jelly roll style adds a stunning and fancy spiral pattern to every slice. You can use any summer squash varieties in this recipe.

CAKE INGREDIENTS

- 3 eggs
- 1 t. vanilla
- 1 c. flour
- ¾ c. sugar
- ½ c. baking cocoa
- 1 t. cinnamon
- ¼ t. salt
- 1 c. zucchini, peeled and shredded (or other summer squash)

FILLING INGREDIENTS

- 1 package cream cheese, softened (8 oz.)
- ¼ c. butter, softened (½ stick)
- 2 t. vanilla extract
- 1 c. powdered sugar

DIRECTIONS

❶ In a large mixing bowl, beat eggs and vanilla.

❷ Add in the flour, sugar, baking cocoa, cinnamon and salt and blend well. Stir in zucchini.

❸ Line a jelly roll pan (15-inch by 10-inch by 1-inch) with lightly oiled waxed paper so that the waxed paper stretches over the pan edge. Spread batter onto pan. Bake at 350° for about 15 to 20 minutes or until cake springs back when gently touched. Turn onto a clean linen towel dusted with powdered sugar. Waxed paper side will be on top.

❹ Peel off waxed paper and roll cake up jelly roll style, starting with a shorter side. Cool cake on wire rack.

❺ While cake is cooling, make filling. In a mixing bowl, beat cream cheese, butter and vanilla until fluffy. Beat in powdered sugar until well-blended.

❻ Unroll cake and spread filling to about 1 inch of edges. Roll up cake again and dust with confectioner's sugar. Refrigerate until serving.

YIELD: 8 servings.

DRINKS

Very Berry Smoothie

Banoffee Toffee Smoothie

Lemon Balm Iced Tea (vegan)

Rhubarb Fizz (vegan)

Homemade Hot Cocoa Mix

Raspberry Cordial (vegan)

Pear Cordial (vegan)

Rhubarb Cordial (vegan)

Frozen Mochaccino

Irish Cream

Rhubarb Strawberry Daiquiri (vegan)

Sipping Peace

There's a concept in construction or manufacturing called embodied energy. Without getting too academic, embodied energy represents all the energy that's used in the digging, processing, manufacturing and shipping of raw materials and their respective final product to an end-user. If something is sold in a retail store, it includes the energy related to shipping it to the store and then getting it from the store to your home. It's the sum of all the energy that goes into making something, even disposing of it at the end of its lifecycle.

What does this have to do with food? Plenty. Not only does shipping our food or ingredients around add carbon dioxide emissions to the atmosphere, it also takes energy to make things grow (depending on the scale of the operations and the need for tractors) and process ingredients into what we may enjoy, like a cup of coffee for breakfast.

"One healthy, mature coffee plant produces about 1,600 cherries each year, which result in 3,200 beans that will eventually become about 1 pound of coffee," says Rodney North, the Answer Man at Equal Exchange. "A pound of coffee will produce about 50 to 60 cups. So each coffee plant will only produce enough for about one cup of coffee per week."

Coffee, savored as far back as the 15th century, is among the top food or beverages in terms of its embodied energy, though it's challenging to reach a final number due to the myriad variables in its growth, processing, transport and use. Close runners-up are tea, chocolate, vanilla extract and bananas. The more processed, packaged and transported the food or drink, the higher the embodied energy; putting things in aluminum or steel cans adds even more energy. By contrast, harvesting some lettuce for a salad cut with a knife from your patio pot would have practically no embodied energy.

So why does coffee have such a high embodied energy? For starters, coffee plants can take up to five years to establish before they produce any cherries. Then the ripe cherries must be harvested, pulped and the various layers of outside skins removed by fermentation. These coffee seeds (aka beans) are then dried and hulled, which removes the final layer of the skin. Now we have green coffee, which still needs to be roasted, often done at a factory far away from the region in which it was grown. After the roasting, usually at temperatures of about 550 degrees, it's shipped again to a retailer and possibly again to our home where we grind it up and brew it in any number of clever, energy-intensive ways.

There's another side to the face of the food we eat: the farmer. More of us are becoming aware that the "free trade" advocated by Washington DC and corporate boardrooms comes at a dire cost to many farmers the world over. Since coffee is often hand-picked, this relationship is ripe for exploitation when corporations squeeze profits from the growers to help offset their shipping costs (rising), roasting costs (increasing) and fancy marketing budgets. Added to this is the fact that these crops are also considered commodities, subject to financial speculation and price swings that may have nothing to do with the actual crop grown.

To address both issues, the process of growing what we eat and accounting for the farmer who's doing the growing, the fair trade movement has come about seeking to support small farmers or democratically organized grower cooperatives by paying them above the price set forth by the "free market"—specifically, on the New York futures market. In much the same fashion as slow food seeks to topple fast food, fair trade is heralded as an option to the exploitative labor and growing practices among food companies operating under the guise of free trade. Fair trade certified products may also be certified organic or shade-grown, where coffee is grown in the shade of other trees which is better for the birds and soil. As for the rich flavors of these coffees, they exceed our expectations in the same way that other organic foods do.

Several non-profit organizations have come about to help inform our food purchasing decisions and inspect and verify the high standards upheld for fair trade certification. This is particularly important for products — like coffee — that both have high embodied energy and lend themselves to multinational corporations manipulating the markets to serve their profit goals. By selecting companies like Equal Exchange (equalexchange.coop), Peace Coffee (peacecoffee.com) and Dagoba Organic Chocolate (dagobachocolate.com), we know that the growers who produced the coffee or cacao beans were paid a fair wage and treated respectfully, not exploited as cheap labor. For the entire fair trade movement, the Fair Trade Federation (fairtradefederation.org) offers a list of trade-certified purveyors of coffee that may roast it near where you live.

With the average supermarket offering over 35,000 choices, sometimes we need a reason to remember to step back and slowly focus on one thing, one taste, one experience — that perfect cup of coffee, not just the buzz we get from it. This beverage chapter gifts us with opportunities to slow down and linger. It's not just what we drink or eat, but how we do so. When go to a coffeehouse, we're the ones you see plopped on the comfy couch with a mocha prepared with organic, Fair Trade coffee, sipping slowly, as we chat about life or read the newspaper.

There's another thing about that pot of coffee or a blender of daiquiris. Drinks, particularly these recipes, beg to be shared. No one makes one glass of lemonade. A pitcher prompts a party. A full coffee pot and a bottle of Irish Cream sit waiting for conversation by the woodstove.

So fill your cup — and your life — to the brim, then slowly savor peace, sip by sip.

"My starting point is that coffee is purely a pleasure thing, as opposed to certain things that are necessary to maintain good health. You don't need it. But if you drink it, it should be a pleasurable experience." —Alfred Peet, Peet's Coffee founded in Berkeley, California.

Very Berry Smoothie

*W*HEN WE FIRST OPENED the B&B, finding a breakfast drink option proved a bit of a challenge as we aspired to keep our meals both seasonal and local. Our solution to a glass of juice at breakfast came in the form of an inherited 1970s yogurt maker. We figured yogurt-based smoothies would showcase our great dairy state. When we have time, we prepare batches of yogurt using organic powdered milk from Organic Valley Family of Farms, then blend into various seasonal breakfast smoothies based on what's ripening in the gardens or what we have frozen in the winter. There's a growing number of regional dairies that also provide artisanal yogurt, a great option if you can't get your hands on a yogurt maker. Because we can't always get ripe organic bananas locally, we stockpile organic bananas when we can find them and freeze the bananas whole. We freeze most of the fruit we grow for these smoothies — using frozen fruit gives the smoothies a shake-like consistency.

INGREDIENTS

3   T. honey
1   c. plain yogurt
½   c. milk
½   c. fresh or frozen strawberries
    (or raspberries, blueberries)
2–3 bananas, depending on size
5   ice cubes (not needed if using
    frozen fruit)

DIRECTIONS

❶ Blend the honey, yogurt and milk first in the blender, otherwise the ice cubes or frozen fruit will solidify the honey, making it difficult to dissolve.

❷ Add remaining ingredients and blend until smooth and creamy, like a thick shake. If too thick, add water until the texture is to your liking.

❸ Pour into serving glasses. Serve in champagne flutes for an elegant touch and garnish with lemon balm or mint leaf.

YIELD: 4 servings.

 COOKING TIP Pour any leftover smoothie into plastic popsicle molds for tasty, healthy frozen treats.

Banoffee Toffee Smoothie

*T*HIS SMOOTHIE DRAWS INSPIRATION from a dessert we discovered in Scotland involving a caramel base made from an unopened sweetened condensed milk can, boiled for several hours. Only in Scotland! Here you'll find a much simpler smoothie version without an explosive accident waiting to happen in the kitchen.

INGREDIENTS

3   T. honey
1   c. plain yogurt
½   c. milk
2–3 bananas, depending on size
1   t. vanilla extract (see page 233)
2   T. peanut butter
    about 5 ice cubes

DIRECTIONS

❶ Blend honey in blender with yogurt and milk, then add remaining ingredients and blend. Blend the honey, yogurt and milk first, or the ice cubes will freeze the honey, making it difficult to blend.

❷ Pour into serving glasses. Champagne flutes add an elegant touch and garnish with a lemon balm or mint leaf.

YIELD: 4 servings.

Standing stones at Calanais, Scotland.

Lemon Balm Iced Tea

OUR LEMON BALM GROWS prolifically and spreads like wildfire. To keep it somewhat under control, we drink it up as a refreshing summertime iced tea. In our efforts to cook in low-energy ways, we pull out our crock pot to slow simmer the lemony flavors out of the lemon balm. On sweltering summer days, we'll start the Crock-Pot during the cooler evening hours, usually set out on our front porch. The Crock-Pot technique works well, but you could also simmer the tea on the stove. Vary these proportions based on your Crock-Pot size and how sweet you like your tea.

INGREDIENTS

- 8 c. water (enough to fill Crock-Pot)
- big bunch of fresh lemon balm stalks with leaves (enough to pack tight into your Crock-Pot)
- ½ c. honey
- ¼ c. lemon juice

DIRECTIONS

❶ Stuff as much rinsed lemon balm into a Crock-Pot as will fit. Cover with water and let simmer about 3 hours on low.

❷ Drain liquid into pitcher.

❸ While still warm, add honey and lemon juice. It's easier to add the honey while the tea is still warm since it readily dissolves.

❹ Chill before serving.

YIELD: 8 servings.

COOKING TIP Growing Lemon Balm

Lemon balm comes from the mint family, easily identified by its square-shaped stem. Mints grow prolifically and are highly invasive. If you have limited growing space, it's best to plant your mint in a container—even if you bury the container underground—to control spreading.

Rhubarb Fizz (with Rhubarb Syrup)

THERE'S STILL A PLACE for soda pop, we think. Try this unique recipe adapted from an old church punch bowl recipe but created for one-glass servings rather than for the whole congregation. We've made it completely organic, avoiding the GMO-corn-derived high-fructose corn syrup that's the sweeter mainstay for the soda pop industry. Like the Lemon Balm Iced Tea recipe, this one takes advantage of a Crock-Pot to simmer the juices out of the rhubarb; this is one recipe, too, that blows through the stalks.

INGREDIENTS

12 c. fresh rhubarb, chopped

2 c. water

3 c. sugar

2 liters unflavored seltzer water

DIRECTIONS

❶ In a Crock-Pot or large saucepan, cook rhubarb and water over low heat for approximately 2 hours or until rhubarb is a soft pulp.

❷ Drain out pulp and place warm liquid in large bowl.

❸ Stir in sugar until completely dissolved. You've just created Rhubarb Syrup (also used in our Rhubarb Strawberry Daiquiri, page 210).

❹ For each individual serving, add ice to glass then pour Rhubarb Syrup to about half full. Top with seltzer water and stir. Experiment with how sweet you like your drink, adding syrup or seltzer water accordingly.

YIELD: 8 servings.

Freezing Rhubarb Syrup is a cinch and allows you to use it at a later point for this soda pop as a juice base (blended with water) or in our Rhubarb Strawberry Daiquiris (see page 210).

Farm Chicks for Change: Four ways Women Instigate an Agriculture Revolution

Quick trivia question: What's the second verse to "The Farmer in the Dell"? Anybody?

Here you go:

The farmer takes a wife,
The farmer takes a wife,
Hi-ho, the derry-o
The farmer takes a wife.

Female scarecrow at Pie Ranch.

Talk about stale lyrics in dire need of an update. Women make up the largest and fastest growing group buying new farms today. So we should be teaching kids something more like:

"The wife took over the farm.
To the land she did no harm,
Hi-ho, times change, you know,
These chicks can really grow."

Consider Iowa farmer Denise O'Brien, chief female-farmer stereotype smasher. Founder of the Women, Food and Agriculture Network (WFAN), she has been organizing and promoting the voice and face of women in agriculture for the past twenty years. "Finally, the tides are starting to turn for women farmers as policies start to change," explains Denise. "There's still much we as women, from growers to grocery shoppers, can do to create a healthy food system for future generations."

O'Brien has a history of seeing opportunity in crisis. Her agriculture advocacy work started back during the farm crisis of the 1980s when many family farms collapsed and were forced into foreclosure. "It was the women on the farms who saw this economic gloom on the horizon since they often kept the accounting books. They could see where things were heading," Denise recalls. "But the problem was that these women still considered themselves 'just farm wives.' Nobody took their voices seriously. We women needed to get out of the role of just making coffee at meetings."

This launched O'Brien on the road to agriculture activism, balancing multiple roles helping run her family's diversified dairy and produce farm, Rolling Acres, raising children and serving as a national advocate and spokeswoman for women in agriculture. "I realized during the farm crisis that if I didn't step to the plate to organize women, if I didn't instigate something, perhaps no one would," adds O'Brien. In 1997 she launched the Women, Food and Agriculture Network to help women farmers develop the organizational and speaking skills to collectively advocate for a stronger voice and representation.

You don't need to be a farmer to support women in agriculture. "Whatever your background, there's a role each of us women can play to support a healthy, green and fair food system," O'Brien explains. Here are some steps women can take to support better food for all:

1. Connect with Kindred Spirits

Start coalition building by connecting with others in your community who share your healthy food values. Denise first met many of her local tribe of kindred spirits by starting a food co-op. It drew people together with a desire to purchase natural foods not available in their rural area. "Turns out we shared other interests as well, such as politics and organic gardening," adds Denise.

2. Be Available

Make yourself available to attend meetings, particularly those that are traditionally dominated by men such as local planning and farm service meetings. When her children were young, O'Brien would often attend meetings with her kids in tow: "I wanted my kids to grow up realizing the importance of being involved and active with the issues you consider important."

3. Support Other Women

Denise took Lisa under her wing, providing an open door for advice, connections and support. "Women need to be each other's cheerleaders," Denise explains. This support led Lisa to launch the Rural Women's Project for the Midwest Organic and Sustainable Education Service (MOSES), championing resources and networks for women farmers and food-based ecopreneurs, working in close collaboration, naturally, with organizations like WFAN.

4. Join Advocacy Groups

Agriculture groups like the WFAN and the National Sustainable Agriculture Coalition synthesize key farming issues, making it easier for you to take action on food and agriculture policy, such as writing letters to representatives threatening programs that help new farmers or dilute the certified organic standards set forth by the National Organic Program, the federal regulatory framework governing organic food administered by the USDA.

Homemade Hot Cocoa Mix

*Y*OU'LL CHUCKLE THE NEXT TIME you see trendy, overpriced hot cocoa mixes at the store after you realize how easy it is to make your own. Plus, homemade hot cocoa made from pure cocoa powder has five times as many antioxidants, known for their cell-protecting properties, than a store-bought mix. We get our organic dry milk powder from Organic Valley Family of Farms and add in cocoa from Equal Exchange.

INGREDIENTS

5½ c. dry milk powder

1¼ c. sugar

¾ c. unsweetened baking cocoa

INGREDIENTS MAKE 1 SERVING

⅓ c. hot chocolate mix

¾ c. water

¼ t. vanilla extract

DIRECTIONS

❶ Combine all ingredients. Ideally combine in a food processor to blend well.

❷ Store in an airtight container in a cool, dry place.

DIRECTIONS TO MAKE 1 SERVING

❶ Bring water to a boil.

❷ Add mix and blend well. Remove from heat and add vanilla.

Raspberry Cordial

V Vegan

*S*INCE OUR RASPBERRY HARVEST lasts until the first frost, this raspberry cordial often seconds as an eerie Halloween decoration. When the raspberries "float" in the vodka during the first step of the raspberry cordial-making process, the vodka turns a rich red color and the clumped together raspberries turn white, resembling a brain floating in blood inside a glass jar. Instead of another pumpkin, set this glass jar on the windowsill to spook the neighborhood kids.

INGREDIENTS

2 quarts raspberries (8 c.)

2 quarts vodka (8 c.)

2 quarts water (8 c.)

2½ c. sugar

DIRECTIONS

❶ Mix raspberries and alcohol and let sit 2 weeks in a sterilized gallon-sized glass jar with a tight-fitting lid. Raspberries will turn white as the alcohol turns red.

❷ After approximately 2 weeks, strain mixture through a sieve to remove raspberries.

❸ Mix water and sugar. Heat until dissolved. Add to strained liquid and stir well.

❹ Pour into sterilized glass containers and age in a dark, cool spot at least 6 months.

YIELD: About 1½ gallons.

Pear Cordial

$\mathcal{W}$ HEN WE'RE UP TO OUR EYEBALLS in summer fruit and have eaten, frozen and canned our winter stash, Lisa starts her homemade hooch-making factory. A "cordial" is a sweet alcoholic beverage where a flavoring (in our case fresh fruit, but you could use, nuts, herbs or even edible flowers) is infused with an alcohol base. Even if you don't care for pears due to their grainy texture, don't let that stop you from trying this recipe, which highlights the smooth, sweet side of pears with a honey-like finish.

INGREDIENTS

- 3 c. sugar
- 2 c. water
- 6 c. pears, peeled and sliced thinly (about 6 large pears or 3 lbs.)
- 1 t. lemon zest
- 2½ c. vodka

DIRECTIONS

❶ Boil sugar and water over medium-high heat, stirring constantly. When mixture is clear, remove from heat and let stand until just warm.

❷ Place pears and lemon zest in a sterilized gallon-sized glass jar with a tight-fitting lid. Pour syrup over pears and add vodka. Stir. Let stand in a cool, dark place for 2 weeks.

❸ Using a fine mesh strainer, strain out solids. Transfer strained cordial to a sterilized glass container, cover and let stand 3 more weeks. Strain through cheesecloth to remove sediment and pour into sterilized final bottles.

YIELD: 6 cups.

Local Liquors

The locavore movement is not just for fruits, vegetables, herbs and honey. The expansive growth of microbreweries allows us to enjoy a local beer; likewise, the spirits industry is experiencing a renaissance of distilled beverages made in small batches with local ingredients. We're loyal to our organic Death's Door Vodka from Death's Door Spirits, using local organic ingredients. Another favorite is mead from White Winter Winery; it's made from honey and various local fruits. Search your community or region for unique and flavorful options.

Rhubarb Cordial

V
Vegan

TALK ABOUT AN UNDERRATED CINDERELLA. On one hand, she's about as sour a vegetable as they come. But dress her up with some sugar bling and Zinfandel, suddenly rhubarb leaps to "belle of the ball" status. Give this to your friends and they'll undoubtedly respond with, "You mean this is rhubarb?" We're for promoting the underdog, so let's give rhubarb some overdue star treatment. Our point: Rhubarb is not just for pie. Just drink up before midnight in case she turns into a pumpkin.

INGREDIENTS

4   c. fresh rhubarb, chopped
1½ c. water
3   c. sugar
1   t. orange zest
1   c. white Zinfandel wine
2   c. vodka

DIRECTIONS

❶ Boil rhubarb, water, sugar and orange zest together over medium heat, stirring constantly.

❷ When sugar dissolves, remove from heat and let stand until just warm. Pour into a sterilized gallon-sized glass jar. Add vodka and wine. Cover with a tight-fitting lid and let stand in a cool, dark place for 2 weeks.

❸ Using a fine mesh strainer, strain out solids. Transfer strained cordial to a sterilized glass container, cover and let stand 2 more weeks. Strain through cheesecloth to remove sediment and pour into sterilized final bottles.

YIELD: 4 cups.

One little thing can revive a guy,
and that is a piece of rhubarb pie;
Serve it up, nice and hot;
Maybe things aren't as bad as you thought.

GARRISON KEILLOR, IN "BE-BOP-A-RE-BOP RHUBARB PIE FILLING,"
A PRAIRIE HOME COMPANION

Frozen Mochaccino

*W*HO NEEDS THOSE un-local coffee franchises overcharging for fancy, frozen gourmet coffee drinks when you have the ultimate tool for a cold, refreshing, whipped afternoon pick-me-up at home: the blender. This recipe affords a perfect way to use up leftover coffee by freezing it in ice cube trays. That way you don't loose the coffee flavor with ice. Instead of brewing fresh, hot coffee only to pour it over ice (and dilute it), take advantage of partial pots of joe by making "java cubes" and chill out when the heat rises.

INGREDIENTS

8   coffee ice cubes (or 1 c. cold brewed coffee plus a few ice cubes)
¼   c. sugar
1   c. milk
⅛   c. cocoa powder

DIRECTIONS

❶ Combine all ingredients in blender and blend until frothy.

YIELD: 2 servings.

Irish Cream

*R*ING IN THE WINTER SOLSTICE with a glass of indulgence! With a decadent cream base, keep this Irish Cream refrigerated and use up within 2 weeks. Trust us, that won't be hard.

INGREDIENTS

1   c. half & half cream
1⅔ c. whiskey (any kind)
1   t. instant coffee powder
1   t. vanilla extract
1   t. almond extract
1   T. cocoa powder
2   T. sugar

DIRECTIONS

❶ Combine all the ingredients in a blender and blend for about 30 seconds. Place in a large glass jar (we use a canning jar).

❷ Keep refrigerated. Give the sealed jar a good shake to remix the ingredients before pouring over ice or adding a splash to coffee.

YIELD: 4 cups.

SHOVEL READY: YOUNG FARMERS BACK IN THE FIELDS

Severine von Tscharner Fleming,
The Greenhorns,
Hudson Valley, New York

Who's feeding America, and how?

Here's the state of the soil. There are only about 2 million farmers left to feed a population of about 309 million people, with the average age of these farmers pushing upwards of 57 years old. Most of the crops grown are government-subsidized commodity crops: corn, soybeans, wheat, cotton and rice. Most of the corn, soy and wheat are the key ingredients for the processed food Americans have acquired a taste for in their breakfast cereals or frozen pizzas. Added to this reality, about 2,880 acres of fertile farmland are being lost every day to build more houses, strip malls and golf courses, according to the USDA. Joni Mitchell's "Big Yellow Taxi" rings truer today than when she first sang it in 1970: we "paved paradise and put up a parking lot."

Enter Severine von Tscharner Fleming, activist-organizer and farm manager for a 100-acre diversified organic farm in the Hudson Valley, growing fruit, vegetables, herbs and flowers, mostly for restaurants and local markets. But she doesn't want to talk about her day job.

She's also at the helm of the non-profit organization she co-founded, The Greenhorns, serving farmers of the under-40 set who are passionate about growing healthy food. That's her focus. Her expanding team of Greenhorns multi-task, throw farmer mixers and blog on The Greenhorns website. Lisa first spotted Severine on a unicycle, weaving in and out of tables at a national Kellogg Foundation Food Conference. Then they got to talking turnips and rabbits.

To spread the news about the future of food in America, Severine has directed a documentary film, *The Greenhorns*, exploring our nation's young farmers, their struggles and their valor in the "everyday drama of entrepreneurship," as she puts it.

Released in 2011, *The Greenhorns* is complemented by *Greenhorn Radio* on the Heritage Radio Network, as well as an online wiki and a map listing new greenhorn farms sprouting up. Everything is for farmers by farmers. There's also a blog on their website (thegreenhorns.net) and a 30-page *Guidebook for Beginning Farmers*, a free resource that can be shared far and wide. With all their gatherings nationally, there's plenty of chance to meet your farmer match, too. Who wants to farm in isolation?

The Greenhorns seek to promote, recruit and support young farmers in America, turning back the clock on the average age of farmers. Severine calls them greenhorns, but don't let the name fool you. While a few of these farmers may be new to the agricultural scene, they're doing just fine, selling fruits or vegetables at farmers markets and finding farm-direct outlets for pastured poultry, beef or rabbits.

"We may do business differently, but we're farm-

ers with real lives, real businesses and real needs," explains Severine, addressing how sustainable or organic farming practices contrast with the "get big or get out" mantra of big agriculture with the chemicals, huge tractors and concentrated animal feeding operations (CAFOs). "Most of our greenhorns are navigating the system, but face financial, infrastructure and regulatory hurdles that result from one-size-fits-all agricultural programs." And relevant to these times, the greenhorns are creating their own green jobs, not relying on the government to step in and provide them.

Severine racked up some real, hands-on experiences as an early career farmer before starting The Greenhorns. She's travelled around the world for seven months, working on farms listed with the World Wide Opportunities on Organic Farms (WWOOF). She's apprenticed at four Swiss alpine dairies and set up an organic farm on the campus of Pomona College in Claremont, California, before picking up her degree in AgroEcology from the University of California, Berkeley, leaving only after the Society for Agriculture and Food Ecology was up and running.

"My mother's family had a farm, and I loved all the animals, the flowers, fruit trees and being outside," says Severine, explaining that her childhood experiences on the farm set the stage for what would follow later in life. It reminds her of the importance and urgency of reaching out to young people today.

"Food is sunshine organized by the labor of our hands," observes Severine, who sees growing food as a way of manifesting our values in what we eat and how we treat the land that feeds us. "Great food is grown out of our durable relationships with the land. While a lot of the greenhorn-owned farms are organic or grow organically, many are not certified organic by the USDA. These greenhorns find that they don't need this certification thanks to the direct relationships they have with their customers."

"A good diet for us is based on what's a good diet for your soil," says Severine. "Manure, not synthetic chemicals, are good for your soil, so keeping animals within a self-sustaining farm system makes for healthier soil. Pigs are great since they fatten up fast, eat just about everything — but seem to particularly enjoy crop residue and food not fit for human consumption — and can work up the soil."

"It's true: Some of the greenhorns that come into farming are vegetarian," she continues, admitting that she's now an omnivore after years of being a vegetarian. "It's a reaction to how little control we have over the food we eat and how it's raised and how the animals are treated. Many of us switch once we have control. We're making our own butter or cheese, as farmers, and since we're in control of our diet and raising our own food, we've been able to let go of the rules we had followed as vegetarians or vegans. We can save the world more directly by how we farm than how we buy."

Severine is also co-founder of the National Young Farmers Coalition, which helps young farmers with the great re-skilling needed for viable, family-scale, sustainable farming after decades of chemical and oil-addicted mega-farming. Besides the practical knowledge of processing chickens or packing CSA boxes, the coalition connects these future farmers of America with policymakers in DC and to fellow farmers across the nation.

"By hook or by crook — through entrepreneurship, policy advocacy, community organizing, barn raisings and blog banter — the greenhorns are coming," affirms Severine. "Eat fresh and win."

Rhubarb Strawberry Daiquiri

V
Vegan

*L*ET'S SAY YOU'RE CRAVING that Strawberry Rhubarb Pie (page 192), but it's late, you're tired and the couch is calling your name. Consider this grown-up pie in a glass, no rolling of dough required. With a rum base and lime, this cocktail makes you feel like you're eating pie in some island tiki hut. Drink two and you'll be joining us in the limbo under the laundry line.

INGREDIENTS

- 2   c. strawberries, fresh or frozen
- ¼   c. rum
- ¼   c. Triple Sec (or any orange liquor)
- 1   T. lime juice
- ¼   c. powdered sugar
- ½   c. Rhubarb Syrup (see page 201)

DIRECTIONS

❶ Combine all ingredients in a blender. If using fresh strawberries, throw in some ice cubes if you're after that slushy, frozen feel. Blend for about 30 seconds or until slushy.

❷ For an informal summer evening, serve in pint-sized canning jars around the campfire.

YIELD: 4 servings.

COOKING TIP · **Pickle Jar Hooch**
Save gallon-sized glass pickle jars for cordial making, then transfer into decorative glass bottles for serving and gift-giving.

LIAM'S FAVORITES & PANTRY STOCKING

Macaroni & Cheese

Freezer Pickles (vegan)

Rolled Pancakes with Fresh Fruit or Chocolate Filling

Liam's Apple Omelet

Tortilla Wraps

Garden Fresh Salad (vegan)

Spring Rolls

Fireballs Energy Snack

Lemonade, with real lemons (or juice from real lemons)

Playdough (not for human consumption)

Crazy Crayons (not for human consumption)

Homemade Graham Crackers

Chocolate Syrup (vegan)

Balsamic Honey Dressing (vegan)

Ranch Dressing (and dip sauce)

Croutons

Pastry Dough

Quick Baking Mix

Homemade Baking Powder

Sweetened Condensed Milk

Vanilla Extract

Lentil and Polish Sausage Soup

Connecting the Dots to Homemade

We get it, we do. "There's planes to catch. Bills to pay. The new job's a hassle, and the kids have the flu," as Harry Chapin bellows. It's as if he possessed some uncanny ability to peer into the future where "getting ahead" meant more than throwing around a baseball with your kid.

Harry Chapin might as well have sung about the trophy kitchens without any spills, or those brushed-steel appliances with no one around to use them. There is many a kitchen table sitting empty with everyone on the run. We've put a man on the moon but can't find the time to feed our kids things other than Lunchables, candy and cartoons.

Over the last eight chapters, we've tried to share how great food doesn't need to be complicated or fussy, that home cooks are just as capable as any celebrity chef at preparing a meal that nourishes and satisfies. It does depend on fresh, seasonal and local ingredients, if not your own, at least from those farmers or growers who walk their talk. Farmstead anything means "from the farm." And homemade, by definition, is something ideally made from scratch in the home. Fresh, seasonal organic food not only tastes better but is better in other ways, too. We're just trying to do everything we can to be on a first name basis with our farmer, not our doctor. If we can avoid the chemicals, hormones, GMOs or preservatives, why not?

This last chapter resembles a bit of a connect-the-dots puzzle: What do recipes for vanilla extract, macaroni and cheese and playdough have in common? On the surface, nothing. Can't even eat all of them. Scratch further and this eclectic lineup sprouts themes of self-reliance, resiliency and frugality found throughout this book and in our lives.

When folks ask, "What do you do?" we ramble off the list of hats we wear: innkeeper, cook, photographer, speaker, parent, farmer, marketing consultant and spouse. Diversity fosters creativity and stability. One role parlays into another, like the cheddar cheese melts into the noodles. Great cooks, like great inventors, spend more time asking "Why not?" than "Why?" So, give it a try.

Embracing diversity, however, doesn't mean shooting off in every direction. You'll need to focus on projects like you follow along on a recipe. Failure is okay; it's how we learn. If you fall, just fall forward, not backward. Compost the disaster and move on. Diversity forges strength. By not putting all our eggs in one basket, we develop more options to tap into, lest one disappears. Eating a diverse diet keeps us healthy in much the same way that a diverse social network — from young kids to elderly seniors — keeps the mind fresh and engaged. Diversity is the antidote to boredom, in food, friends and life.

Frugality is a reality we savor every time we prepare a meal better than anything we've ever tasted at a restaurant, or bite into as we realize that our monthly grocery bill rarely breaks $100. Sure we could go out and buy playdough, sweetened condensed milk and boxed macaroni and cheese (they even make organic these days). But by making our own, we're reclaiming our kitchen and the satisfaction we get from making it at home. Homemade and homegrown belong in the lexicon of our national identity, instead of the slick marketing messages wrapped around processed food. We the people, we the farmers and we the eaters can be producers and conservers, not merely consumers.

So, if you're going to make homemade vanilla, make a double batch, add a bow to the jar and share

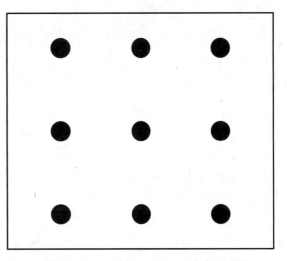

Connect the dots with four consecutive straight lines without picking up your pencil or pen. Clue to solve: Think outside the box.

it with a neighbor. Or head outside for a picnic in a park, patio or garden. For some fry-your-brain fun, try connecting the dots of the puzzle that introduces this chapter.

Just don't forget, there's no rule in life that says you can't draw outside the lines.

Macaroni & Cheese

*T*HE MOST KID-FRIENDLY RECIPE around yet still "gourmet" enough for grown-ups, this mac and cheese has graced the table at many of Liam's birthday parties.

INGREDIENTS

1   package elbow macaroni (10–12 oz.)
6   T. butter, divided
3   T. flour
2   c. milk
1   package cream cheese, cubed (8 oz.)
2   c. cheddar cheese, shredded
2   t. Dijon mustard
½   t. salt
¾   c. bread crumbs (see crouton recipe, page 230 for tips on making your own)

DIRECTIONS

❶ Cook macaroni according to directions on package.

❷ Meanwhile, melt 4 T. butter in a large saucepan. Stir in flour until smooth. Gradually add milk. Bring to a boil; cook and stir for 2 minutes. Reduce heat; add cheeses, mustard and salt. Stir until cheese is melted and sauce is smooth.

❸ Drain macaroni; add to the cheese sauce and stir to coat.

❹ Transfer to a lightly oiled shallow 3-quart baking dish. Melt the remaining butter; toss with bread crumbs. Sprinkle over macaroni.

❺ Bake, uncovered, at 400° for 15 to 20 minutes or until golden brown.

❻ Serve immediately but without any garnish, since some kids can get freaked out by "green stuff" on top.

YIELD: 12 servings.

What do snowmen eat for breakfast? Snowflakes.

UNKNOWN

Freezer Pickles

L isa's Baltic roots genetically transferred to Liam — they share a love of pickles. We're all for ease. This recipe produces great crunchy pickles, no canning required.

INGREDIENTS

14 c. cucumbers, thinly sliced
2 c. onions, sliced
2 c. vinegar
3 c. sugar
2 T. celery seed
3 T. salt
3 T. fresh dill (3 t. dried)

DIRECTIONS

❶ Mix cucumbers and onions in a clean one-gallon glass jar.

❷ In a separate bowl, mix vinegar, sugar, celery seed, salt and dill. Pour over cucumber mixture.

❸ Refrigerate one week, stirring every day.

❹ After one week, cucumbers will taste like pickles. Pack in freezer containers and freeze, draining off some of the liquid.

YIELD: About 6 pints.

If I had influence with the good fairy who is supposed to preside over the christening of all children, I should ask that her gift to each child in the world be a sense of wonder so indestructible that it would last throughout life. If facts are the seeds that later produce knowledge and wisdom, then the emotions and the impressions of the senses are the fertile soil in which the seeds must grow. If a child is to keep alive his inborn sense of wonder, he needs the companionship of at least one adult who can share it, rediscovering with him the joy, excitement and mystery of the world we live in.

Rachel Carson, *The Sense of Wonder*, 1965

Rolled Pancakes with Fresh Fruit or Chocolate Filling

*D*ON'T FREAK WHEN WE SUGGEST try cooking with your parents — or in-laws. That's what happened after Lisa's mom took a tumble and busted up her hand. Flipping a pancake with two hands is awkward enough; try it with one. So during a family visit, we stepped to the plate and took over the flippin'. That's when we found this rolled pancake recipe, an easy standby to the French crepes we'd normally make with special gear and some techniques we've still not completely mastered. After a quick lesson from Lisa's mom on how to swirl around the batter in the 10-inch skillet, we were good to go. One more thing: it's best to use their kitchen when cooking with your parents. They know where everything is — most of the time.

INGREDIENTS

1   c. flour
1   c. milk
3   eggs
½   t. salt
1   T. sugar
2   T. butter, melted
1   c. fresh fruit filling or ½ cup chocolate syrup (see recipe page 227)

DIRECTIONS

❶ Blend all ingredients in a blender. Let batter sit on counter for about 1 hour.

❷ Melt an additional 1 t. butter in pan. Pour approximately ¼ c. batter into pan for one pancake. Cook on both sides untill brown.

❸ Remove pancake from pan and spread fruit filling or chocolate on pancake.

❹ Roll up pancake and place on heatproof serving plate in a warm 200° oven until all pancakes are made. Sprinkle with powdered sugar before serving (an exception to the "no garnish for kids" rule since kids love sugar and recognize it instantly).

YIELD: 12 pancakes.

COOKING TIP Instead of chocolate syrup, try Nutella, that European standby. It's a spread made with hazelnuts (100 per jar) and cocoa; it has zero artificial preservatives or colors and doesn't need to be refrigerated after opening (so you don't need to eat the whole jar in one sitting).

Liam's Apple Omelet

*M*AYBE IT'S JAMIE OLIVER'S NO-NONSENSE, you-can-do-it, make-a-cloud-of-flour–in-the-kitchen approach. Or maybe it's Liam's keen sense of flavor paired with his insatiable Hobbit-like appetite — with first breakfast and second breakfast and so on. But one morning he laid siege to the kitchen (with permission), and his apple omelet is the result. Cooking is not a science, it's an art. And kids know art; they produce it by the wall-full. Like the zillions of paint strokes on a canvas, let your spatula, chef's knife and your imagination run wild with new concoctions in the kitchen. That's how our son came up with his apple omelet. Don't forget the "pinch of baa-zil" (say it with Oliver's accent!).

INGREDIENTS

- 4   eggs
- 1   apple (crisp, tart apples work best), peeled
- ½   c. cheddar cheese, shredded
- 2   T. fresh basil, or 2 t. dried basil
- 1   t. salt
- 1   t. seasoning salt
- 2   T. butter, divided

DIRECTIONS

❶ Peel apple and remove the core, then dice into small, ⅛-inch square pieces.

❷ Crack eggs into bowl, add salt and beat until smooth. Heat an 8-inch skillet over medium heat. Add 1 T. butter. Pour half of the egg mixture into the skillet.

❸ Once eggs have firmed up slightly on top, about 2 minutes, scatter half the diced apples into the cooking eggs, so that the apples cook into the egg mixture for about another 1 minute.

❹ Sprinkle half the cheese and basil over the egg-apple omelet, and cover for 1 minute. Remove cover then fold over in half. Slide onto a warmed plate.

❺ Repeat for second omelet.

YIELD: 2 servings.

Bloom where you're planted.

ALICE WALKER

Tortilla Wraps

A TRAY OF THESE KID-FRIENDLY wraps disappears quickly at potlucks. We'll sometimes skip slicing the wraps into ½-inch sections and keep the whole tortilla wrap intact. We call them our "travel sandwiches" since they make great road food, allowing us to continue our boycott of fast food. If they get squashed, no problem — the taste is the same.

INGREDIENTS

1   package cream cheese, softened (8 oz.)

½   t. salt

½   t. seasoning salt

¼   t. garlic powder

1   t. dill

2   t. parsley

½   t. onion powder

approximately 6 whole wheat flour tortillas

assorted crunchy, washed fresh veggies like lettuce, pea pods, cucumbers and grated carrots

DIRECTIONS

❶ Mix cream cheese, salts, garlic powder, dill, parsley and onion powder. Chill at least a couple of hours.

❷ Let come back to room temperature to soften. Spread evenly on tortillas, right up to the edges.

❸ Add in fresh, raw washed veggies evenly up to edges of tortillas.

❹ Tightly roll up tortillas and slice in ½-inch sections. Store in refrigerator or in cooler for sandwiches to go.

YIELD: 12 as an appetizer.

Selecting Tortillas

Tortillas are one store-bought item we like to have handy in the fridge. Look for a tortilla without hydrogenated oils and pick one with higher fiber through ingredients such as flax seed, whole oats and whole wheat flour. Tortillas in the refrigerated case will often have fewer preservatives.

Garden Fresh Salad

Kids know fresh when they see it — and taste it. As parents, we relish the fact that our son can plop himself in our strawberry patch for a snack every June, since nothing we grow is sprayed with poisons or doused in chemical fertilizers. Often, when we're busy working away in the spring, Liam — unnoticed by us — takes a break from climbing trees or hanging out on top of our chicken coop to prepare a fresh salad for us for dinner, enjoyed after we're forced inside on account of darkness. It's easy to lose track of time when there's compost to be spread, rows to be tilled and weeding to be done (as if we're ever done with the last one). When we arrive inside, perhaps after taking a quick solar shower outside by the greenhouse, we're greeted by his smile and a proud nod toward the front porch where three perfect salads sit waiting for us, complemented by some fresh lemonade (see recipe on page 222, so easy a kid can make it). With a little Balsamic Honey Dressing (see page 228), this salad is like eating sunshine. That it's prepared by our son, all the better.

INGREDIENTS

- ½ c. sweet pea tendrils (young, green tops of sugar snap sweet peas)
- 1 c. tender mesclun salad mix (small, young leafy lettuces, chervil, arugula, endive)
- ½ c. sugar snap sweet peas, strings removed
- ¼ c. young Swiss chard leaves
- ¼ c. young dandelion greens
- ¼ c. nasturtium flowers (edible)
- ¼ c. bee balm flowers (edible)
- ¼ c. homemade croutons (see page 230)

DIRECTIONS

❶ Wash the delicate salad greens and give the edible flowers a quick shake, checking for insects that might be hanging on. Pat dry the mesclun greens.

❷ Arrange, with the creativity of a child, the delightful colors and textures of the ingredients on the plate, topping with a few croutons and a drizzle of salad dressing.

YIELD: 4 servings.

Serving Up Kid-inspired Humor with Your Fruits and Vegetables

What is a scarecrow's favorite vegetable?   Strawberries.

What vegetable has rhythm?   Beets.

What is the kindest vegetable?   Sweet potatoes.

Spring Rolls

*D*ON'T LET THE NAME FOOL YOU. We savor spring rolls in the middle of the summer as an alternative way to enjoy fresh lettuce and mint — or in the fall, when we have carrots coming out of our ears. Of course you can eat them in the spring, too, or anytime, like our son does. What's not to like about eating a salad like finger food? With a potted mint plant in the house, this herb can be savored fresh any time of year. The spring roll wrappers are made from rice and on our list of items to stock up on at the Asian grocery store in the city. Have a bunch of small bowls on standby for each of the cooking steps for this recipe and a bamboo sushi mat (if you have one) to drain water off the wrappers.

INGREDIENTS

- 6 oz. extra-firm tofu (half a 1 lb. container)
- ¼ c. soy sauce
- 6 oz. of rice noodles (small noodle size)
- 8 rice paper wrappers
- 48 fresh mint leaves, whole (optional—use only if in season)
- 2 c. lettuce, mesclun mix or other non-iceberg type, shredded
- 1 carrot, shredded

DIRECTIONS

❶ Slice tofu in ½-inch sections. Remove any moisture with a towel. Place tofu on non-stick baking pan with a lip. Pour soy sauce on top of tofu. Bake for 45 minutes at 325°, turning the tofu sections until they are dry and browned. Remove and cut the tofu into strips the size of French fries, then set aside in bowl.

❷ Place the rice noodles into boiling water and cook for about 2 to 3 minutes until tender. Pour into colander and rinse with cool water to quickly cool them. Set aside in a bowl.

❸ Place about 2 inches of cool water in a large enough skillet to hold the rice paper wrappers. Separate the wrappers and place them in the skillet while making sure they're completely covered with water before adding the next one. Leave the wrappers in the water for about 3 minutes, until they are flexible. Once the wrappers are flexible, immediately start assembling the spring rolls. Leaving the rice paper wrappers in too long will make them mushy.

❹ Remove a wrapper from the water, gently let as much water as you can drip off and then lay it flat, ideally on top of a bamboo sushi mat if you have one (a baking sheet if you don't). No stress here, but work quickly: place 4 mint leaves, 1 strip of tofu and a pinch of rice noodles, lettuce and carrots onto the center of the spring roll wrapper.

❺ Fold the bottom of the wrapper over the fillings, then fold the two sides and continue to roll it up tightly. The key is to keep the wrappers moist and the fillings dry. If one busts apart, just eat it, don't plate it.

❻ After all the spring rolls are completed, serve immediately with sweet sauce (below). No additional cooking needed. We've found spring rolls best eaten immediately; they don't keep well once rolled.

YIELD: 8 spring rolls.

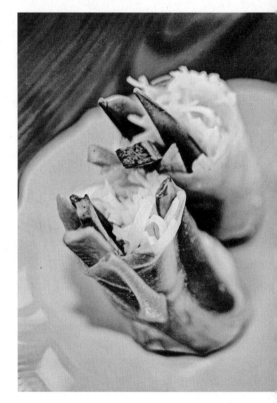

SAUCE INGREDIENTS

4	T. sugar
¼	c. soy sauce
1	c. chicken broth
2	T. cornstarch
¼	c. cold water
1	clove garlic, minced

SAUCE DIRECTIONS

❶ Combine sugar, soy sauce and broth in pot. Bring to boil. Mix the cornstarch with the cold water and add to broth mixture. Cook until smooth and thickened.

❷ Reduce heat and simmer for 1 minute, stirring in garlic.

❸ Serve at room temperature. The sauce can be refrigerated for up to five days.

YIELD: 1½ cups.

Fireballs Energy Snack

*A*s a toddler, Liam dubbed these "Fireballs" because he claims they give him energy. They do pack a wallop for grown-ups, too, thanks to the honey and peanut butter.

INGREDIENTS

about 45 graham crackers (see recipe page 226)

⅔ c. honey

½ c. dry milk powder

1 c. peanut butter

DIRECTIONS

❶ Crush graham crackers in a food processor.

❷ Add honey, milk powder and peanut butter. Mix until blended.

❸ Roll into balls about the size of a walnut. Store in refrigerator. Will keep for about a week.

YIELD: Makes about 35 snacks.

Lemonade, with real lemons (or juice from real lemons)

*W*e blush with embarrassment every time someone asks for our "secret recipe" for lemonade. Um, lemons, sugar, water? Due to this high request demand, here are more specific proportions. You'll never go back to the mix stuff again.

INGREDIENTS

1 c. lemon juice (3 to 4 fresh lemons, juiced)

1½ c. sugar, or less to taste

8 c. water

DIRECTIONS

❶ Combine lemon juice, sugar and water in a large pitcher. Mix thoroughly.

❷ Add more sugar or lemon juice to taste.

YIELD: half gallon.

We are living in a world today where lemonade is made from artificial flavors and furniture polish is made from real lemons.

ALFRED E. NEWMAN

Playdough

*T*HE MOST ADDICTIVE RECIPE in this cookbook may just be calorie free. You can't eat it, but put a batch of this playdough in front of anyone and watch how they start rolling, pinching and creating. No need to deal with that smell of the commercial variety. When it hardens or you're ready for fresh colors, just send it to the afterlife on the compost pile, since it's non-toxic. Make a multi-colored batch for a fun birthday gift for kids of any age. **Note: Not for human consumption.**

INGREDIENTS

1   c. flour
¼   c. salt
2   T. cream of tartar
1   T. vegetable oil
1   c. water
    food coloring

DIRECTIONS

❶ Mix the flour, salt and cream of tartar in medium pot.

❷ Add food coloring, oil and water. Stir over medium heat 3–5 minutes. Don't worry if the mixture gets lumpy; keep stirring and it will turn into dough.

❸ When the mixture forms into a ball in the center of the pot, take off stove and let it cool. Lightly knead on a floured surface.

❹ Store in a closed container in the refrigerator. When things get dry and crumbly, it's time for a new batch.

YIELD: 2 cups.

Crazy Crayons

*T*HEY KIND OF LOOK LIKE colorful candies, but don't eat the crayons! These "crazy crayons" take creative recycling to new levels, transforming those old crayon bits into funky new drawing tools. Use an old garage-sale muffin tin for this project since the wax tends to leak — definitely not a flavor enhancer for your morning muffin making. **Note: Not for human consumption.**

INGREDIENTS

miscellaneous crayon pieces
foil
old 12-cup muffin tin

DIRECTIONS

❶ Line muffin cups with foil.

❷ Remove paper wrappers from crayons. Break into pieces to fill each tin half full. Experiment with various color combos; mixes of light and dark colors work well.

❸ Place in a preheated low oven (200°) for about 5 minutes or until crayons just start to melt and blend together. Watch the oven carefully because if crayons fully melt, the crayon color turns in into a dark brown.

❹ Remove from oven and let cool thoroughly. Remove foil.

YIELD: 12 crazy crayons.

Stock up on Convenience:
Farmstead Pantry Checklist

Artists keep stocked with paint, pencils and other supplies so they can craft a masterpiece whenever the creative muse hits. Likewise, as someone passionate about food and cooking, your palette is your kitchen pantry. We keep ours stocked with the core ingredients necessary to whip up anything from bag lunches for our son to an impromptu dinner party. Stocking the pantry saves time and money — two non-renewable resources. With a little planning and organization, your pantry will never let you down.

When we moved from our Chicago apartment to our Wisconsin farm, we traded convenience for countryside. No more quick runs to the mini-mart at the end of the block for a missing ingredient. We've learned to have the staples on hand to do anything from feeding a round of B&B guests to whipping up pear pies for our neighbors down the road who just helped replace our leaking sink.

Keep the following items on hand, and with some basics from the refrigerator and garden, you can whip up anything from coffeecakes to a jam-making marathon. This list covers just about everything you'll need for this cookbook!

Bulk Basics

Arrowroot powder	Dry milk
Flour (unbleached)	Nutritional yeast
Whole wheat flour	Oats (whole)
Unbleached sugar	Pasta (variety of whole
Bread crumbs	grain)
Brown sugar	Popcorn
Powdered sugar	Raisins
Beans (dried: chickpeas,	Rice (brown, sushi,
lentils)	arborio)
Chickpea flour	Sea salt
Cornmeal (regular &	Rice noodles
self-rising)	Soy flour
Cornstarch	Wheat germ
Couscous	Bulk yeast

Baking Basics

Baking soda	Honey
Baking powder	Instant coffee powder
Cocoa powder	Molasses
Chocolate chips	Nuts (almonds, walnuts,
Coconut	pecans, peanuts, pine)
Cream of tartar	Peanut butter
Crushed pineapple	Nutella hazelnut spread
(can)	Soy milk
Extracts (vanilla, lemon,	
almond, peppermint)	

Oils

Canola oil	Sesame oil
Extra-virgin olive oil	

Dried Spices & Herbs

Allspice	Mustard powder
Basil	Nutmeg
Bay leaves	Onion flakes
Celery seed	Onion powder
Chili powder	Onion salt
Cilantro	Orange zest
Cinnamon	Oregano
Cumin	Paprika
Curry	Parsley
Dill	Peppercorns
Fennel seed	Red pepper flakes
Garlic powder	Rosemary
Garlic salt	Sage
Ginger, ground	Seasoning salt
Lemon zest	Tarragon
Marjoram	Thyme
Mint	

Vinegars*

Apple cider vinegar	Rice vinegar
Balsamic vinegar	White wine vinegar
Red wine vinegar	

Canned Goods & Snacks

Crackers	Rice paper wraps
Tahini paste	Seltzer water
Olives (kalamata)	Sesame seeds
Capers	Sunflower seeds
Anchovies	Nori wraps
Cooking wines:	
white, red, sherry &	
Kirschwasser	

store in refrigerator after opening

Seasonings & Condiments

Barbeque sauce *	Worcestershire sauce*
Ketchup*	Fish sauce
Lemon juice*	Vegetable, beef &
Lime juice*	chicken stock*
Mayonnaise *	(frozen)
Mustard (Dijon &	Maple syrup*
yellow)*	Red curry paste*
Salsa*	Hoisin sauce*
Applesauce*	
Soy sauce*	

Homemade Graham Crackers

*M*OST GRAHAM CRACKERS you'll find on the supermarket shelves don't contain a gram of graham flour. This recipe cooks up the real cracker, based on Sylvester Graham's work back in the early 1800s to develop a "health cracker" made with self-dubbed graham flour, a combination of fine-ground white flour and coarse-ground wheat bran and germ. Apparently Graham attempted to create a cracker to suppress "carnal urges." Not sure about that part, but they definitely assist in the internal plumbing department.

INGREDIENTS

- 2 c. graham flour
- ½ c. flour
- ¼ c. brown sugar, firmly packed
- ¾ t. baking powder
- ½ t. baking soda
- ½ t. salt
- ¼ t. cinnamon
- ¼ c. butter (½ stick)
- ⅓ c. honey
- ¼ c. milk
- ½ t. vanilla extract

DIRECTIONS

❶ In a food processor, mix flours, brown sugar, baking powder, baking soda, salt and cinnamon. Add in the butter and mix until crumbly. Add the honey, milk and vanilla and process until dough becomes a ball. Cover dough in plastic wrap and refrigerate 1 hour.

❷ Unwrap dough and place on lightly floured surface. Roll out dough to ¼-inch thickness. Cut with cookie cutters.

❸ Bake at 350° for about 15 to 20 minutes or until edges just start to darken. Cool on a wire rack.

YIELD: 2 dozen.

COOKING TIP

Graham Cracker Crust

To make a graham cracker crust, take about 10 crackers and crush them in a food processor. You can also place crackers in a plastic bag and crush them with a rolling pin. This should result in about 1⅓ cups of graham crackers. Keep crumbs in food processor and mix in ¼ c. sugar. Drizzle in ⅓ c. melted butter until crumbs clump together. Press into a lightly oiled 9-inch pie pan or other pan as needed.

Chocolate Syrup

*H*ONEY, I SHRUNK THE PANTRY. An interesting perk on the road to self-reliance: the more basic staples we have on hand, the fewer items we need to buy. Like chocolate syrup. We have the cocoa powder, sugar, salt and vanilla extract, so why do we need to buy any chocolate syrup? From the pocketbook to the pantry, there's more space and resources opened up for more-pressing things, like preparing the ultimate banana split made with homemade ice cream and topped with this syrup.

INGREDIENTS

- ½ c. cocoa powder
- 2 c. sugar
- 1 c. water
- ½ t. salt
- ½ t. vanilla extract

DIRECTIONS

❶ In a saucepan, whisk together cocoa powder, sugar, water and salt over low heat until cocoa and sugar are thoroughly dissolved. If cocoa and sugar are not fully dissolved, the syrup will be grainy.

❷ Once cocoa and sugar are dissolved, heat to a boil over medium heat and boil for 3 minutes. Be sure to watch syrup carefully as it has a tendency to boil over and make a big sticky mess on your stove. If it looks like it is about to boil over, immediately take it off the heat and stir. Replace over lower heat.

❸ After 3 minutes, remove from heat and stir in salt and vanilla extract.

❹ Let cool completely and skim off a skin that may form on the top of the syrup.

❺ Pour into a clean sterile jar (we like to use wide-mouth glass canning jars) and store covered in the refrigerator. Will keep for about 2 weeks.

YIELD: 2 cups.

Balsamic Honey Dressing

WITH JUST THE RIGHT AMOUNT OF KICK, this dressing showcases summer salad greens. Store any leftover dressing in a glass canning jar in the refrigerator, but use it up within about a week or two. Give the jar a shake before serving to ensure the ingredients blend nicely.

INGREDIENTS

½ c. balsamic vinegar

¼ c. onion, chopped (1 small onion)

1 T. soy sauce

3 T. honey

1 T. sugar

2 cloves garlic, minced

¼ t. crushed red pepper flakes

½ c. extra-virgin olive oil

DIRECTIONS

❶ Purée the vinegar, onion, soy sauce, honey, sugar, garlic and red pepper flakes in a blender on high.

❷ Gradually add the olive oil. Continue puréeing until thick, about 2 minutes.

YIELD: 1 cup salad dressing.

Making your Salad Dressings

Prepare the dressings at least a few hours before you use them to let the flavors marinate. Shake well before using and store in the refrigerator. The fresh flavor and lack of preservatives mean you'll only want to whip up what you need.

Ranch Dressing (and dipping sauce)

SKIP THE POWDERED AND PROCESSED version that's loaded with preservatives and make your own Ranch Dressing. Ranch Dressing works well both in salads and as a dipping sauce for prepared foods or fresh veggies. We recommend it with the Squash Fritters and Vegetable Tempura. It's best to make this the day before you need it to fully release the flavors.

INGREDIENTS

½ t. parsley (dried)
½ t. dill (dried)
½ t. garlic powder
½ t. onion powder
¼ t. salt
⅛ t. pepper
½ c. mayonnaise
¼ c. sour cream
¼ c. water

DIRECTIONS

❶ In a small bowl, combine parsley, dill, garlic powder, onion powder, salt and pepper.

❷ In a large bowl, whisk mayonnaise, sour cream and water.

❸ Add spice mixture to mayonnaise mixture and blend well.

YIELD: 1 cup of dressing.

COOKING TIP

Mix 'em Up
Live on the edge. Take a few spoonfuls of this Ranch Dressing and drizzle some of our Balsamic Honey Dressing over the top for a remarkably tasty dressing blend for a fresh salad.

Croutons

*C*ONSIDER CROUTONS the wonder drug of the farmstead pantry. True, life will go on without croutons on the salad or sprinkled in soup, but life is too short to miss out on any crunchy opportunities. We use these in a variety of dishes, like our summer staple Tomato Crouton Casserole (page 101). Only use dried herbs; fresh herbs don't stick to the bread as well.

1   loaf French baguette, cut into ½ inch squares (8 c.)

¾   c. olive oil

1   T. dried oregano

1   T. dried basil

1   T. garlic powder

½   T. seasoning salt

DIRECTIONS

❶ Toss bread chunks with olive oil, and then sprinkle with seasoning.

❷ Spread on baking sheet (ideally use a jelly roll pan with sides in case any oil leaks over).

❸ Bake at 350° about 10 to 15 minutes until golden brown and crispy.

YIELD: 8 cups of croutons.

COOKING TIP

Bread Crumbs Anyone?
Make your own preservative-free bread crumbs by crushing these croutons in a food processor. Four cups of croutons will crush down to about three cups of bread crumbs. We keep the crumbs in the freezer for added freshness.

Pastry Dough

*E*XPAND THE CONCEPT OF "pantry staples" to your freezer: What processed items we typically buy can have a homespun, versatile version? This simplified version of pastry dough, inspired by a King Arthur Flour recipe, provides a light and flaky butter dough.

INGREDIENTS

1½ c. flour
½ t. salt
½ t. baking powder
1 c. butter (2 sticks)
½ c. sour cream

DIRECTIONS

❶ In a large mixing bowl, mix flour, salt and baking powder.

❷ Cut in butter until crumbly. Stir in sour cream.

❸ Turn dough onto a lightly floured surface and work with hands to bring it together into a ball.

❹ Roll into an 8-inch-by-10-inch rectangle. Dust both sides of the rectangle and, starting with the shorter side, fold it in 3 like a business letter.

❺ Roll again into an 8-inch-by-10-inch rectangle and repeat the process.

❻ Chill dough for at least 30 minutes before using. Dough can be frozen. Defrost in refrigerator overnight.

YIELD: Equivalent to one 17 oz. box of frozen puff pastry sheets.

The greatest fine art of the future will be the making of a comfortable living from a small parcel of land.

ABE LINCOLN

Quick Baking Mix

THE IDEA BEHIND a quick mix like Bisquick stems from premixing flour, shortening, salt and baking powder together to quickly make certain kinds of baked goods like biscuits, pancakes and dumplings. Unfortunately, a lot of chemicals and preservatives go into the mix as well, to make it shelf-stable. Keep the convenience while improving the quality of the ingredients that go in the mix by making your own.

INGREDIENTS

9 c. flour
⅓ c. baking powder
1 c. powdered milk
4 t. salt
1½ c. vegetable oil

DIRECTIONS

❶ Mix flour, baking powder, powdered milk and salt. Cut oil into flour mixture until it resembles coarse cornmeal.

❷ Store, well covered in cool dry place. We store ours in the freezer. No need to defrost before using; just add it in.

YIELD: 9 cups.

Homemade Baking Powder

WHO HASN'T ACCIDENTALLY switched baking powder and soda in a recipe? Whoops. Both are leavening agents, which means they have sodium bicarbonate producing carbon dioxide that enables the dough to rise. But baking soda is pure sodium bicarbonate, while baking powder also contains cream of tartar and a drying agent like cornstarch. Unfortunately, most commercial baking powders also contain unnecessary aluminum (sodium aluminum sulfate) that you can avoid by making your own.

INGREDIENTS

1 t. cornstarch
1 t. baking soda
2 t. cream of tartar

DIRECTIONS

❶ Mix cornstarch, baking soda, cream of tartar until well combined.

YIELD: 1 tablespoon.

Sweetened Condensed Milk

SWEETENED CONDENSED MILK represents the ultimate pantry mystery ingredient: What is it, why does it taste so good and why does it come in a can? It's basically milk with about 60% of the water removed and sugar added, hence it adds a creamy richness to baked goods. Historically it comes in a can to give it a long shelf life and transportability, but who needs that if your goal is lemon meringue pie in your kitchen right now?

INGREDIENTS

1   c. dry milk powder
⅓   c. hot water
⅓   c. sugar
3   T. butter, melted

DIRECTIONS

❶ Combine all ingredients in a blender, layering wet and dry ingredients. Blend until smooth.

YIELD: 1 standard-size can sweetened condensed milk (14 oz.).

Vanilla Extract

IT'S A PANTRY GIFT that keeps on giving. Invest a little time (each batch takes 6 months to make) and use quality whole vanilla beans. Make sure the vanilla beans are slightly pliable and not fully dried out. Store your vanilla extract in a dark place and always give it a good shake before using.

INGREDIENTS

1   whole vanilla bean
¾   c. vodka

DIRECTIONS

❶ Split vanilla bean lengthwise with a sharp knife.

❷ Place in jar with vodka. Be sure bean is completely covered with the vodka.

❸ Seal tightly and store in a dark, cool place for a minimum of 4 months before using. Shake jar occasionally during the time that the vanilla is being absorbed by the vodka to help the release the flavors from the vanilla beans.

❹ Use as you would store-bought vanilla extract.

YIELD: ¾ c. vanilla extract.

COOKING TIP

Shortcut Tips & Substitutions

1 oz. unsweetened chocolate = 3 T. unsweetened cocoa plus 1 T. butter or canola oil
1 c. cake flour = 1 c. flour, take out 2 T. of the flour and add 2 T. cornstarch
1 c. buttermilk = A wee bit less than 1 c. fresh milk with 1 T. vinegar or lemon juice. Let sit 5 minutes (will curdle).

CULINARY COMMUNITY ACTIVISTS HOST SOUP NIGHTS

The Carus Family, Monroe, Wisconsin

"The kids liked it, all four of them," laughs Brenda Carus, an urban homesteader at the helm of the kitchen and gardens for her family of four kids and her husband, Luis, who excels at tinkering with things until he gets them to work.

Less than two blocks off the Historic Downtown Square of Monroe, Wisconsin, their 1906 5-bedroom, brick Victorian home is surrounded by bountiful gardens that yield a dizzying array of fresh fruits, vegetable and herbs, most of which are either consumed fresh or canned for year-round use. "Luis loves lentils, so the lentil and Polish sausage soup recipe seemed like a perfect blend of savory, with some flavorful chunkiness of the sausage added in," she continues, with her youngest son, Simon, on her lap.

It's this pragmatic approach that likewise guides Brenda's gardening in her five 4- by-10-foot raised beds, interspersed with meandering gardens that wrap around the house. "What my family eats is what I decided to grow," she admits, knowing that while kale may be a nutrient-packed vegetable, there's a reason the number one use of it is to line the salad bars at restaurants. "I have limited space, so I grow mostly for fresh consumption for every meal during the growing season. Besides preserving fruits in jams and jellies to last the entire year, I grow enough for canning salsa and tomato sauce, eating winter squash until around the New Year, drying herbs, making and freezing pesto and using our garlic for most of the year."

"I started planning the garden before Luis and I even purchased the house in 2001," she confides. "Home produce is what I grew up with, and I prioritized that for my own family. The best part of it is knowing that the carrots, asparagus and broccoli are all yours. With four kids, though, some of it never makes it into the kitchen, like the sugar snap sweet pea pods." Since moving in, they've replaced more than half the lawn with fruit trees, herb beds and kitchen gardens.

Our paths crossed with the Carus family, not by gardening happenstance, but through our interest in breastfeeding Liam. Before Liam came along, we were welcomed into the local La Leche League group, of which Brenda was also a member. From there, our friendship grew.

But Brenda also recognized the power of food during one gathering. "A friend was sharing a story about potlucks and how it brought neighbors together and helped build a sense of community around food," she explains. "Autumn came and with it, soup season. So we hosted a soup night at our place."

Ever the pragmatist, Brenda and the entire Carus family have a contrarian tradition of throwing a party to give them a focus to clean up the house. While most of us fear the mess after the party is over, the Carus family believes differently. "We call it the 'cleaning-via-entertaining' approach to keeping a clean house, and it works," affirms Brenda. "It gives us a deadline, a focus and a tasty reward at the end: a delicious meal with friends. Luis does the vacuuming, the kids dust, and I put on a few pots of soup and two types of bread. Part of being a good hostess is having a clean house for your guests and making sure they feel comfortable," says Brenda, known for setting out a few extra sets of slippers for those who attend.

And soups there are: chicken soup prepared with free-ranging broilers, five-bean vegan soup with a mild curry base, and Brenda's Lentil and Polish Sausage Soup. There are pumpkin spice muffins, corn bread, French baguettes and sourdough along with comforting macaroni and cheese for the kids and chocolate zucchini bread for dessert, often enjoyed while playing a game of dominoes on the cleared dinner table. With raw wind howling outside, we can't tell if we're warmed inside by the soup, the kids running around or the feeling of security and happiness that comes from knowing you're amongst friends.

Perhaps a key to their soup night success is the convivial nature of the gathering, matched by the selection of choice local ingredients for most of the soups, sides and desserts shared by guests equally committed to serving their families healthy meals, featuring the local, organic and fresh. "If the animals live the life they are meant, in the fields or pastures, and the vegetables grow in a soil that is alive and full of nutrients, who can argue against great taste?" asks Brenda.

"This isn't radical," she continues, matter-of-factly. "What we're doing is traditional, going back to my roots, having grown up on a farm. It's what my grandmother did, and their grandmothers before them. We've just chosen to do it in the city, instead of the country, because of our community's walkability." Besides growing upwards of twenty-five percent of everything they eat year-round, the Carus family drives about 5,000 miles per year—around half the American average.

That leaves plenty more time for cooking, canning, gardening—and hosting soup nights.

Brenda and Luis Carus, hosts of the community soup nights and urban homesteaders in Monroe, Wisconsin.

Lentil and Polish Sausage Soup

*T*HE RECIPE CAME ABOUT, as many great recipes do, based on what Brenda Carus had in the house at the time, and a degree of cooking creativity, to which we all can lay claim. You need not be a chef to make a great meal, or pot of soup that your family loves. "I've made the recipe numerous times since, and it works every time," Brenda beams. Soup's on.

INGREDIENTS

- 6 c. leeks, cleaned and thinly sliced (2 large leeks)
- ½ c. onion, sliced
- 2 c. carrots, sliced and diced (3 carrots)
- 2 T. olive oil
- 2 cloves garlic, minced
- 3 c. red potatoes, diced small (3 medium potatoes)
- 2½ c. lentils
- 8 c. chicken stock
- 1 t. caraway seed
- ½ t. salt
- ½ t. pepper
- 4 slices bacon
- 3 smoked Polish kielbasa sausages

DIRECTIONS

❶ Sauté leeks, onions and carrots in a pot with olive oil for about 15 minutes, until the leeks and onions are translucent and carrots have a nice golden color. Add the garlic to the sautéed vegetables after about 7 minutes of cooking.

❷ Add just a little stock to cool down the pan slightly. Add the remaining stock, lentils, potatoes and caraway plus salt and pepper to taste. Simmer covered for about 30 minutes, until lentils and potatoes are soft. If necessary, add a little more stock. When making lentil soup, you may be tempted to purée part of it, although it's not necessary with this soup. Just be sure the lentils are fully cooked (very soft).

❸ While the soup simmers, fry the bacon until crisp. Cool the bacon, crumble and set aside in a small bowl.

❹ Slice the sausage and fry it in the remaining bacon grease in the skillet until hot. Then add the sausage to the soup.

❺ Just before serving, add the crumbled bacon to the soup. Serve immediately.

YIELD: Serves 6.

COOKING TIP

Making Chicken Stock

Since we eat such little meat, making chicken stock doesn't make sense (the Superior Touch Better than Bouillon brand works fine for the few times we need it). Brenda's family, however, likes their chicken. Making stock is how they use up their leftover parts that don't get eaten. To a pot containing a poultry carcass or two and 3 cups of water, add sliced onions, carrots and celery. Bring to a boil, possibly adding some garlic, your favorite herbs for seasoning (dried oregano or cumin) and a little dry white wine. Reduce the heat so the pot simmers, uncovered for about 3 hours. Keep adding water to keep the contents covered and feel free to skim off the fats that may float to the top. Add salt to taste. When you get a flavorful taste, strain the liquid from the pot and then freeze in 2-cup-size portion containers.

Recipe Index

Index

About the Authors

LISA KIVIRIST is an innkeeper of the nationally recognized Inn Serendipity Bed & Breakfast, completely powered by the wind and the sun. With her husband, John Ivanko, Lisa co-authored the award-winning book *ECO-preneuring* as well as *Rural Renaissance*. Lisa is a distinguished Food and Community Fellow and leading national advocate for women in sustainable agriculture. She directs the Rural Women's Project for the Midwest Organic and Sustainable Education Service (MOSES), championing women farmers. Lisa is also a national speaker and a contributor to Hobby Farm Home and Edible Madison. Based on her family's organic farm in southwest Wisconsin, Lisa can usually be found pickling, parenting or pecking away at the keyboard.

JOHN IVANKO is an innkeeper of the nationally recognized Inn Serendipity Bed & Breakfast. Together with his wife, Lisa Kivirist, John is a national speaker, marketing consultant and co-author of the award-winning *ECO-preneuring* as well as *Rural Renaissance*. He is also the co-author and photographer for six award-winning multicultural children's books for the Global Fund for Children, including *To Be a Kid*, *Be My Neighbor* and *To Be an Artist*. As a freelance writer and photographer, John contributes to *Urban Farm*, *Mother Earth News*, *Natural Home*, *Hobby Farms*, *Natural Awakenings* and *E Magazine*, among many others. Based in Browntown, Wisconsin, he shares his organic farm with his wife and son, millions of ladybugs and a 10 kW Bergey wind turbine.

For more about Farmstead Chef, please visit farmsteadchef.com or join the book Facebook page at facebook.com/farmsteadchef

For more about Inn Serendipity Bed & Breakfast, visit innserendipity.com

If you have enjoyed *Farmstead Chef,* you might also enjoy other

BOOKS TO BUILD A NEW SOCIETY

Our books provide positive solutions for people who want to
make a difference. We specialize in:

**Sustainable Living • Green Building • Peak Oil
Renewable Energy • Environment & Economy
Natural Building & Appropriate Technology
Progressive Leadership • Resistance and Community
Educational & Parenting Resources**

New Society Publishers

ENVIRONMENTAL BENEFITS STATEMENT

New Society Publishers has chosen to produce this book on recycled paper made
with **100% post consumer waste,** processed chlorine free, and old growth free.

For every 5,000 books printed, New Society saves the following resources:[1]

35	Trees
3,210	Pounds of Solid Waste
3,532	Gallons of Water
4,607	Kilowatt Hours of Electricity
5,835	Pounds of Greenhouse Gases
25	Pounds of HAPs, VOCs, and AOX Combined
9	Cubic Yards of Landfill Space

[1]Environmental benefits are calculated based on research done by the Environmental Defense Fund
and other members of the Paper Task Force who study the environmental impacts of the paper
industry.

For a full list of NSP's titles, please call 1-800-567-6772 *or check out our website* at:

www.newsociety.com

NEW SOCIETY PUBLISHERS